T0288184

On Changes in Jewish Liturgy

Options and Limitations

On Changes in Jewish Liturgy
Options and Limitations

Daniel Sperber

Urim Publications
Jerusalem ◆ New York

On Changes in Jewish Liturgy:
Options and Limitations
by Daniel Sperber

Copyright © 2010 by Daniel Sperber

Printed in Israel
First Edition

ISBN: 978-965-524-040-5

Urim Publications, P.O. Box 52287, Jerusalem 91521 Israel
Typeset by Ariel Walden

Lambda Publishers Inc.
3709 13th Avenue Brooklyn, New York 11218 U.S.A.
Tel: 718-972-5449 Fax: 718-972-6307, mh@ejudaica.com

www.UrimPublications.com

CONTENTS

INTRODUCTION   9

The Complexity of the Hebrew Prayer Book   21
The Constant Evolution of Our Liturgical Text   24
The Variety of Liturgical Versions   31
Blessings Offensive to Women   33
Recommended Changes   41
The Legitimacy of Change   51
New Prayers and Innovative Creativity   54
Talmudic Sources Forbidding Change in the Liturgy and
    Maimonides's Understanding of Them   57
Limits of Flexibility in Change   66
The Dynamic Process of Change in Our Liturgy   70
The Main Reasons for Change   72
Examples of Internal Censorship   86
The Talmudic Sources Revisited   93
The Positions of Geonim and Rishonim   96
Attempts to Fix a Single, Crystallized Version, and Their Failures   99
Nusah ha-Ari and the Hasidic Position   103
The Response of the *Mitnaggedim*   108
The Impact of Printing on the Hebrew Prayer Book   114
The Permissibility of Making Changes   120

AFTERWORD   131

CONTENTS

APPENDICES

1. On the Liturgical Theories of Hasidei Ashkenaz   143
2. Seven Versions of *Birkat Nahem*   161
3. The *Ha-Siddur ha-Meduyak* Affair   168
4. Corrupt Versions or Alternate Versions?   174
5. The *Piyyutim* Controversy   181
6. The *Avodah* Prayer – An Example of the Complex
   Development of a Benediction   192
7. "For Your Covenant which You Sealed in Our Flesh"   199
8. On R. Meir's Three Benedictions   204

Index of Primary Sources   209
Index of Prayer Books   211
Index of Prayers, Benedictions and Piyyutim   213
General Index   215

🕎 Mishnah *Berachot* 4:4: R. Eliezer says: He who treats his prayer as a perfunctory obligation (*keva*) – his prayer is no true supplication.

🕎 BT *Berachot* 29b: What does *keva* mean? Rav Yosef [explains] . . . He who cannot make some innovation [in his prayer] (i.e., cannot direct his heart to request his needs – Rashi).

🕎 And when you pray, add to each and every benediction something suitable to its essence relating to your own needs.

INTRODUCTION

In recent years, there has been a growing number of initiatives in the Orthodox Jewish community to make certain changes in the text of our liturgy. Orthodox feminists have felt that it is too male-oriented or, as Tamar Ross expressed it, it has an "androcentric bias."[1] Others have asserted that it does not take into account major events that have taken place in our recent history. To cite several examples, the Holocaust is hardly represented in the prayers of our fast days, the establishment of the State of Israel receives hardly any mention (other than a single prayer for the state[2]), nor does the reunification of Jerusalem

---

1   Ross, Tamar. *Expanding the Palace of Torah: Orthodoxy and Feminism*. Waltham, MA: 2004, 21, 37–38. There (21) she writes:

> Standard prayers are also phrased with reference to men only. The female pronoun appears only in brackets, if at all. This same androcentric bias also applies to all classics of Jewish thought. Thus, women reading the traditional sources are likely to have the sense of eavesdropping on a male-only conversation. Women's opinions do not figure in the discussion.

On p. 257, n. 95, she refers us to Rachel Adler, "I've Had Nothing, So I Can't Take More" (*Moment* 8:8 [September 1983]: 22–23).

On Tamar Ross's book, see the review by Aryeh Frimer in *BDD* 18 ([2007]: 67–106), Ross's rejoinder in *BDD* 19 ([2008]: 93–123), and Frimer's reply (ibid., 125–126).

2   On the question of the authorship of the prayer for the State of Israel, there has been a great deal of controversy. Some suggested Agnon, others Rabbi Herzog, still others Rabbi Uziel. See the articles by M. Hovav in *Ha-Tzofeh* (11/10/02) and Shaul Schiff (ibid., 18/10/02), etc.

However, most recently Yoel Rappel published an article (*Makor Rishon*, 19/9/2008, *Shabbat* 6–7), proving most assertively and convincingly that it was

(other than on Jerusalem Day). Some of those who live in Israel recite in the Grace after Meals: הרחמן הוא ... יוליכנו קוממיות בארצנו, and not לארצנו – "May the Merciful One . . . lead us upright *in* our land," rather than "*to* our land."[3] Others have expressed the unsuitability of the formulation of the *Nahem* prayer, which is recited in the afternoon prayer on the Ninth of Av: ואת העיר האבלה והחרבה והבזויה והשוממה – "the city [i.e., Jerusalem] in mourning, in ruins, defiled and empty" (i.e., a ruined ghost town), in view of the radical historical changes that have altered the face of modern-day Jerusalem.[4] Further examples could be given.[5]

Rabbi Herzog who composed the prayer and that Agnon made only the most minor editorial changes. He also lists several earlier attempts by various rabbis to formulate such a prayer. He states that his book on this subject will appear shortly.

3   This change appears in *Ha-Siddur ha-Meduyak* (see below app. 2), and apparently was first introduced by R. Shlomo Goren, the Chief Rabbi of Israel. Needless to say, this emendation was also bitterly attacked in the pamphlet *Kovetz li-Gedor-Peretz*, 42 (app. 3).

Furthermore, in *Kuntres Ish Matzliah*, published in *Va-Yaan Shmuel* (vol. 3, 2000, 332) the author points out that this is the version found in R. Moshe Hagiz's manuscript responsum, cited by R. Hayyim Sithon, in his *Eretz Hayyim*, sec. 60, who writes that R. Moshe ben Haviv also had this version. So, too, is R. Yaakov Hagiz's *Halachot Ketanot* (vol. 1, sec. 185). Hence, this version has a fine pedigree indeed.

4   See app. 2.

5   I should like to quote from Rabbi Jules Harlow's essay. "The *Siddur* and the Contemporary Community" (in *Prayer in Judaism: Continuity and Change*, edited by G. H. Cohen and H. Fish, 203. Nashville, New Jersey and London: 1996):

A concern for contemporary relevance is not something invented only with the appearance of these booklets [i.e., the 175 booklets containing experimental services and readings, from Reform and Conservative congregations in the United States that he collected; see ibid., 201]. If you will consider prayer books published with English translations in the United States in this century, including the Sabbath and Festival *Prayerbook* published for the Orthodox Rabbinical Council of America in 1960 and edited by Rabbi David De Sola Pool, you will see that they contain supplementary prayers, usually set up as responsive readings, on various topical subjects of general as well as Jewish concern. Such readings are generally found collected at the end of the book, or at the end of sections. The booklets are different, however, in that their compilers obviously feel that the new material should be integral to the fabric of a service, that you should not have to look to the back of the book for the relevant readings, that they are part of the service itself.

I would like to run through some of the most popular themes in the new

Indeed, there seems to be evidence for the legitimacy of such change in a passage in the Talmud (BT *Yoma* 69b):

> R. Yehoshua ben Levi said: Why were they called *Anshei Kenesset ha-Gedolah* (Men of the Great Assembly)? For they returned the crown to its erstwhile [glory]. Moses came and said, "God, the great, the mighty, and the awesome (Deut. 10:17). Came Jeremiah and said, "Gentiles are cackling in His holy sanctuary. Where is His awesomeness?" He did not say "awesome." Came Daniel and said, "Gentiles are subjugating His children. Where is His might?" He did not say "mighty." Then they came and said, "On the contrary, this is the strength of His mightiness: that he overcomes His inclinations and shows prolonged mercy to the wicked. It is His awesomeness, for were it not for His awesome nature, how could a single people survive among the nations?"

The meaning is that they reinstated Moses's original formulations. Surely from here we may learn that at certain times, changes in the liturgy could be

---

material: *Self-understanding*. Often found as a sort of *kavvanah*, or devotional introduction to a service. *Brotherhood*. This reflects the situation in the United States, not so much at this moment, but certainly in previous years. There were a number of readings on brotherhood, trying to reflect the fact that black and white, rich and poor, are brothers. *Democracy*. All men are created equal. *Ghettoes*. Interestingly, in the United States these days, ghetto does not mean a place where Jews live. And whenever the word appears in these booklets, as in the newspapers, it refers to the "black ghettoes." *Poverty. Love. Holiness. Pollution*. Ecology and pollution are very much on the minds of children and adults. The threat of ecological disaster is more real for them than the threat of extinction by a crusade. Concern over and reaction to pollution articulates something that people feel. *War*. Especially the war in Vietnam. *Peace. Violence*.

For more strictly Jewish themes: Soviet Jewry, Jews in Arab lands, Israel, Jerusalem, the Six Day War, the Holocaust, and Jewish commitment head the list.

We may, for example call attention to the addition found in the Conservative *siddur*, *Sim Shalom* (New York: 1989), 414–415, in the *mi-she-berach* after the Torah reading on Shabbat, which has:

| And all who devotedly involve themselves with the needs of this community *and the Land of Israel*. | וכל מי שעוסקים בצרכי צבור ובבנין ארץ ישראל באמונה... |

See the introduction by the editor, Rabbi Jules Harlow, ibid., xxii.

and were made (albeit by prophets, according to this passage) in view of the contemporary circumstances.[6]

On the other hand, there is a commonly accepted notion that one may not make any change in our standard liturgy. This notion was very clearly and forcefully articulated by Rabbi Hirz Scheur, rabbi of Minz, in his letter, which was printed in *Eleh divrei ha-brit* (These Are the Words of the Covenant), a document published by order of the Orthodox Community of Hamburg, in Altona in 1819:

> No changes in prayers are permitted. This pertains not merely to prayers established more than two thousand years ago by the Men of the Great Assembly, but also to later traditional prayers of Ashkenazim and Sefaradim. By the least change, the originally intended meaning would be altered . . . . Changing the content and text of our prayers *is the worst aberration from the Jewish faith* [emphasis mine – D. S.], since the regular prayers constitute our basic service in place of the sacrifices. Changing the prayers would split Judaism into two religions.[7]

---

6   See R. Hayyim Navon's remarks on this passage in *Tzohar* 32 (2008): 58. Some great scholars did indeed suggest radical changes in their prayers. Thus, R. Yehiel Michel Epstein, in his work *Aruch ha-Shulhan, Orah Hayyim* 425:2, writes:

> Know that I have always questioned our version as it appears in *Ata yatzarta* (from the *mussaf* prayer of Shabbat Rosh Hodesh), in which after the phrase למחילת עון one says: ושבת קדשך . . . כי בעמך ישראל בחרת, etc. Why does one not say: קדשנו במצותיך ותן חלקנו בתורתך . . . והנחילנו . . . וינוחו בו ישראל מקדשי שמך . . . , continuing: כי בעמך ישראל. For surely on every festival that falls on Shabbat, and so on Rosh ha-Shanah and Yom ha-Kippurim that fall on Shabbat, we recite this text, which is the essence of *kedushat Shabbat*, at the end of the middle benediction, and why should we not recite it on Rosh Hodesh that falls on Shabbat? In the Sefardi version, this indeed is the version. In my opinion, this is missing from the Ashkenazic editions, and I am accustomed to saying it, for I see no reason not to do so. But I have found no one who commented on this issue.

> In other words, this great authority wished to add some twenty-five words to the commonly accepted version!

> See further in the discussion, and an explanation for this "lacuna," in *Mavo le-Siddur Maharsha* by R. Yitzhak Satz (Baltimore: 2002, 464–478).

7   I have followed the translations of Alexander Guttmann, in his *The Struggle over Reform in Rabbinic Literature during the Last Century and a Half* (Jerusalem and New York: 1977, 210–211).

This notion was reiterated in varying formulations in several other statements by prominent Orthodox leaders that were also published in *Eleh Divrei
ha-Brit*.[8] One rabbi whose statements were published was R. Jacob of Lissa,
who maintained, inter alia, that "changing the versions [i.e., the text of the
prayers] is bitter poison,"[9] and in the various responsa of the Hatam Sofer
and R. Moshe Shik.[10] However, we should remember that such statements
were made in response and opposition to the newly emerging Reform movement, which sought to excise any mention of the coming of the Messiah, the
return to the Land of Israel, the reestablishment of the Temple service as it was
conducted in ancient times, and so on. The vehemence of their style is ample
testimony to their strong opposition to these trends.[11]

This attitude may be found in the writings of the early geonim of
Babylonia. Thus we find in a manuscript version of the work *Shibolei ha-leket*
(ms. Oxford 659, published by I. Ta-Shma in *Tarbiz* 53/2 [1984]: 287–288)
in which Rabbi Natronai ben Rabbi Hilai, head of the Academy at Mata
Mehasia, writes as follows:

You have asked concerning *hazanim* who appear to be punctilious [in their liturgy], and delete and add to the version which the sages estab-lished, and make changes. Thus have we seen: that what they do is not seemly in that they change the custom of the two Yeshivot [i.e., Sura and Pumbedita] and all Israel. And their exami-nation (*iyyun*) [of the text] is worthless.	וששאלתם חזנין שנראין כאילו מדקדקין, וגורעין ומוסיפין על מטבע שטבעו חכמים, ומשנים. כך ראינו, שלא יפה הם עושים שמשנים מנהג של שתי ישיבות וכל ישראל. ועיון שלהם – לא כלום הם מעיינים. חזנים אלו גורעין ומוסיפין ומשנים, ועם כל זה הם נראין כאילו הם מדקדקין.

Even more radical is the statement we find cited by Rabbi Yohanan b.
R. Reuven of Ochride in his commentary to the *Sheiltot* (*Parshat Yitro*, ed.
Mirsky, Exodus, Jerusalem: 1964, 140):

Said R. Amram [Gaon, author of the great *Siddur Rav Amram Gaon*]: Said Rav Nahshon in the Academy: In all places that have rabbis, we make no	וכן אמר רב עמרם ז"ל: אמר רב נחשון במתיבתא, בכל אתר דאיכא רבנ' לא משנינן כלל

---

8   Ibid., 209–233.
9   Ibid., 227.
10 Ibid., 242 et seq.
11 Guttmann, *passim*.

changes in the prayers established by the sages, nor do we introduce into the synagogue a *hazan* who knows [i.e., who inserts into the liturgy] *piyyut*. The members of a synagogue in which *piyyutim* are recited demonstrate thereby that they are unlearned. Rav Amram said: We do not change that which the sages in the Talmud said [be it in the weekday (liturgy) or on the festivals]. If we find ourselves in a place where the *hazan* recites something that does not accord with the text established by the sages, we remove him. Rav Zemah, a great judge and cantor, [said:] Whoever adds to the text established by the sages in the liturgy and lengthens the prayer (*marbeh be-devarim*) should be excommunicated, and must be removed.

מתפילות דרתקינו רבנן, ולא אמרי' פיוט, ואין מכניסין לבית הכנסת חזן שיודע פיוט. ובירת כנסת שאומרין פיוט מעידין עצמן שאינן תלמידי חכמים. ואמר רב עמרם: אין אנו משנים על מה שאמרו חכמים בתלמוד [בין בחול] בין ביו"ט, ורא'י [אק] לעינן לאתרא דאמר חזן מאי דלא דמי למטבע שטבעו חכמים מסלקינן ליה. ורב צמח דייאנא רבא שליח ציבור שמוסיף על מטבע שטבעו חכמים בתפילה ומרבה דברים בר נידוי, ומתבעי לעבוריה.

(See below, and in Appendix 5, on the issue of the insertion of *piyyutim*.)

This, then, is the position of the Babylonian geonim, as opposed to that of the contemporary Palestinian authorities, who allowed and practiced greater flexibility in changing formulations and modulating the liturgy, as we shall see below. (For an in-depth analysis of the issue of inserting *piyyutim* in the body of the liturgy, see Yitzhak Shilat, *Rosh devarecha* [Maaleh Adumim: 1996, 241–256].)

It is interesting to find a similar position in the second half of the twentieth century, though for a completely different reason. Apparently, this was the position of Rabbi Yosef Dov Soloveitchik, as expounded by David Hartman in his work *A Living Covenant: The Innovative Spirit in Traditional Judaism* (New York and London: 1985). Because of the importance of this discussion, I shall cite Hartman's analysis in extenso (145–147):

> According to Soloveitchik, it is because human beings are so insignificant and helpless before God that they are dependent upon precedent in order to dare to pray at all. For that reason, Soloveitchik considers it impossible to make the slightest change today in the forms of prayer. This not only excludes the innovations introduced in Reform Jewish worship, but even *tefillat nedavah* – spontaneous voluntary prayer. The three fixed daily prayers, in the morning, the afternoon, and the evening, are all that are permitted to a Jew.
>
> Since it is only the distant past that legitimates prayer today, there must be

absolute commitment and conformity to the prayer forms of the tradition. In utilizing the fixed forms of the tradition, I admit my own unworthiness to pray. The words of the prayer book are a gift of the tradition – I pray because my ancestors prayed. My thoughts and feelings are sacrificed on the altar through my voluntary renunciation of the possibility of introducing new prayers. By submitting to the prayer forms that the tradition has given me, I both acknowledge the absolute urgency to stand in prayer before God and confess my sense of personal unworthiness to do so.

Soloveitchik does not portray the absolute authority of *halakhah* as enslavement to tradition or as crushing human poetic passion and creativity. The willing renunciation of innovative or spontaneous prayer expresses the heroic self-sacrificial feature of Soloveitchik's dialectical anthropology. Jews submit to the halakhic form of prayer because of the existential terror that finite man feels before the infinite God, not because Judaism enslaves one to the past ....

... In *Ra'ayonot al ha-tefillah*, [he writes:] "There is no place for *tefillat nedavah* in Soloveitchik's approach to prayer. *Nedavah*, the free, spontaneous gift, would presuppose that God is easily approachable. Only one who feels welcome to stand before God could look upon *tefillat nedavah* as a legitimate form of prayer. For Soloveitchik, however, there is no one alive today who is qualified to act in that spirit. As individuals with their own particular religious longings, Jews have not been able to pray for centuries. They can pray only collectively as the children's children of the patriarchs, whose unique ability to initiate prayer was consolidated by the scribes and sages of the tradition. Only within the ordered framework of ritual prayer is one given the legitimacy to express petitional needs. Any outpouring of the soul that is not grounded in total subordination to the liturgical form of the Amidah must be viewed as egocentric expressions by an arrogant individual who has forgotten that prayer is a gift from the tradition and not a normal expression of covenantal consciousness.

If it is not within the worshiper's ability to present before God the whole arrangement of the prayer in its original formulation, to arrange the praise of the Lord and to request permission for his daring approach, to recall the merit of the patriarchs and also the gracious deeds of the Holy One, blessed be He, Who is responsive to the needs of all creatures – the worshiper does not have permission to ask for his own needs. An egoistic supplication which falls outside the form of prayer that was instituted by the men of the Great Assembly is forbidden.

Soloveitchik's covenantal man sees himself as able to stand before God exclusively because he is a remote descendant of those who received the Torah

at Sinai. In his view, the covenantal community, which extends across the generations, redeems the individual Jew from an existence that is fundamentally worthless and empty of significance. It keeps us from being overwhelmed and crushed by a divine reality that seems to repulse human beings and negate their right to approach God in prayer. According to Soloveitchik, we must use the absolutely immutable forms of Judaic prayer because we can pray only as tiny components of a vast historical drama, not as contemporary individuals with our own sentiments and concerns. If we dare step outside the fixed structure and language of prayer handed down by the tradition, we lose the right to speak. Of course, the question is which "tradition" we must follow.

Hartman, in his subsequent discussion, or rather critique, of Soloveitchik's position, completely rejects this approach to prayer (ibid., 151–159), encouraging spontaneity within structure and what he calls *kavvanat ha-lev*, as opposed to *kavvanah latzet* – prayer that expresses a personal relationship rather than prayer that is recited merely out of a sense of duty (165–170).

This study will attempt to examine the possible parameters of change in the liturgy within the framework of normative halachic thinking, drawing upon classical sources and rabbinic precedents, and viewing the evolution of our liturgy in its historical perspective.[12]

---

12 This study deals with rabbinic liturgy mostly from the destruction of the Second Temple onwards. It does not touch upon biblical prayer, intertestamental-apocryptal liturgic evidence or Qumranic liturgy. There is a considerable body of scholarly literature on these subjects, but I do not feel it is germane to our thesis. See, for example, the fine study of Daniel K. Falk, *Daily, Sabbath, and Festival Prayers in the Dead Sea Scrolls* (Leiden, Boston, Köln: 1998), especially his introduction (1–9). Thus, Ezra Fleischer, for example, argued forcefully that in the generation after the destruction of the Second Temple, Rabban Gamliel II introduced without precedent the novel institution of prayer as obligatory for individuals and as service to God for the community, together with fixed formulations for the central components of the synagogue liturgy (ibid., 3, referring to E. Fleischer, "On the Beginnings of Obligatory Jewish Prayer." *Tarbiz* 59 [1990]: 397–401, 414–415, 426–427). Falk (5) also quotes S. Reif, *Judaism and Hebrew Prayer: New Perspectives on Jewish Liturgical History* (Cambridge: 1993, 66) as follows:

> The situation at Qumran, at least physically separated from worship, prayer, praise and benediction were in the process of merging. The question that has yet to be asked, let alone answered, is whether that process is to be understood

꿈

This book began as a lecture given at a conference of the Jewish Orthodox Feminist Alliance (JOFA) on Feb. 11, 2007. The lecture was recorded and then transcribed. I edited it, and the end-product was put on the JOFA website under the title "Our Dialogue with God: Tradition and Innovation."

When I later reread my own words, I realized that there was a great deal more to say on the subject. Over the years, I had dealt with numerous liturgical questions, as will be evident from even the most cursory perusal of my eight volumes of *Minhagei Yisrael* (Jerusalem: 1989–2007). I was most fortunate to have had very close personal relationships with three of the foremost authorities on liturgical history of the last half-century, all of whom are unfortunately no longer with us: Prof. Ezra Fleischer, Prof. Josef Heinemann, and Prof. Naftali Wieder. My debt to them is greater than may be apparent from references in the footnotes. From them, as also from my own studies,

---

as a unique feature of the way of life represented at Qumran, which was later adopted and adapted by the rabbinic inheritors of Jewish religious practice, or as an example of popular liturgical piety that was common to various Pharisaic and Essenic groups and subsequently survived in the tannaitic traditions.

He then adds:

Here, Reif has put his finger on the key issue: not just whether individual prayers originated in a secluded sect or not – a question which is being asked more frequently in recent years – but whether the system of formal communal liturgy reflects a wider phenomenon in the Second Temple period. Uncertainty on this question has lent itself to uncertainty about the relevance of the Dead Sea Scrolls for the history of Jewish prayer.

See also his discussion (ibid., 73–75) in *Tahanunim* in the *Words of the Luminaries* (DJD 7 [1982]: 168–175) and our *Tahanun* (which we have discussed below in "Recommended Changes" ad fin.). Some scholars saw numerous parallels between them, while others felt it unnecessary to posit any direct relationship, rather explaining that they both make use of common themes found in biblical scrypticatory texts (e.g., E. Chazon, "A Liturgical Document from Qumran and Its Implications: Words of the Luminaries." 4QDibNani, Hebrew University Dissertation, 1991, 109–112). For my part, I do not enter into the very interesting discussions, which I feel are not relevant to the central message of this study.

I became keenly aware of the extreme complexity of the textual history and nature of our liturgy. Already in 1989, in the introduction to the first volume of *Minhagei Yisrael* (page 13), I noted that there was, thus far, not even a preliminary bibliography of all liturgical literature, *siddurim* and *mahzorim* both in print as well as in manuscript (see ibid., n. 8). Since then much important work has been done, such as J. Tabory's "Jewish Prayer and the Yearly Cycle: A List of Articles" (*Kiryat Sefer*, Supplement to vol. 64, 1922–1993), and J. Tabory and M. Raffeld's bibliography in the booklet they published in 1994, entitled *Siddur Hanau* (1628); and of course Yeshayahu Vinograd's invaluable *Thesaurus of the Hebrew Book* (Jerusalem: 1995), which in the first volume has two indices to liturgical literature (343–376). A great deal of work has also been done in the areas of textual and historical research, as well as through the publication of a number of important editions of classical prayer books. Needless to say I have benefited greatly from all these valuable resources.

Nonetheless, much basic research is still to be done, such as clear, but detailed guides to the standard prayer books, with historical introductions to each section, discussions on their halachic status, clarifications of the various versions, explanations for customs and laws relating to the various prayers, such as when and why one stands, when and why one bows, stepping backwards and onwards, taking little jumps, what one says silently, what out aloud, what the cantor repeats and what not, when is it sufficient to hear the cantor's recitation, and when one must recite things on one's own, what is private prayer, what is communal, when and where may one add one's own personal prayers into the body of the standard text, etc. Textual groundwork for some of these requirements is being done by Prof. Yonah Fraenkel, in his preparation for a critical edition of the *siddur Nusah Ashkenaz*, which promises to be a work of outstanding importance.

I have been a communal rabbi here in Jerusalem for over four decades. Nonetheless, I never served as a *hazzan*, a *sheliah tzibbur*. And the main reason for that is that, because of my knowledge of the complex variety of versions, and their rationale, I was never quite sure of my own *nusah*, and often stumbled even when reading a standard prayer book. Perhaps this is what the great Sanzer Rebbe, Rabbi Yekutiel Yehudah Halberstam of Sanz-Klausenburg,

meant when he reportedly said that he wanted to establish a fixed text for the
Amidah, listened carefully to his father's recitation of it and recorded each
benediction in faithful detail. However, he was astounded when he heard a
completely different version several days later, and after a few times realized
that the versions changed each time. So finally, he accepted for himself versions of the Shinyever Rebbe, which was in accordance with *Nusah Ashkenaz*.
And he continued:

> I was delighted when I found in *Shaar ha-Kavvanot* (59a), and in the early
> authorities that no one day has been identical to the next since the creation of
> the world, and the version of the prayer (נוסח התפילה) changes every day, and
> on each day for each prayer. There is a different version of *shaharit*, *minhah*
> and *aravit* . . . .
>
> See *Sefer halichot hayyim: hilchot ve-halichot mi-Maran*
> *mi-Sanz, seder ha-yom* (edited by A. Y. Kluger, 146–148,
> introduction 10–11, 146–148, 2008).

He added that this is how he understood the Mishnah (Avot 2:13) which
states:

> אל תעש תפילתך קבע – "Do not make your prayer a fixed form," meaning: You
> cannot pray in a fixed formulation, for there is no fixed formulary, since it con-
> stantly changes . . . .

In view of all of the above, I decided to expand my original article, seeking to demonstrate convincingly the complexity, fluidity and variety in our
liturgy, and to discuss the possible parameters of change, be it in additions,
deletions, alterations, and/or corrections, so as to reflect the contemporary
situation and its sensitivities. And hopefully this will stimulate thought and
discussion and lead to a deeper appreciation of the nature of our liturgy, and
an ability to find greater meaning in our prayer.

Here I would like to express my sincere thanks to Mrs. Esther Drenger,
who with care, loyalty and great perseverance prepared this manuscript, suffering silently my never-ending changes and additions, and finally producing
a clean copy. I owe an undying debt of gratitude to my dear deceased par-
ents, who imbued in me the love of learning and the spirit of prayer, and to
my paternal grandparents, whose great wisdom and deep but simple faith

left a permanent mark on my way of thinking. My parents-in-law, Nana and Papa, have been a constant source of encouragement, and merit my deepest appreciation.

And finally my immeasurable thanks to my dear wife, Chana, for her unflagging love and support, without which none of this would have been possible.

—Daniel Sperber
Jerusalem, 2010

I

The Complexity of the Hebrew Prayer Book

The Hebrew prayer book (*siddur*) is probably the most complex, and perhaps the least researched, book in rabbinic literature[1] – there is as yet no full

---

1   The best introduction to the history of the Hebrew prayer book is Ismar Elbogen's
    Ha-tefillah be-Yisrael be-hitpathutah ha-historit (translated from the original
    German, Leipzig: 1913; edited by Y. Amir, and revised and updated by J. Heinemann,
    Tel Aviv, 1971). A useful addition to it is Stefan C. Reif's *Judaism and Hebrew Prayer:
    New Perspectives on Jewish Liturgical History* (Cambridge: 1993). Invaluable infor-
    mation may be found in N. Wieder's *Hitgabshut nusah ha-tefillah ba-mizrah u-va-
    maarav* (*The Formation of the Jewish Liturgy in the East and the West*) (two vol-
    umes, Jerusalem, 1998). Partial Hebrew bibliographies on studies of prayer were
    published by J. Tabory in *Areshet* 4 (1984): 101–112; ibid., 5 (1985): 85–112; idem,
    Siddur Hanau, 1628 (with Meir Raffeld; Bar-Ilan University, 1994), with a fine
    characterization of the literary complexity of the *siddur*, and also 55–86 ibid., and
    in *Kiryat Sefer* – Supplement to vol. 64 (1991–1993) for a bibliography of articles
    on liturgy and festivals (by Tabory). A good overview of the history of the *siddur*
    may be found in S. Tal, *Ha-siddur be-hishtalsheluto* (Jerusalem: 1985), 1–34. For the
    history of the printed prayer book from the first edition (Prague: 1513) to Z. W.
    Heidenheim's edition (Rödelheim: 1813), see A. Berliner, "*He'arot al ha-siddur*," in
    his *Ketavim Nivharim*, vol. 1 (Jerusalem: 1945). The classic works of L. Zunz, *Die
    Ritus des Synagogalen Gottesdienste Geschichlich entwickelts* (Berlin: 1919), and *Die
    Synagogale Poesie des Mittelalters* (edited by A. Freimann, Frankfurt am Main: 1920),
    are still invaluable. We should also mention the valuable book by Levi Yerahmiel
    Klatzki, *Erech Tefillah* (Warsaw: 1868), which contains much valuable material and
    original insights.
         It is a little odd to read in the preface to *The Story of the Prayer Book* (by Philip
    Arian and Azriel Eisenberg, Hartford: 1968), the following: "Strange as it may seem,
    there has been up to now no single volume in any language on the development of
    Jewish Liturgy through the ages."
         Elbogen's classic was published in 1913, and Zunz's works first appeared even

bibliography of *siddurim* and *mahzorim* in manuscript and print![2] Its multitude of layers come from different periods, which are often interwoven one within another: verses and passages from all sections of the Bible, notably the Book of Psalms, alongside formulations by the rabbis of the Second Temple period, passages from the Mishnah, the Talmud, the geonim, the rishonim, the kabbalists of Safed and even portions from the nineteenth, twentieth and possibly twenty-first centuries. Although it is often difficult to unravel the intertwining strands, certain passages can be dated approximately.[3]

Thus, some clearly identifiable portions date from the latter part of the Second Temple period. Other passages date from the period of the Mishna – in other words, the first two centuries of the Common Era, and the Talmud. Still other portions date from the following three centuries of the Common

---

earlier (Berlin: 1831). And Abraham Idelsohn's *Jewish Liturgy and its Development* first appeared in New York in 1932.

2   See my remarks in *Minhagei Yisrael* 1 (Jerusalem: 1989), 13, n. 8.

3   Jacob J. Petuchowski, at the beginning of his *Prayerbook Reform in Europe: The Liturgy of European Liberal and Reform Judaism* (New York: 1968, 23), has a fine formulation describing this situation:

> Biblical psalmists, Pharisaic interpreters, Rabbinic sages, medieval bards, commentators and philosophers, and more recent mystics and poets – all had their share in the formation of the *siddur*. Moreover, the existence of various rites – such as the Sepharadi, the Ashkenazi, the Italiani, the Yemenite, etc. – within the Tradition itself testifies to the important role played by local needs as well as by local talent. Yet all of the rites, with all their divergences and unique minhagim (local customs), have enough basic material in common to be recognizable as mere varieties of the same fundamental structure of Jewish prayer which was laid down in Mishnah and Gemara, and formalized in the Geonic period.

The complexity of the texts may in some way be appreciated by examining closely the varying versions cited in R. Aryeh Leib Gordon's pioneering *Otzar ha-Tefillot* (Vilna: 1915, in two versions, *Nusah Ashkenaz* and *Nusah Sefarad*), with its supercommentaries and notations, *Iyyun Tefillah and Tikkun Tefillah*, and in the magnificent commentary on parts of the *siddur* by R. Menachem Mendel Hayyim Landau and R. Yaakov Verdiger, in Verdiger's *Tzelota de-Avraham*, vol. 1 (Tel Aviv: no date, but probably 1957), vol. 2 (Tel Aviv: 1961). This unfinished oeuvre, which covered the weekday services and some additional issues, benedictions, etc., has been continued by R. Yaakov Verdiger's son, R. Avraham Verdiger, on the basis of his father's notes covering part of the Sabbath service, in three additional volumes (Jerusalem: 1991–1993). However, these latter volumes are more in the nature of collecteana than developmental analysis.

Era; the period of the *geonim*; additions and accretions that occurred in the time of the Baalei ha-Tosafot; and, of course, numerous additions from the period of the kabbalists of Safed – namely, the latter part of the sixteenth century, such as the whole of the *Kabbalat Shabbat* prayer service on Friday night that includes psalms and other sections.[4] As we go along, we can see that additional prayers were added[5] in the seventeenth, eighteenth and nineteenth centuries. In addition, there are whole sections, small additions within existing prayers, and changes in accordance with what was deemed necessary in specific times or in a specific place. There are also prayers that were penned in the last sixty years or so, such as the Prayer for the State of Israel, the Prayer for Soldiers of the Israel Defense Forces, the prayer for the Royal Family in Britain, the prayers for the government in the United States, and some beautiful prayers that were composed within the past few months for the missing soldiers, the three soldiers abducted prior to the Second Lebanon War.

Chief Rabbi Sir Jonathan Sacks, in his introduction to the new *Authorised Daily Prayer Book* (fourth edition, London: 2006, 81), expressed the above most eloquently, even lyrically:

> The Siddur is the choral symphony the covenantal people has sung to God across forty centuries from the days of the patriarchs until present day. In it we hear the voices of Israel's prophets, priests and kings, its Sages and scholars, poets and philosophers, rationalists and mystics, singing in calibrated harmony. Its libretto weaves together texts from almost every part of the vast library of Jewish spirituality: Torah, the Prophets, the Writings, the classic compendia of the Oral Law – Mishnah, Midrash and Talmud – together with philosophical passages like Maimonides's Thirteen Principles of Faith and extracts from the *Zohar*, the key text of Jewish mysticism.

---

4   See I. J. Cohen's classic study, *Seder Kabbalat Shabbat u-Pizmon Lecha Dodi* (Jerusalem: 1969). Republished in his *Mekorot ve-Korot* (Jerusalem: 1982, 74–106); R. Kimelman. The Mystical Meaning of *Lekhah Dodi* and *Kabbalat Shabbat* (Jerusalem: 2003) (Hebrew).

5   Such as, for example, *Shaarei Tziyyon*, by Rabbi Natan Nata Hanover (ed. Princ. Prague: 1642) (*Tefillot ve-Tikkunim al pi Kitvei ha-Ari*), which has been republished over fifty times. In a similar genre, we find *Likkutei Tefillot*, based on the teachings of Rabbi Nachman of Braslav, edited by his disciple Rabbi Natan Sternhart (two volumes, Breslau: 1824–1827). There are innumerable examples of single prayers or collections of prayers written by rabbis both in the East and the West, a subject that requires further research and documentation.

2

The Constant Evolution of Our Liturgical Text

Thus, we see that our liturgy has always been evolving.[1] There was never a

---

1   It is of interest to note a classic example of the understanding of the dynamic of liturgical change. Norman Lamm, in his magisterial *The Religious Thought of Hassidism: Text and Commentary* (Hoboken, NJ: 1999, 197–198), cites a passage from R. Levi Yitzhak of Berdichev's *Kedushat Levi ha-Shalem* (Munkacz: 1939, reprint New York 1962), to *Parshat Va-Ethanan*, as follows:

> The Talmud (Berachot 4b, 9b) concludes that the words "God, open Thou my lips" [recited at the beginning of the *Amidah*] are not considered an interruption between [the benediction of] Redemption (*Geulah*) and the *Amidah* even during the Shaharit service, for inasmuch as the Rabbis decreed that it is to be recited, it is regarded as an extension of the Amidah. But then the [Talmud's] statement should have been, "The Rabbis decreed it as prayer." One must conclude that this phrase was not included in the original enactment [of the liturgical text] by the Men of the Great Assembly, and when its recitation was decreed later, it was regarded as an extension of the Amidah [rather than as part of the original enactment].
>
> Thus, "God, open Thou my lips" should be understood as a prayer for the ability to pray. The tannaim and their predecessors had no need to pray for this, for surely their prayers were pure. Only later, when "hearts diminished," did they feel compelled to add a prayer that our prayers [i.e., the prayers we are about to recite] should be pure.
>
> Hence there are two aspects to prayer: the prayer itself, and a prayer for the ability to pray [properly].

What R. Levi Yitzhak is saying is that originally, when people were pure, there was no need to invoke the ability to pray. But when "spirituality had so declined that it was difficult to sustain purity of intention in prayer" (Lamm, ibid., n. 89), it was necessary to add an additional opening verse. Even though this would appear to run counter to the rule of סמיכת גאולה לתפילה, that there should be no interruption

fixed text or a *tefillat keva* (a set liturgy) in which everything was fully formed so that no further changes could be introduced. Surely this is the meaning of R. Shimon's statement in *Avot* 2:13: "When you pray, do not make your prayer in a fixed form (*al taas tefillatecha keva*), but [a plea for] mercies and supplications before the Lord . . . ."

Let me give some examples just to demonstrate the degree to which our liturgy was in a state of flux even in the eighth and ninth centuries of the Common Era. We are all familiar with the daily *Amidah* prayer. Let us look at three examples of *berachot* (benedictions) with which we are certainly acquainted. I shall cite different versions from Eretz Yisrael during the geonic period.[2]

Hear our voice, O Lord our God. Have compassion on us and accept our prayers with mercy. Blessed are You, O Lord, Who hears prayer.	שמע קולנו ד'י א־לוהינו ורחם עלינו וקבל בר־חמים א־ת תפילתינו. בא"י שומע תפילה.

That is very close to what we normally say in the Ashkenazic *nusah* (liturgy).

Please listen to us and please hear our prayers. Have compassion on us and please carry out what we have requested because You are compassionate and merciful. Blessed are You, O Lord, Who hears prayer.	שמע בקולנו ושמע תפילתינו ורחם עלינו ועשה מ־הרה בקשתינו כי א־ל חנון ורחום אתה. בא"י שומע תפילה.

This version has been expanded, with additional sections in it, and it certainly is not identical to the first version that we just read.

Hear our voice, O Lord our God. Have pity and compassion upon us and accept our prayers with mercy, for You are a God who listens to prayers and entreaties. Blessed are You, O Lord, Who hears prayer.	שמע קולינו, ד'י א־לו־ד־ינו, וחוס ורחם עלינו, וקבל בר־חמים את תפילתינו, כי א־ל שומע תפילתינו ותחנונינו אר־תה. בא"י שומע תפילה.

---

between *Geulah*, the last benediction before the *Amidah*, and *Tefillah*, the *Amidah* itself. This implies that changing needs require and justify textual modifications. See also R. Hayyim Navon's remarks on this passage in *Tzohar* 32 (2008): 58.

2　See Y. Luger, *Tefillat ha-Amidah le-hol al pi ha-Genizah ha-Kahirit* (Jerusalem: 2001), 167, 135, 105–106, and his detailed discussions following the text and apparatus. On the Palestinian liturgy as revealed in the Cairo Geniza in general, see E. Fleischer, *Eretz-Israel Prayer and Prayer Rituals as Portrayed in the Geniza Documents* (Jerusalem: 1988) (Hebrew).

This latter prayer is fairly close to the so-called *Nusah Sefarad* (the Sefaradic version used by Ashkenazic Jews).

Hear our voice, O Lord, our God. Have pity on us and show mercy toward us. Receive with compassion our prayers, which we hope will find favor in Your eyes, because You are a God who listens to prayers and entreaties. Please do not turn us away empty-handed, for You are a father who is full of abundant compassion. Please listen to us, our King, as we recite our prayers before You, and please hear our moans, just as you heard the moans of our ancestors. Blessed are You, O Lord, Who hears prayer.

שמע קולנו, ה' אלודהינו.
חוס וחמול ורחם עלינו וקבל
ברחמים וברצון את תפילתינו.
כי אל שומע תפילות אתה
ותחנונינו אתה וריקם מלפניך
אל תשיבנו כי אב מלא רחמים
רבים ארתה והעתר לנו מלכינו
בתפילותינו ושמע נאקרתינו
כאשר שמערת את נאקת
אבותינו. בא"י שומע תפילה.

Here we have a version that is much longer than the one most of us have probably heard and that is very similar to the Sefardic version. So we can see that even in this simple *berachah* (benediction), which is part of one of the most crystallized prayers, the *Amidah*, there has been a gradual process of expansion in different periods of time, and in different places. We will not go into the history of the evolution of this *berachah*, but it is sufficient to note that it has been expanded in a period that extends from the eighth to the thirteenth or fourteenth century. Perhaps a more significant example of an earlier *berachah* is the one concerning heretics *("ve-la-malshinim")*, called *birkat ha-minim* in early sources.[3] Again I will start with the shorter version.

---

3   See *Tzelota de-Avraham*, vol. 1 (290–294) for an extended examination of this benediction, including a version beginning *ve-la-kofrim*, "and the heretics or infidels,"
mentioned in *Magen Avraham* 126:1, in the name of the *Kenesset ha-Gedolah* by
R. Hayyim Benvenisti, sec. 118. See *Siddur . . . R. Shabtai Sofer*, vol. 1 (edited by
Y. Satz, 20, n. 15. Baltimore: 1987) and vol. 2 (Baltimore: 1994, note to 148, additions, 59). See further *Beer ha-Golah* by R. Judah Loew, the Maharal of Prague
(Warsaw 1838, 48ab), and R. A. Weiser's article, "*Nushaot ha-Tefillah*," *Ha-Maayan*
12/3 (1972): 35–36. Most recently, this benediction has been examined exhaustively
by Yaakov Y. Teppler in his book *Birkat ha-Minim* (Tübingen: 2007, in the series
Texts and Studies in Ancient Judaism 120), 9–124. Also see David Rokéah's discussion in his *Justin Martyr: Dialogue with Trypho the Jew*, translated from the Greek
with introduction and commentary (Jerusalem: 2004, 4–7) (Hebrew), on the issue of whether Justin makes reference to *birkat ha-minim*. See also the remark of
R. Hayyim Elazar Shapira, the Munkaczer Rav, in his work *Hamishah Maamarot*
(Beregsas: 1922, reprinted Jerusalem: 1981, 168) (in *Maamar Nusah ha-Tefillah*), on

This one, from the Cairo Geniza, dates from the sixth or seventh century and represents *Nusah Eretz Yisrael* (the Palestinian version):

May the apostate Jews have no hope and may the evil kingdom be uprooted quickly and be destroyed in our day. Blessed are You, O Lord, Who destroys evildoers and defeats villains.	למשומדים אל תהי תקוה ומלכות זדון מהרה תעקר ותשבר בימינו. בא"י שובר רשעים ומכניע זדים.

This is a very short version that refers to a specific situation, presumably that of individuals who converted to Christianity.

Another version:

May the apostate Jews have no hope if they do not return to Your Torah, may the Christians and heretics instantly perish, may the days of their lives be erased and may they not be counted among the righteous. Blessed are You, O Lord, Who defeats villains.	למשומדים אל תהי תקוה אם לא ישובו לתורתיך, הנוצרים והמינים כרגע יאבדו ימחו מספר חיים ועם צדיקים אל יכתבו. בא"י מכניע זדים.

Here we have the phrase "if they do not return to Your Torah" – that is, if they do not repent. Furthermore, both Christians and other heterodox people are included with a request that they "instantly perish, may the days of their lives be erased."

Here is yet another version:

May the apostate Jews have no hope, may the evil kingdom be uprooted quickly and be destroyed, and may you defeat it in our day. May the Christians and heretics instantly perish and may the enemies of Your people and those who are hostile to it be quickly sent to their deaths, and may You break the yoke of the Gentiles that weighs upon our bodies (necks?). Blessed are You, O Lord, Who destroys evildoers and defeats villains.	למשומדים אל תהי תקוה ומלכות זדון מהרה תעקר ותשבר ותכניע בימינו והנוצרים והמינים כרגע יאבדו וכל אויבי עמך וצורריהם מהרה יכרתו ושבור עול הגויים מעל צורינו (צוארינו?). בא"י שובר רשעים ומכניע זדים.

Once again we see that, at each stage in the development of this *beracha,* additions have been made. The original version started with *meshumadim*

the effect of the censors on this benediction. All of section 11 (164–171) on the *Amidah* is full of highly illuminating comments. Finally, see David Flusser, *Judaism of the Second Temple Period*, vol. 1 (Jerusalem: 2007, 70–118), a chapter entitled "4QMMT and the Benediction against the Minim."

(apostate Jews), and then *notzrim* (Christians) and *minim* (heretics) were added. Next, the phrase *oyvei amcha ve-tzorereihem* (the enemies of Your people and those are hostile to it) was introduced. Here again we see that, even in this *berachah,* which we consider to be a fully crystallized part of the *Amidah,* there has been a constant evolution. The early, brief text was expanded and at each stage, and in each region, in accordance with the particular sufferings of the Jews in a particular community, additional sections appeared. When the Jews felt that they were being persecuted, they spoke of *ve-chol oyvei* (and all the enemies of). (See also L. Ginzberg's discussion in his work, *A Commentary on the Palestinian Talmud,* vol. 3 [New York: 1941, 279–283] [Hebrew]), for a further discussion on this benediction.)

To give yet a third example, let us look at *birkat ha-shanim* (the blessing of the years).

1. Bless us, O Lord, in all our endeavors. Blessed are You, O Lord, Who blesses the years.

١. ברכינו, ה' א-להינו, בכל מעשה ידינו. בא"י מברך השנים.

2. Grant us this, O Lord: Bless this year so that it will be a good and blessed year. Bless it as You have blessed all the good years. Impart a blessing on our endeavors. Blessed are You, O Lord, Who blesses the years.

٢. ברכה עלינו, ה' א-להינו, את השנה הזאת לטובה ולברכה וברכה כשנים הטובות ותן ברכה במעשה ידינו. בא"י מברך השנים.

3. [Grant us this, O Lord] our God: Bless this year so that it will be a good year. Bless all its crops and quickly bring near the year of our redemption. Grant ... welcome rain and dew for the surface of the earth and grant that Your world will be satisfied with Your blessings. Blessed are You, O Lord, Who blesses the years.

٣. [ברך עלינו ה'] א-להינו השנה הזאת לטובה כל מיני תבואתה וקרב לנו מהרה שנת גאולתנו ותן ... וממטר וטל ברצון על פני האדמה ושבע עולמך מברכותיך. בא"י מברך השנים.

4. [Grant us this, O Lord our God: Bless this year so that it will be a good year. Bless all its crops] and grant dew and rain for the surface of the earth for the sake of Your name, and grant that the entire world will be satisfied with the blessings of Your bounty. Saturate the surface of the world with the wealth of the gifts of Your hands. Guard and save this year, O Lord, from all kinds of destroyers, from all kinds of

٤. [ברך עלינו ה' א-להינו את השנה הזאת לטובה ואת כל מיני תבואתה] ותן טל ומטר על פני האדמה למען שמך ושבע את העולם כולו מברכות טובך ורוה פני תבל מעושר מתנות ידיך ושמרה והצילה ה' אלקינו את השנה הזאת מכל מיני משחית

disasters. Treat us and all the fruits of this year with pity, mercy and compassion. May the year end in abundance, peace and a blessing like the blessing of all the good years. Bless all our endeavors because You are a good God Who grants good things to others. Blessed are You, O Lord, Who blesses the years.

מכל מיני פור—ענות וחום וחמול ורחם עלינו ועל כל פרותיה ותהא לאחריתה שבע ושל—ום וברכה כברכת השנים הטובות ותן ברכה במעשה ידינו כי א-ל טוב ומטיב אתה. בא"י מברך השנים.

5. Grant us this, O Lord our God, this year and all kinds of its crops that they be good, and grant dew and rain for a blessing upon all the earth. Saturate the surface of the world, and grant that the whole world will be satisfied with Your bounty. And fill Yourself with good hope and an ending in peace, and have mercy upon us and upon all crops and fruit, and blessing for bounteous rains. And may its end be one of life, satisfaction and peace as the years of good and blessing. For you are a good God who grants good things and blesses the years. Blessed are You, O Lord, Who blesses the years.

5. ברך עלינו ה' א-להינו את השנ—ה הזאת ואת כל—ל מיני תבואתה לטובה, ותן טל ומטר לברכה על כל פני ד—אדמה ורוה פני תבל ושבע את העולם כולו מטובך, ומל—א לך תקוד—ה טובה ואחרית שלו—ם, ורחם עליה ועל כל—ל תבואתה ופיד—ותיה, וברכה בגשמי רצון ונדבה, ורהי אחרית—ה חיים ושבע ושל—ום כשנים הטובות לברכה, כי קל טוב ומטיב אתה ומברך השנים. בא"י מברך השנים.

(See Y. Tzuberi, *Siddur Kenesset ha-Gedolah*, vol. 1 [Tel Aviv: 1976, 113–118], for the Yemenite versions. Tzuberi cites many early sources for the component parts of this expanded composite version.)

Again, even in what we would regard as one of our standard liturgical texts, which we think of as having been crystallized at the time of Simon Hafakuli (according to BT *Megillah* 17b, in the Tannaitic period), we see, nevertheless, that it was altered and that it evolved, resulting in several different versions. Hence the differences between the Ashkenazic version, the Sefardic version, *nusah Edot ha-Mizrah* (the version used by Oriental Jews) and the Yemenite version, among others.

If we could somehow enter a Palestinian synagogue of the geonic period, we would surely feel lost, since we would not recognize the liturgy. Thus, during a Friday night service, instead of the familiar *hashkivenu* prayer, we would hear something like this:[4]

---

4 According to A. I. Schechter (*Studies in Jewish Liturgy*, Philadelphia: 1930, 105), this is only said on weekdays because on the Sabbath we are protected from evil

We shall lie down with Your benevolence and awaken to and be satisfied with Your faithfulness, and fear and affliction and Satan shall not have sovereignty over us during the nights, as is it stated, "When you lie down, you shall not be afraid. You shall lie down, and your sleep shall be sweet" (Proverbs 3:24). Watch over us and save us from all evil, for You are our guardian and our savior. Blessed are You, Who spreads the canopy of peace over us and over all the congregations of His people Israel and over Jerusalem.

נשכבה בחסדך ונקיצה
ונשבעה באמונתך ופחד וצרה
ושטן בלילות אל ימשול בנו,
כאמור "אם תשכב לא תפחד
ושכבת וערבת שנתך" (משלי
ג' כד) ושומרנו והצילנו מכל
דבר רע, שומרינו ומצילנו
אתה. בא"י פורש סוכת שלום
עלינו ועל כל עדת עמו ישראל
ועל ירושלים.

As we continue into the Friday night *Amidah* prayer, we will not see the familiar *va-yechulu*, but rather the following prayer:

And out of Your love, O Lord our God, that You love Your people Israel, and out of Your mercy that You have bestowed upon the children of Your covenant, You gave us, Lord our God, the seventh day, this great and holy [day] with love, for greatness, strength, holiness, for rest, worship and acknowledgement, for a sign and a covenant and for glory, and to grant us your blessing and peace . . . .[5]

ומאהבתך ה' א-להינו שאהבת את
ישראל עמך ומחמלתך מל-כינו
שחמלת על בני ברייתך נתת לנו
ה' א-להינו את יום השביעי הגדול
והקדוש הזה באהבה לגדולה
ולגבורה לקדושה ולמנוחה לעבודה
ולהודאה לאות ולברית ולתפארת
ולתת לנו ברכה ושלום מאתך . . . .

One can imagine how lost a modern-day Jew well acquainted with the standard contemporary prayers would feel in this unfamiliar liturgical atmosphere.

---

spirits by the holiness of the day. That version also contains: השמד שטן מלפנינו ומאחורינו ושמור צאתינו ובואינו מעתה ועד עולם – and destroy the Satan before us and behind us, and protect our exiting and entry from now unto all eternity. See also J. Mann, "Genizah Fragments of the Palestinian Order of Service" (HUCA 2 [1925]: 304, n. 83, 313, 324). I have cited the version in S. Assaf, *Gaonica* I (Jerusalem: 1933) [*Mi-sifrut ha-geonim*], "Mi-toch seder tefillah kadmon," 75–76.

See further E. Fleischer, *Eretz-Israel Prayer and Prayer Rituals as Portrayed in the Geniza Documents* (Jerusalem: 1988) 83–84, nn. 150, 155 (Hebrew).

5   *Seder Rav Amram Gaon*, ed. Goldschmidt, 63; *Seder Rav Saadya Gaon*, III, with slight variations. We are citing Fleischer, ibid., 22.

3

The Variety of Liturgical Versions

Therefore, one cannot speak of a single crystallized version of the liturgy. In fact, even within the Sepharadic and Oriental versions and that of the Hasidim, there are numerous versions, as one can see from the following example from the *Amidah*:[1]

1. And provide (lit. raise up) complete healing for all our wounds.	1. והעלה רפואה שלמה לכל מכותינו.
2. And provide (lit. raise up) a balm and complete healing for all our wounds.	2. והעלה ארוכה ורפואה שלמה לכל מכותינו.
3. And provide (lit. raise up) a balm and complete healing for all our ills, all our pains and all our wounds.	3. והעלה ארוכה ומרפא לכל תחלואינו ולכל מכאובינו ולכל מכותינו.
4. And provide (lit. raise up) a balm and a cure for all our ills and all our pains, complete healing for all our wounds.	4. והעלה ארוכה ומרפא לכל תחלואינו ולכל מכאובינו רפואה שלמה לכל מכותינו.
5. And provide (lit. raise up) a balm and a cure for all our ills and all our pains and all our wounds, complete healing for all our wounds.	5. והעלה ארוכה ומרפא לכל תחלואינו ולכל מכאובינו ולכל מכותינו רפואה שלמה לכל מכותינו.

---

1 See M. Medan's article *"Nusach 'Sefarad' ve-shel hasidim: tivo ve-gilgulav"* (*Tagim* 5–6 [1975]: 117–126, especially 118), and Weiser (ibid., 37). See additional examples in Weiser, 38.

Consider the following versions in the third blessing of the Grace after Meals (*rahem*):

כי אם לידך המלאה הפתוחה הקדושה והרחבה ...

לידך הקדושה והמלאה והרחבה ...   (*Or Zarua,* section 199)

לידך המלאה והרחבה העשירה והפתוחה ...   (Sepharadim)

לידך המלאה הרחבה הקדושה והפתוחה ...   (*Leket Yosher*)

לידך המלאה הרחבה והפתוחה והשבעה והטובה[2]   (Italian version)

Without going into a detailed analysis to explain these various versions, we may note the fluidity – or perhaps even tangled jumble of words – in the formulation of this passage. Such examples can be multiplied almost endlessly.

---

2   See *Tzelota de-Avraham*, vol. 2, 521; Friedman, Yisrael Hayyim, *Likkutei Mahariah*, vol. 1 (New York: 1964, 118a–b), noting that this whole section is absent in many early versions, such as *Mahzor Vitry* and *Abudarhim*, and so too in the Yemenite versions (see, for example, *Siddur Kenesset ha-Gedolah*, by R. Yosef Tzuberi, vol. 1, Tel Aviv-Jaffa: 1976, 649). Some authorities questioned the word קדושה and suggested reading גדושה (*Likkutei Mahariah*, ibid.).

    For an additional example, the fourteenth benediction, *boneh Yerushalayim*, see my work *Minhagei Yisrael*, vol. 4 (Jerusalem: 1995), 13–17, and A. Ashkenazi, "*Elohei David u-Boneh Yerushalayim*" (in *Beit Aharon ve-Yisrael* 38 [1992]: 134–138).

    On the halachic status of this blessing, and indeed of the first three blessings of the Grace after Meals, whether of biblical (*mi-de-oraita*) or rabbinic (*de-rabbanan*) authority, see most recently the succinct survey of opinions in Eric Blum, *Birkat Yitzhak* (Brooklyn: 2000, 59–61).

4

Blessings Offensive to Women

Nowadays, certain *berachot* (blessings) are particularly disturbing to women in general and to feminists in particular. Perhaps one of the most famous is one of the three *berachot* that we say in the morning, *she-lo asani ishah* (that He [that is, God] did not make me a woman). It is particularly disturbing because the Tur (Rabbi Jacob ben Asher, 1268–1340), in explaining the meaning of this particular *berachah,* or even more so in explaining the meaning of the phrase *she-asani kirtzono*[1] (that He [that is, God] made me in accordance with His will), states that when women recite the latter *berachah,* they must come to terms with the unfortunate situation of their status. In other words, "What can we do? This is the way that God made us." Indeed, Rabbi David Abudarhim says that, in reciting this female version, Jewish women are performing *tzidduk ha-din* – making peace with their divinely decreed "sentence," ("*Siddur shel Hol,*" Jerusalem: 1907, 39–40). We know that many women

---

[1] This variant does not appear in all *siddurim*. The Ashkenazic tradition in the name of R. Yisrael Isserlein has:

> And he said: A woman says instead of "Who has not made me a woman" – "Who has not made me a beast (*behemah*)." However, I have heard from a woman who says instead of "Who has not made me a woman" – "Who has made me in accordance with His will." (But it appears to me that the Gaon [R. Yisrael Isserlein] did not agree to this, for his holy mother, of blessed memory, during the Austrian decree, may the Lord avenge her blood, used to say, "Who has not made me a beast." (*Leket Yosher*, by R. Yosef ben R. Moshe [written c. 1460, ed. J. Freimann, Berlin: 1903; reprinted Jerusalem: 1964]. Part 1, 7). See *Siddur Hanau*, 28, for their observation on this benediction.

considered this prayer very offensive.[2] Some rabbis were so keenly aware of this that one prominent halachist of the late eighteenth century, Rabbi Aaron ben Abraham Wermish of Metz, recited it silently because he considered it an offense to women to say it aloud.[3] It is also possible that certain amoraim felt

---

2   Wieder also points out in *Hitgabshut* (vol. 1, 213–214, n. 70) that this blessing is absent in several manuscripts. He notes that he has not found explicit criticism of this blessing until relatively late, when the censor of the *Mahzor* (Prague: 1710) deleted it for moral reasons. He refers us to Steinschneider's Bodleian Catalogue (*Catalogus Librorum Hebraeorum in Bibliotheca Bodleiana*, Berlin 1852–1860), col. 385 [no. 2521a], and *Hebraeische Bibliographie* (vol. 5, 1892, 128).

      Indeed, women would have been even more offended had they been aware of what is written in *Derashot al ha-Torah* on Tazria-Metzora by R. Yehoshua ibn Shuaib (Cracow: 1573, 48b, ed. Z Metzger, 258 [Jerusalem: 1991], vol. 1, 258):

> Therefore every day we say the blessings: who has not made me a Cuthean, and who has not made me a slave, and who has not made me a woman . . . . For the souls of [men of] Israel are holier than those of the [other] nations and of Canaanite slaves who are [even] less [holy] (הפחותים), and even of women, and [even] if they observe mitzvot (שייכי במצוות) and are of Israelite offspring (מזרע ישראל), their souls are not like the soul of a male [Jew] who is obligated (השייך) to the Torah and all the mitzvot, both positive and negative.

That is to say: regarding the status of holiness, women are inferior to men.

3   *Beer Sheva: On the Blessings of Shabbat and Eruvin* (Mainz: 1819). See most recently Rabbi Dr. Joel S. Wolowelsky, *Tradition* 29:4 (Summer 1995): 61–68, and again in his *Women, Jewish Law and Modernity: New Opportunities in a Post-Feminist Age* (Hoboken: 1997, 14–84), who also advocated following this suggestion. His view was vigorously rejected by Rabbi Emanuel Feldman in *Tradition* (ibid., 69–74), who stated that doing so "became a daily confession to or accusation that is not true; that there is something intrinsically offensive to women in this *berachah*." Feldman instead suggests "Interpreting it properly."

      See further Rabbi Moshe Meiselman's discussion in his work *Jewish Woman in Jewish Law* (New York: 1978, 49–51). He writes, inter alia:

> The woman, when reciting her blessing, acknowledges that the role differentiation implicit in her exemption from certain mitzvot [i.e., the time-related ones, *mitzvot asei she-ha-zeman geraman*] is part of the overall divine plan for the world, whose justification lies in the will and wisdom of God.

He further quotes a passage from the *Hinah Siddur* (Jerusalem & New York: 1932), relating to the three morning blessings:

> These three aspects of our own [male] status impose upon us duties much more comprehensive than the rest of mankind. And if our women have a smaller number of mitzvot to fulfill than men, they know that the tasks which they must

uncomfortable with it even as far back as talmudic times. Thus, in *Menahot* 43b, we read:

> It was taught: R. Meir says: A person must say three benedictions every day, and these are they: who has made me an Israelite (i.e., a Jew); who has not made me a woman; who has not made me an ignoramus. Rav Aha bar Yaakov heard his son reciting the blessing, "Who has not made me an ignoramus." He said to him: Why do you recite this blessing? Surely the ignoramus is also obligated in mitzvot (Rashi, ibid.). [The son replied: What, then, should I say in order to complete the three benedictions? (Rashi) Who has not made me a slave? That is the same as a woman . . . .

This difficult passage was interpreted by R. Hayyim Hirschensohn, in his work, *Malki ba-kodesh,* vol. 4 (St. Louis, 206), as follows:

> But in truth I will tell you something to which all the earlier and later decisors were not sensitive . . . . And that is that indeed, the Babylonian Talmud [also] objected to this benediction . . . and that the discussion [in *Menahot,* ibid.] demonstrates the opposition to it . . . . For it is clear that both Rav Aha bar Yaakov and his son objected to this blessing . . . . For these saintly elders sensed the feeling of affront to the dignity of women, and Rav Aha bar Yaakov was not willing to recite this benediction, and [therefore] his son said "Who has not made me an ignoramus" instead . . . .

See the continuation of his interpretation (and what I wrote in *Darkah shel halachah* [Jerusalem: 2007, 103, n. 148], and on greater sensitivity to women's feelings, ibid., pass.).

We find this kind of sensitivity in yet another talmudic liturgical context. Thus in BT *Berachot* 49a, we read the following:

> Rabbi Zeira said to Rav Hisda, "Come and teach!" Rav Hisda answered, "I have not even learned *birkat ha-mazon* properly, and you want me to teach?" Rabbi Zeira said, "What are you talking about?" Rav Hisda responded: "When

---

discharge as free women are no less in accordance with the will and the desire of God than those of their brothers. Hence their blessing is "who has created me in accordance with His will."

These are the sorts of arguments – apologetic – put forward to explain, or justify, such blessings. See further *Expanding the Palace of Torah*, 38, on Rabbi A. I. Kook's justification for this blessing.

I visited the house of the Exilarch and recited *birkat ha-mazon*, Rav Sheshet un-coiled his neck at me like a snake." [He was very angry.] "Why?" "Because I did not mention *brit* [the covenant of circumcision], Torah or [David's] kingship." "Why not?" "I followed Rav Hananel in the name of Rav, as Rav Hananel said in the name of Rav that whoever did not say "covenant," "Torah" and "kingship" [nevertheless] fulfilled the obligation. I omitted "covenant" because it does not apply to women, and I omitted "Torah" and "kingship" because they do not apply to women and slaves." Rabbi Zeira exclaimed, "You rejected all the tannaim and amoraim and followed Rav?!"

The majority of rabbis did not accept Rav Hisda's version, nor do we follow it here. However, Rav Hisda's sensitivity to everyone who recites the grace after meals and his desire to avoid using language that does not apply to everyone equally are surely significant. (See Afterword, n. 9.)

Closer to our own day, Rebbetzin Rayna Batya, the granddaughter of Rabbi Hayyim Volozhiner (1749–1821) and the first wife of Rabbi Naftali Zvi Judah Berlin (the Netziv, 1816–1893) is said to have been deeply offended by this blessing. Her nephew, Rabbi Baruch Halevi Epstein (the author of the *Torah Temima* and the son of the *Aruch ha-Shulhan*), writes as follows in his memoirs, *Mekor Baruch* (part 4, chap. 46, sec. 3 [Vilna: 1928, 981], as cited by Ross (ibid., 37–38):

How bitter was my aunt that, as she would say from time to time, "Every empty-headed, ignorant man," every ignoramus who hardly knew the meaning of the words and who would not dare to cross her threshold without first obsequi-ously and humbly obtaining her permission, would not hesitate to boldly and arrogantly recite to her face the blessing of *she-lo asani isha*. Moreover, upon his recitation of the blessing, she was obliged to answer "Amen."

"And who can muster enough strength," she would conclude with great an-guish, "to hear this eternal symbol of shame and embarrassment to women?"

Furthermore, it was the same R. Meir who commented (BT *Bava Batra* 16b) on the verse in Genesis 24:1, "and the Lord had blessed Abraham *with all*" (בכל, *ba-kol*):

What is "with all" – *ba-kol*? ... That he had no daughter. R. Yehudah says: That he had a daughter. And others said: He had a daughter and Ba-kol was her name.

And in Midrash ha-Gaddol ad loc.: "Said R. Meir: He *definitely* had no daughter" (שלא היתה לו בת כלל). (R. Meir's conclusion accords with his understanding of a text in Job 42:12–13, as we learn from JT *Hagigah* 2:1, 77b. See Lieberman, *Mehkarim be-Torat Eretz Yisrael* [Jerusalem: 1991], 114, and see M. A. Friedman in *Teudah* 4 [1886]: 79, in his article "*Iyyunim be-midrasho shel R. Meir*," in which he shows conclusively [page 82] that the blessing *she-lo asani ishah* may indeed be attributed to R. Meir.)

The same R. Baruch ha-Levi Epstein, whom we cited above, comments on R. Meir's statement in his *Torah Temimah* on Gen. ibid. (217, n. 6):

Also, one might say concerning this view of R. Meir that he is [here] consistent with his ruling in BT *Menahot* 43b that one must recite the blessing every day "that He has not made me a woman," and one may suggest that women were of lesser value in his eyes because of their inferior intelligence (קלות דעתן), as is apparent from BT *Avodah Zarah* 18b [where we are told] that he fled in shame because of his wife Beruriah . . . and also that he fell into temptation at the hands of a certain woman, as we learn from his biography in *Seder ha-dorot*.

גם יש לומר בדעתיה דר' מאיר דאזיל לשיטתיה שרתיקן לברך בכל יום שלא עשני אשה, כמבואר במנחות מ"ג ע"ב, וזה יש לומר **שערך הנשים היה קל בעיניו מפני קלות דעתן**, כמבואר בעבודה זרה י"ח ע"ב שברח מחמת כסופא מפני ברוריה אשתו ועיין שם, וגם מפני שנכשל על ידי אשה אחת כמבואר בתולדותיו בסדר הדורות. . . .

This view is very different indeed from the one expressed by the late Rabbi Professor Emanuel Rackman in his classic article "Arrogance or Humility in Prayer" (*Tradition* 1 [1958]: 13–26), in which he criticizes the Conservative and Reform movements' radical rewriting of the *siddur*:

It is interesting that the author of these blessings was Rabbi Meir, whose wife was not only his beloved, but also his peer – a woman who was so scholarly that her view in opposition to the majority of rabbis is cited by the Talmud in connection with a very difficult Halakhic problem (and her view prevailed). She was one of the many to be credited with the literature of the Mishnah.

And when an Orthodox Jew recites the blessing Rabbi Meir composed, he hesitates to emend it and make himself appear more chivalrous than the great sage, and more appreciative of his own wife than Rabbi Meir was of his. (18)

But clearly, this apologetic statement is part of the general polemic theme of his article. (For further examples of such apologetic justifications

see I. Jacobson, *Netiv Binah,* vol. 1 (Tel Aviv: 1976 [fifth Impression], 166), referring to R. S. R. Hirsch, etc., and in E. Munk, *Olam ha-Tefillot,* vol. I (Jerusalem: 1994 [ninth impression], 35–36). However, Munk's argument with R. Meir's statement in BT *Sanhedrin* 59a is irrelevant because it refers only to gentiles, and the additional reference to *Yalkut Shoftim* 4.4, 705b is to a statement by R. Pinhas ben Eliezer, not R. Meir.)

If we accept the *Torah Temimah*'s suggestion that R. Meir had an anti-feminist attitude for whatever reason and that he adopted the ancient blessing *she-lo asani ishah* because of it, we may ask ourselves whether we must follow his apparent prejudice in our day. After all, we do not necessarily accept his view that Abraham had no daughters. The rabbinic consensus is actually that he had one daughter who may even have been called *Ba-kol*!

Parenthetically, we may comment that his opinion that Abraham had no daughter is very strange, since it would mean that he had not satisfied the requirements of the mitzvah of procreation (*periah u-reviah*). According to the Mishnah in *Yevamot* 6.2, one fulfills this mitzvah only after having both a son and a daughter (according to Beit Hillel, while Beit Shammai requires two sons and a daughter; see also *Shulhan Aruch Even ha-Ezer* 1:4). Can it be that the patriarch Abraham, who according to the sages of the Talmud (BT *Yoma* 28b) kept all 613 *mitzvot* (!), neglected the first and perhaps the most important one? (See Maharsha, R. Shmuel Eliezer ha-Levi Eideles, *Hiddushei Aggadot* on BT *Bava Batra* 16b, and *Perushei Maharal mi-Prag le-Aggadot ha-Shas*, vol. 3, edited by M. S. Kasher and Y. Y. Belchrowitz, 78, Jerusalem: 1966.)

Returning to R. Aharon Worms's (Wermish) statement that he recited the *beracha "she-lo asani ishah"* silently, this view was more recently advocated by Rabbi Dr. Joel S. Wolowelsky in *Tradition* (29:4 [1995]: 61–68) and re-peated in his book *Women, Jewish Law and Modernity: New Opportunities in a Post-Feminist Age* (Hoboken: 1997, 75–84). In the same issue of *Tradition,* R. Emanuel Feldman, in a section entitled "An Articulate Berakhah" (69–74), states that doing so "becomes a daily confession to an accusation that is not true: that there is something intrinsically offensive to women in this *berakhah* and R. Feldman advocates instead 'interpreting it properly.'" Although R. Dr. Ephraim Bezalel Halivni, in his recently published book, *Distinctions between Men and Women in Halakha* (Jerusalem: 2007, English section, 8–10), ap-pears to accept R. Feldman's position, he adds:

Nowadays, there is no reason for the *shaliah zibbur* to recite any of the *birkhot hashahar* aloud; indeed in many congregations the *shaliah zibbur* does not recite the *birkhot hashahar* aloud. Of course, in that case, the issue of reciting "*she-lo asani ishah*" aloud becomes moot.

R. Feldman's "proper interpretation" of the *berachah* is neither that of the Tur nor, apparently, of R. Aharon Worms, whose interpretation is really the *peshat* – the simple, straightforward and correct interpretation. It parallels to the other two *berachot, she-lo asani nokhri* and *she-lo asani aved.* Saying it silently was a sign of sensitivity to the feelings of others, if not an ideal solution. Indeed, feminist dissatisfaction with this formulation will undoubtedly continue as long as it remains in the prayer book.

Perhaps a more radical suggestion is simply to omit the benediction. Thus, for example, the Rambam strongly rejected *birkat dam betulim,* to be recited after first intercourse with a virgin (*Shulhan Aruch Even ha-Ezer* 63:2), since he saw in it a lack of modesty (*Responsa*, edited by Blau, 364, 366. Jerusalem: 1958) and later on by the Maharshal, R. Shlomo Luria. It is already absent from *Siddur Saadya Gaon,* though since it is a post-talmudic benediction, it is easier to reject and omit it. (See N. Wieder, *The Formation of Jewish Liturgy in the East and West: A Collection of Essays* [Jerusalem: 1998, 619–621 (Hebrew)]; B. Z. Groner, *Berachot she-nishtaku* [Jerusalem: 2003], 29–34.)

Similarly, the blessing *magbiah shefalim* ("who raises up the lowly"), which is talmudic according to some opinions (*Ba"h* [*Bayit Hadash*], by R. Joel Sirkes, on *Tur Orah Hayyim,* sec. 4b) and used to be found in many *siddurim*, fell into disuse. (See in detail for all aspects of this blessing in M. Hallamish, *Kabbalah in Liturgy, Halakhah and Customs* [Ramat Gan: 2000, 465–473]. For many other examples of blessings that fell out of use, see ibid., 436–445.) Yet perhaps even more significant is the fact that many early authorities rejected the clearly Tannaitic blessing *she-lo asani bur* ("who has not made me an ignoramus") (see S. Lieberman, *Tosefta ki-fshutah* [New York: 1955], 119–120), which is one of R. Meir's three blessings (in BT *Menahot* 43b and Tosefta *Berachot* 6:18, in the name of R. Yehudah, and Yerushalmi ibid., 9, 2, 13b) on the basis of the continuation of a discussion in *Menahot,* ibid., and it gradually disappeared from our liturgy (Hallamish, ibid., 440–441) (see Appendix 8 below).

We should also note that the blessing "Who has not made me an

ignoramus," which was also a blessing of R. Yehudah and appears in many early *siddurim* (see Hallamish, ibid., 440–441), was rejected as far back as early medieval times. R. David Kochavi, a Provençal scholar of the early fourteenth century, writes as follows in his work, *Sefer ha-Batim* (*Beit Tefillah,* edited by M. Hershler, 216 [Jerusalem: 1983]):

Some customarily recite a blessing, "Who has not made me an ignoramus." It seems to me that they are mistaken, since this blessing should not be recited.	יש נהגו לברך שלא עשני בור, ונראה לי שטעות הוא בידם, שאין מברכין ברכה זו.

The editor, ad loc. (n. 802) refers us to additional early authorities from the school of Rashi who also rejected this blessing, all basing themselves on BT *Menahot* 43b, when we read that when Rav Aha bar Yaakov heard his son reciting the blessing "Who has not made me an ignoramus," he said to him: "So much so!" – כולי האי, indicating that he was criticizing him for saying it (see Rashi's two explanations ad loc. and the continuation of the passage). Thus, on the one hand, despite Rav Aha bar Yaakov's dissatisfaction with this blessing, it survived to make its way into many early prayer books. On the other hand, there was a good talmudic precedent for rejecting it, which was adopted by many early authorities, so that eventually it dropped completely out of use. (See also below Appendix 8.)

Eventually, this may happen to שלא עשני אשה as well. It, too, may join the many benedictions that faded into oblivion (see Groner *passim*). Only time will tell.

5

Recommended Changes

There were also various attempts at various times to rectify the situation. We are not referring to the changes suggested by representatives of Conservative, Liberal or Reform Judaism in our own time. We are speaking of classical times. Thus, for example, we find that in 1476, Rabbi Abraham Farissol wrote a prayer book in Ferrara, Italy, which can now be found at the Jewish Theological Seminary Library in New York, in which he provided alternative versions for these blessings: *baruch she-asani ishah* (blessed is He Who made me a woman) instead of *kirtzono* (in accordance with His will). This was a private *siddur*. Since Rabbi Farissol was a scribe, he presumably wrote such *siddurim* for wealthy Jewish women of the Renaissance period who specially ordered them. He also wrote there:

Blessed are You, Who has not made me a handmaid or slave.	ברוך ... של'א עשני אמה ושפחה.

In a second *mahzor* that was written four years later, in 1480 – a beautiful illuminated manuscript of which may be found in the Jewish National Library in Jerusalem – we read as follows:

Blessed are You ... Who did not make me a handmaiden. Blessed are You ... Who made me a woman and not a man. Blessed are You ... Who did not make me a Gentile woman.[1]	ברוך ... של'א עשני אמה. ברוך ... שעשרתני אשה ולא איש. ברוך ... של'א עשני גויה.

---

1   See Y. H. Kahn's article, "*Baruch she-asani ishah,*" in *Baruch she-asani ishah?* (ed. D. Y. Ariel, M. Leibovitz, Y. Mazor, 124–126. Tel Aviv: 1999 [in Hebrew]).
   See *Treasures Revealed 1925–2000: From the Collections of the Jewish National and*

These three blessings, which we normally recite during the *shaharit* (morning) prayer services and which are found in the Tosefta,[2] are actually

---

University Library, Jerusalem: 2000, 98–101. On p. 99, we read the following description: "A prayer book for year-round, according to the Italian rite (*Mahzor Bnei Roma*), written by R. R. Abraham ben Mordecai Farissol in Mantua, 1480."

The prayer book was written for a wealthy lady, apparently from the banking family of Judah and Jacob Norsa, Farissol's patrons during his sojourn in Mantua. For this worthy lady, Farissol changed the wording of the morning blessings: "Blessed be He [. . .] Who made me a woman and not a man" (see p. 101).

Abraham Farissol was born in Avignon in 1452, and in 1470 moved with his family to Mantua. His career as a scribe, which began while he was still at Avignon under his uncle's guidance, continued for some sixty years. Farissol, who was learned in philosophy and sciences, wrote commentaries on books of the Bible and on Ethics of the Fathers, as well as his book *Magen Avraham*, a disputation with Christians written in the wake of an actual disputation in Italy to which Farissol was delegated as Jewish representative in 1487–1489. At the end of his life, in 1525, he even wrote a cosmological-geographical work, *Iggeret orhot olam*, in which he also describes America shortly after its discovery.

2   Tosefta *Berachot* 6 (7): 18 (ed. Lieberman, 38); parallels in JT *Berachot* 9.2, 13b; BT *Menahot* 42b, etc. See S. Lieberman, *Tosefta ki-fshutah*, vol. 1 (New York: 1955, 119–121), with bibliographic references. Lieberman himself is somewhat skeptical of the Greco-Hellenistic influence on these *berachot*. See the interesting suggestion of I. S. I. Hasidah, in his article "*Le-havanat shloshah berachot* . . ." (*Sinai* 99/1–2 [1986]: 95–96), where he tries to find a biblical source in Psalms 100:3 for these three benedictions. Although his argument is clever, it is not convincing.

There were apparently various traditions as to the exact version of these benedictions. In the Palestinian Genizah we find several expanded versions, and there are some very different readings of the whole of *birkot ha-shahar*. See Dalia Sara Marx, "The Early Morning Ritual in Jewish Liturgy: Textual, Historical and Theological Discussion in Birkot Hashakhar (The Morning Blessings) and an Examination of the Performative Aspects," PhD diss., Hebrew University (April: 2005), 176–216. Here we shall cite two examples from the Cairo Genizah:

Ms. Antonin 993, fol. 16–2a, published by S. Assaf, "*Mi-seder ha-tefillah be-Eretz Yisrael.*" *Sefer Dinburg* (Jerusalem: 1956, 122):

Blessed art Thou . . . Who hath created me	ברוך אתה ה' אלקינו מלך העולם אשר ברא אותי
A human being and not an animal	אדם ולא בהמה
A man and not a woman	איש ולא אשה
Male and not female	זכר ולא נקבה
An Israelite and not a gentile	ישראל ולא גוי
Circumcised and not uncircumcised	מהול ולא ערל
Free and not a slave	חופשי ולא עבד
Pure and not impure	טהור ולא טמא

בּ﯁ֵי אמה שעשיתני אשה ולא איש
בּ﯁ֵי אמה שלא עשיתני
בּ﯁ֵי אמה המעביר
וכל שינת מעיני ותנומה מעפעפי
יהי רצון מלפניך יֵ﯁ אלהי ואלהי אבותי
שתרגילני לדבר מצוה ואל תרגילני
לדבר עברה ושון ותשלט בי יצר טוב
ואל תשלט בי יצר רע וחזקני במצותיך
ותן חלקי בתורתך ואל תביאני לא לידי
נסיון ולא לידי בזיון ויכוף את יצרי
להשתעבד לך ותכנע את ערפי לשת
אליך ותחיש כליותי לשמור פקודיך
וכול את לבבי לאהבה ולכבד ולירא את
את שמך ולעשות וליטב והישר בעיני

parallel to Greek benedictions that are found in Greek classical sources, specifically in the writings of Plato and Aristotle, and in other Greek sources from the fifth century B.C.E.

> Blessed are You Who has made me an Athenian and not a barbarian.
> Blessed are You Who has made me a man and not a woman.
> Blessed are You Who has made me a free man and not a slave.

Since the Jewish prayers were deemed offensive to women, alternative versions were written in Italy as early as the fifteenth century. These versions actually appear later on in other places such as Bavaria. They were used and apparently were quite acceptable.[3] Indeed, we may well be surprised when we read the following discussion of these three first morning benedictions in Berliner's classic *He'arot al ha-siddur*[4] (part 1, 21–22):

And in ms. Cambridge 3160/b, published by J. Mann, "Genizah Fragments of the Palestinian Order of Service" (*HUCA* 2 [1925]: 277), we read:

Blessed art Thou . . . who hath created me	ברוך אתה ה'. . . אשר ברא אותי
A human being and not an animal	אדם ולא בהמה
A man and not a woman	איש ולא אשה
An Israelite and not a gentile	ישראל ולא גוי
Circumcised and not uncircumcised	מל ולא ערל
Free and not a slave	חופשי ולא עבד

It is surely evident that the first version we quoted (and the second to a lesser degree) is a conflation of different traditions, for "a man and not a woman" is actually the same as "male and not female," and so too "Israelite and not a gentile" is much the same as "circumcised and not uncircumcised, and also "pure and not impure." "Circumcised and not uncircumcised" may refer to Christians as opposed to Moslems, who are circumcised. See Mann's comment (ibid., 274). Mann (ibid., n. 19) cites yet another version from JTS Cod. Turin 51), which reads as follows:

שלא עשני גוי כגויי הארצות מל ולא ערל שלא עשיתנו עבד לבריות
שלא עשיתני אשה שלא עשיתני בהמה

. . . Who hath not made me a gentile like the gentiles of the world, circumcised and not uncircumcised, Who hath not made me a slave to people, Who hath not made me a woman, Who hath not made me an animal.

Mann rightly notes that "The influence of the Palestinian rite is obvious."

3   Kahn, ibid.
4   *He'arot al ha-siddur* is a Hebrew translations of a series of articles in German: *Randbemerkungen zum taeglichen Gebetbuch*, vol. 1 (Berlin: 1909), vol. 2 (Berlin: 1912); *Die Einheitsgesang* (Berlin: 1910); *Literatur-geschichtliche Belege über die*

... In the ancient and current versions, "Who has not made me a *goy*," the meaning of the word *goy* is, as it is found in the Talmud – a non-Jew.

The versions that were "corrected," for reasons of censorship, contain the suggested *nochri* instead of *goy* and are totally incorrect, since in talmudic parlance the word *nochri*, which means someone from a foreign land, may refer even to a Jew who is not local. For this reason, in the mid-eighteenth century, they began to read: "Who has not made me an *akum*" (עכו"ם) – idolator.

It is to be recommended in the most forceful manner to institute in all *siddurim* the [following] formulation: שעשני ישראל – who has made me an Israelite, as is clearly to be found in printed prayer books, such as the Mantua edition of 1558, Tihingen 1560, Prague 1566, Venice 1566 and 1572, Dyhrenfurth 1694, Benvenisti's *Kenesset ha-Gedolah*, vol. 1., fol. 46, etc., all of whom demand that this be the version . . . .

If this version should be accepted and become the norm throughout all Jewish communities, then, ipso facto, the two other benedictions, "Who has not made me a woman" and "Who has not made me a slave," become superfluous (בטלות מאליהן), and we will no longer be obligated to justify them in whichever way [was required in the past]. Moreover, there is no place for the late formulations "Who has not made me a *goyah*" or "*nochrit*" (non-Jewish woman), "Who has made me according to His will," "Who has not made me a maidservant" or even "Who has not made me a beast" (as in *Leket Yosher,* part 1, 7, and in several other manuscripts).

If, after all these proofs and reasons, there still remain serious doubts and hesitations in one's heart that prevent one from accepting [this] version, which already in ancient times underwent change and alteration, let us bring a conclusive example from our sages, who, in order to leave no place for misunderstanding, even changed the formulation of a biblical verse: I refer to that which is said in BT *Berachot* 11b, where we are told that they altered the blessing *Yotzer*; for in Isaiah 45:7 it is written, "I form the light and create darkness, I make peace and create *evil*," and they changed it to end "and create *all*."

He then cites additional evidence in order to support his argument. This

christliche Orgel im jüdischen Gottesdienste, apud *Zur Lehr' und Wehr* . . . (Berlin: 1904, 40–63). The translations were by Y. A. Zeidman and Y. Blumberg. Note that R. Yitzhak Vaneih in his *siddur* (*Tichlal*), *Paamon Zahav* (ms.) has: ברוך שעשני יהודי. See A. Gaimani, *Temurot be-Moreshet Yahadut Teiman* (Changes in the Heritage of Yemenite Jewry), Ramat Gan: 2005, 123. On this *siddur* see M. Gavra, *Teima* 4 (1994): 55–65. This reading was known to R. Yihye Tzalah (Maharitz), but rejected. See his *Tichlal Etz Hayyim*, vol. 1 (edited by S. Tzalah, 43b. Jerusalem: 1979).

is not the only place where he strongly recommends changes in the prayer. Thus, on page 20 (ibid.), he writes:

> The following version is recommended (in *Yigdal*), הינו אדון עולם וכל יוצר יודה גדולתו ומלכותו, instead of what is found in our editions, [הינו אדון עולם לכל נוצר יורה גדולתו ומלכותו]. Several testimonia bear out this version, and it is suited to the thirteen principles of faith, as set out by Maimonides in his commentary to Mishna Sanhedrin, and the beginning of chapter *Helek*.

Berliner (1853–1915) was not a Reform rabbi. On the contrary, he was a staunch supporter of Orthodoxy and an opponent of Reform. He supported Hildesheimer in the establishment of the *Adas Israel* secessionist congregation and acted as chairman of the council for many years. It is said that he was such a strong traditionalist he refused to call up to the Torah those not wearing "cylinder" top hats. Yet he was willing to recommend changes in prayers, texts and customs that were not to the liking of his Orthodox colleagues.[5]

Another passage which I have often heard to be offensive to women is found in the long *tahanun* prayer beginning with the words הפותח יד בתשובה – "You who hold out an open hand of repentance." In the passage there are verses that run as follows:

God, see how low our glory has sunk among the nations. They abominate us as much as the ritual impurity of the menstruant woman. How long will Your strength be held captive, and Your glory in the hand of the foe?

א־ל, הביטה, דל כבודנו בגוים, **ושקצונו כטומאת הנדה**, עד מתי עוזך בשבי ותפארתך ביד צר.

Clearly, in modern terms the phrase ושקצונו כטומאת הנדה – "They abominate us as much as the ritual impurity of the menstruant woman" is not "politically correct," to put it mildly.

Here it should be noted that this whole prayer derives from the *Mahzor Vitry*, from the school of Rashi. In the Horowitz edition of this work (Berlin 1889–1897), these two verses are absent (70). Apparently, there was a gap in the editor's manuscript, indicated in his edition by three dots. (The manuscript he used was ms. Brit. Mus. No. 655, from c. 1242.) It seems clear that

---

5   See *Encyclopaedia Judaica*, vol. 4 (Jerusalem: 1971, 665), and A. Ferziger, *Exclusion and Hierarchy* (Philadelphia: 2005, 24–29). For a fuller evaluation of Berliner's religious positions, see Yishayaha Wolfsberg's introduction to *He'arot*, 5–10.

this lacuna is the result of (internal) censorship. Maybe it is for this reason that these lines are absent in the *siddurim* that are in accordance of the Lurianic tradition. Thus, they do not appear in *Siddur ha-Ari Kol Yaakov* of R. Yaakov Koppel (Slavita: 1784, reprinted Jerusalem: 2004, 71a); *Siddur Tefillah al pi Nusah ha-Arizal, in Perush Mahari"d*, vol. 1 (=R. Yitzchak Dover) (Kfar Habad: 1991), 124; nor in the standard Habad *siddurim*. They do not appear in *Siddur Hegyon Lev* (Königsberg: 1845, 89–90, and see editor's comment ad loc.), or in a manuscript from 1344 where many sections of the *tahanun* that are now found in our prayer books are absent.

On the other hand, it is found in the manuscripts of the *Mahzor Vitry* used by A. Goldschmidt in his edition (Jerusalem: 2004, vol. 1, 118). It is also found in *Perush Siddur ha-Tefillah la-Rokeah*, vol. 2 (edited by Hershler, 394. Jerusalem: 1892), in *Siddur R. Herz Shatz* (Tihingen) and, more surprisingly in *Siddur ha-Arizal* (Zolkiev: 1771, 79b), and in the *siddur* printed in Yampol in 1950, 52b. Nonetheless, in *Siddur Tzelota de-Avraham* (vol. 1, 353–354), in *Nusah Ashkenaz* these verses appear in brackets. And, as an interesting observation, we note that in the *siddur* printed in Turin (Torino) in 1525, the text reads: ושקצונו כטומאת (!) with the word נדה absent.

In view of the above, it would seem to be perfectly acceptable to follow the version found in the *siddurim* of Habad and the prayer books that omit these verses, particularly since they also do not really reflect the contemporary situation of the Jewish people.

In this connection, it would serve well to recall the rabbinic tradition that seeks to explain the institution of the *Tahanun* prayer. We shall cite the text as it appears in *Perush Siddur ha-Tefillah la-Rokeah* (vol. 2, edited by Hershler, 369–370, Jerusalem: 1992):

מצינו בתשובת הגאונים:

תיקון **והוא רחום** שאנו קורין בחמישי ושני ובחמישי מעומד יסדו אנשי השם שהוגלו מירושלים בשעת חורבן הבית והגלה אותם אספסיינוס שחיק עצמות, וצוה לעשות להם אניות והכניסן בתוכם בלא רב החובל ובלא שום מלח והגרישם בים, ועמד עליהם הרוח והשליכם ליבשה בכל פלך ופלך. ספינה אחת נתיישבה במדינת ליידון והאחרת במדינת ארלדו והשלישית במדינת בורדיל. אותה שנתיישבה במדינת בורדיל יצאו מן הספינה ונתיישבו שם וקיבלם שר העיר בסבר פנים יפות ונתן להם שדות וכרמים, והיו שם ימים רבים עד שמת אותו שר וקם עליהם מלך חדש. מה שתיקון להם מלך הראשון סתר השני, וזה מחדש עליהם גזירות רעות שלא היה להם צד להפנות, כי גבר עליהם יד המציק וכח אין לילידה. והיו שם ב' אחין יוסף ובנימין ובן דודם היה ביניהם ושמואל

שמו והם היו בעצמם מאנשי ירושלם. ויצעקו אל ה' בצר להם וממצוקותיהם הוציאם, וישבו בצומות
ובתעניות ולבשו שקים על בשרם ושיחרו לא-ל, ויסדו והוא רחום שלשתן. יוסף יסד והוא רחום עד
כי א-ל מלך חנון ורחם אתה, ובנימין אחיו יסד מן אנא מלך רחום וחנון עד אין כמוך, ושמואל בן דודם
יסד מן אין כמוך עד שמע ישראל ה' א-להינו ה' אחד. לאחר שהושיעם וגאלם גואל ישראל מחמת
המיצר שלהם במיתה מרה וקשה, כתבוהו בכתב ועל ידי המעשה, שלחו בכל מקומות ישראל לקבל
עליהם לומר והוא רחום בשני ובחמישי, וכל קהילה שקיבלה על עצמה לאומרו בשני ובחמישי עדיין
היא רגילה ומתמדת בו. וכמו שהושיעם צור ישראל וקדושו כן יושיענו מכל צרתינו הא-ל המושיע.

According to this tradition, after the destruction of the Second Temple, Vespasian seized the leading personalities in Jerusalem and exiled them by placing them in boats and casting them adrift with no captain or sailors to steer them. A wind came and drove each of the boats to a different shore, to Bordil (Portugal), Leiden (or: Lepanto), and Arlado (Arles). The survivors who arrived at Bordil, were welcomed by the local ruler, who granted them fields and orchards. They lived there for a long time until a new leader arose who did away with all the former favors and enacted harsh decrees. Living in the Jewish community were two brothers, Yosef and Binyamin, and a cousin named Shemuel, all of whom were Jerusalemites. They cried out to God, fasted and donned sackcloth, and instituted the three *Ve-hu rahum* prayers ("He is merciful"). Yosef established כי א-ל מלך רחום אתה to והוא רחום, Binyamin his brother from אנא מלך רחום וחנון to אין כמוך, and Shmuel from אין כמוך to שמע ישראל ה' א-להינו ה' אחד. After the decrees were nullified and they were saved from their terrible plight, they sent messages to all the Jewish communities throughout the world telling them to recite these three prayers on Mondays and Thursdays, and all communities that took it upon themselves to do so continue the practice to this day. The passage ends with a brief prayer that just as the Rock of Israel saved them from their afflictions, so may the God of salvation save us from all our misfortunes. In some versions they were placed in a fiery furnace, like Hananya, Mishael and Azariah, and were miraculously saved, and there they formulated the three sections of *Ve-hu rahum*.

(For a further analysis and comparisons to this text see *Siddur Otzar ha-Tefillot* [907–410] in *Tikkun Tefillah*; *Baer Siddur*, 112–113; and full references in *Sefer ha-Manhig* [edited by Raphael, 102, n. on line 88]; Elbogen [60–61, 403, n. 17]; Berliner [66–67]. The text appears with variations in *Sefer ha-Machkim* [sec. 14]; *Kol Bo* [sec. 12]; *Tanya* [sec. 5]; *Orhot Hayyim* [sec. 1]; *Abudarhim*, 127, and so on.)

אָנָּא בִּי בֶּן דַּרְכְּךָ עַד שֶׁהֶחָסֵד חִינָם בְּכָל דּוֹר וָדוֹר חוּסָה
עַל עַמְּךָ וְהַצִּילֵנוּ מִזַּעֲמֶיךָ וְהָסֵר מִמֶּנּוּ מַכַּת הַמַּגֵּפָה
וּגְזֵרָה קָשָׁה כִּי אַתָּה שׁוֹמֵר יִשְׂרָאֵל   לְךָ יְיָ הַצְּדָקָה וְלָנוּ
בֹּשֶׁת הַפָּנִים מַה נִּתְאוֹנֵן מַה נֹּאמַר מַה נְּדַבֵּר   וּמַה
נִּצְטַדָּק נַחְפְּשָׂה דְרָכֵינוּ וְנַחְקוֹרָה וְנָשׁוּבָה אֵלֶיךָ כִּי יְמִינְךָ
פְּשׁוּטָה לְקַבֵּל שָׁבִים אָנָּא יְיָ הוֹשִׁיעָה נָּא אָנָּא יְיָ הַצְלִיחָה
נָּא אָנָּא יְיָ עֲנֵנוּ בְּיוֹם קָרְאֵנוּ   לְךָ יְיָ הִבַּנְתָּ לָךְ יְיָ קַוִּינוּ
לָךְ יְיָ   בְּיַחֵל אַל תַּחְשֶׁה וְתַעֲנֵנוּ כִּי נִמּוֹ גּוֹיִם אֲבָדָה
תִקְוָתָם כֹּל בְּרֹד וְכָל קוֹדְמָה לָךְ לְבַד תַּשְׁתַּוָה:
הַפּוֹתֵחַ   יָד בִּתְשׁוּבָה לְקַבֵּל פּוֹשְׁעִים וְחַטָּאִים נִבְהֲלָה
נַפְשֵׁנוּ מֵרֹב עַצְבוֹנֵינוּ אַל תִּשְׁכָּחֵינוּ בְּצֶח
קוּמָה וְהוֹשִׁיעֵנוּ בִּי חֲסִיבוּ בָּךְ   אָבִינוּ מַלְבֵּינוּ יְדַעֲנוּ כִּי
אֵין בָּנוּ מַעֲשִׂים צְדָקָה עֲשֵׂה עִמָּנוּ לְמַעַן שְׁמֶךָ זְכוֹר לָנוּ
אֶת בְּרִית אֲבוֹתֵינוּ וְעֵדוּתֵנוּ בְּכָלַיִם יְיָ אֶחָד   הַבִּיטָה
בְּעֵינֵינוּ כִּי רַבּוּ מַבְאוֹבֵינוּ וְצָרוֹת לְבָבֵנוּ   חוּסָה יְיָ
עָלֵינוּ בְּאֶרֶץ שִׁבְיֵנוּ וְאַל תִּשְׁפָּךְ חֲרוֹנְךָ עָלֵינוּ כִּי אֲנַחְנוּ
עַמְּךָ בְּנֵי בְרִיתֶךָ אֶל בִּטְחָה דַל כְּבוֹדֵינוּ   וְשַׁקְּרֵצִינוּ
בְּטוּמְאַת   עַד מָתַי עֻוֹךָ בַּשְּׁבִי וְתִפְאַרְתְּךָ בְּיַד צָר
עוֹדֵד גְּבוּרוֹתֶךָ וְאַתָּה יְיָ עַל שׂוֹנְאֵינוּ הֵם יֵבֹשׁוּ וְיֵחַתּוּ
מִבְּוּדְתָם וְאַל יִמְעֲטוּ לְפָנֶיךָ תְּלָאוֹתֵינוּ מַהֵר יְקַדְּמוּנוּ
רַחֲמֶיךָ בְּצָרוֹתֵינוּ לֹא לְמַעֲנֵינוּ כִּי אִם לְמַעֲנֶךָ פְּעוֹל וְאַל
תַּשְׁחִית זֵכֶר שְׁאֵרִיתֵנוּ וּכְבוֹד אֱלֹהִים הַמְּיַחֲדִים שִׁמְךָ פַּעֲמַיִם
בְּאַהֲבָה וְאוֹמְרִים שְׁמַע יִשְׂרָאֵל יְיָ אֱלֹדֵינוּ יְיָ אֶחָד :
רַחוּם   וְחַנּוּן חָטָאתִי לְפָנֶיךָ יְיָ מָלֵא רַחֲמִים רַחֵם
עָלַי וְקַבֵּל תַּחֲנוּנַי יְיָ אַל בְּאַפְּךָ תוֹכִיחֵנִי

It is generally accepted that *Ve-hu rahum* dates back to the geonic period and was composed during a period of severe persecution (perhaps during the seventh century, so Zunz surmises; see Berliner, ibid. and above Introduction, n. 12). In any case this prayer, with its component parts, is evidence of a dire threat to the Jewish community at a particular place and time. Many subsequent generations, who saw it as reflecting their own condition, also used it. It was always regarded as a personal prayer to be recited silently, with the status of *minhag* (custom), rather than obligatory prayer. Perhaps it should have this status in our time.

6

The Legitimacy of Change

When we ask ourselves about the legitimacy of change, we can demonstrate that changes in the liturgy took place at all times. Sometimes the changes were minor, sometimes there were additions, and sometimes completely new prayers and benedictions were composed.[1] For example, who would have thought that the central sections of the four Sabbath *Amidah* prayers are actually post-talmudic embellishments that were not necessarily accepted by all communities during the geonic and early post-geonic periods? Saadya Gaon writes in his *siddur* (111) as follows: "I found the custom that the middle benedictions of the four Sabbath prayers are not identical." He had to "find" this fact, which apparently was by no means obvious to him. Rav Natronai Gaon writes (cited in *Sefer ha-Ittim,* 174):

---

1   On the subject of new, post-talmudic benedictions, see Groner (29–33). Groner (29–30) shows that already in geonic times there was a difference of opinion as to whether it was permissible to formulate new benedictions that had not been mentioned in the Talmud. Pirkoi ben Baboi (*Ginzei Schechter,* 550) is adamant that "one is forbidden any benediction that is not in the Talmud." This is also the view of various rishonim, such as the *Manhig* (*Hilchot Sukkah,* 61), Rosh (*Kiddushim* chap. 1, sec. 41 ad fin.), etc. This is also the ruling of the Beit Yosef of R. Yosef Caro (*Orah Hayyim,* sec. 46). On the other hand, R. Amram Gaon and R. Saadya Gaon, accepted some post-Talmudic benedictions, and Rabbenu Tam (*Sefer ha-Yashar,* Responsa responsum 45:4, 82) wrote: "We have found several benedictions . . . even though they are not written [in the Talmud], which we accept." Among the later authorities, the *Turei Zahav* (called Taz) on *Orah Hayyim,* sec. 46 also recognizes the legitimacy of some post-Talmudic benedictions. Groner, in later chapters of his book, discusses specific examples of this phenomenon (e.g., 171 et seq., 259 et seq., etc.).

As to your question regarding whether the *arvit, shaharit* and *minhah* prayers on Shabbat are identical, just as are the prayers we pray on Yom Kippur and the festivals: the custom in the two Yeshivot and in the house of our Master in Babylonia is [as follows]: in *arvit* we say "*U-me-ahavatecha,*" in *shaharit* we say "*yismah Moshe,*" and in *minhah* "*Ata ehad ve-shimcha ehad.*"

Even in Rashi's time, these embellishments were not altogether accepted, as we hear from *Sefer ha-Pardes* (ed. Ehrenreich, 310):

> Strictly speaking, it would appear that one should not add in the Sabbath prayers anything after *Ha-El ha-kadosh* (the end of the third benediction of the *Amidah*), but go straight on to *retzeh* .... However, they are accustomed to say *Ata kiddashta* (in *maariv*), and in the morning *yismah Moshe,* and in *minhah Ata ehad* before saying *retzeh*. They also found a reason [or pretext] to lengthen the prayer.... And you too, "Do not forsake the instruction of your mother" (Proverbs 1:8).

R. Avraham ben Natan Ha-Yarhi tells us the following in his *Sefer ha-Manhig* (ed. Raphael, 150):

> R. Shlomo (i.e., Rashi) did not say *Ata kiddashta* ... but R. Yaakov (i.e., Rabbenu Tam) ... returned it to its erstwhile estate ....

We see, then, that what we believe to be basic components of the Sabbath *Amidah* prayers were actually additions composed in order "to lengthen the prayers" (see on this in detail in Wieder, *Hitgabshut,* 295–319).

Since we have mentioned new benedictions, let us take a look at a fascinating example that Wieder discovered in the Cairo Genizah (*Hitgabshut* 1, 323–347). It is a long anti-Karaite benediction that was recited before the recitation of the Mishnayot of *Ba-meh madlikin* (M. Shabbat, chap. 2), which is recited in the Friday night service. As it is a most interesting and instructive benediction, I shall cite it in extenso:

Blessed are You, Lord our God, King of the universe, Who chose the sages and their disciples and gave them the Torah at Mount Sinai through our teacher Moses, and commanded us to read the Torah, the Mishnah, the Talmud, the Halachah, in order to acquire the two worlds, and chose our master Moses of all the prophets, speaking with him	ברוך אתה ה' אלקינו מלך העולם אשר בחר בחכמים ותלמידיהם ונתן להם התורה מהר סיני על ידי משה רבנו וצוה אותם לקרא בתורה במשנה בתלמוד בהלכה לקנות חיי שני עולמים. ובחר במשה רבנו מכל הנביאים ודבר

face to face, as it is said, "With him will I speak mouth to mouth" (Numbers 12:8). After him He chose his disciple Joshua and the seventy elders and prophets and sages and their disciples and commanded them to keep the Sabbath and light the Sabbath candle – *Ba-meh madlikin* .... (With what does one light ...?).

עמו פנים בפנים שנאמר, "פה אל
פה אדבר בו וגו'" (במדבר יב ח),
ואחריו בחר ביהושע תלמידו
ושבעים זקנים ונביאים וחכמים
ותלמידיהם, וצוה אותם בשמירת
שבת ובהדלקת הנר של שבת –
במה מדליקין וגו'.

Wieder (ibid., 335–336) analyzed this long text, showing it to be a conflation of two different blessings (cf. chap. 17, n. 1, last paragraph, on this phenomenon), and found yet another similar benediction (332) in A. Neubauer's *Mediaeval Jewish Chronicles* (vol. 2, Oxford: 1895, introduction, xiii), though with a different liturgical context – a blessing over the Torah:

ברכתא לדברי חכמים ז"ל
ברוך אתה ה' א‑להינו מלך העולם
אשר בחר בחכמים ובצדיקים
ומסר להם רזי תורה ונתן להם
תורה, הוא בר‑חמיו הרבים יזכה
אותנו לכל מדה טובה ללמוד
וללמד לשמור ולעשות. ברוך
אתה ה' נותן התורה.

Blessed are You, Lord our God, Ruler of the universe, Who has chosen the sages and the righteous ones and given them the secrets of the Torah and given them the Torah. May He in his great mercy grant us every good measure to learn and to teach, to keep and to practice. Blessed are You, O Lord, Who gives the Torah.

We have here clear and unambiguous evidence of the creativity that the rabbis felt free to exercise in formulating new liturgical elements when they saw an urgent need for it. Similarly, we know of a long, complex and totally new prayer that R. Elazar of Worms composed, probably at the end of the thirteenth century.[2]

---

2   See J. Dan, apud *Temirin* 1 (edited by L. Weinstock, 90–91. Jerusalem: 1981).

7

New Prayers and Innovative Creativity

Since we have mentioned new prayers, let us consider the example of a fairly recent, completely innovated prayer. On Tu bi-Shevat, some of us may recite a special prayer written by Rabbi Yosef Hayyim of Baghdad, the Ben Ish Hai, one of the major halachists of the late nineteenth and early twentieth centuries. Let us look at several passages from its text:

Dear God, please rescue us on this day dedicated to trees, on this day of the New Year. Dear God, please help us succeed in our endeavors on this day dedicated to trees, on this day of the New Year. Dear God, please provide us with prosperity on this day dedicated to trees, on this day of the New Year. Dear God, please be our benefactor on this day dedicated to trees, on this day of the New Year. Dear God, please bless us on this day dedicated to trees, on this day of the New Year.

אנא ה' הושיעה נא, היום הזה לאילן, הוא ראש השנה. אנא ה' הצליחה נא, היום הזה לאילן, דהוא ראש השנה. אנא ה' הרויחה נא, היום הזה לאילן, הוא ראש השנה. אנא ה' הטיבה נא, היום הזה לאילן, הוא ראש השנה. אנא ה' ברך נא, היום הזה לאילן, הוא ראש השנה.

We recognize that this passage is based on the Hallel, the song of praise that we recite on festivals and on Rosh Hodesh (the new moon); Rabbi Yosef Hayyim has, in effect, introduced a new type of Hallel for the trees on the festival of the trees. This is the beginning of the year for the trees, ראש השנה לאילנות. He then continues:

And may it be Your will, dear God, our Lord and the Lord of our ancestors, that You bless all the different varieties of trees and may they bring forth an abundance of luscious, wholesome fruit. Bless the grapevines, so that they may bring forth an abundance of

ויהי רצון מלפניך ה' א-לוהינו וא-לוהי אבותינו, שתברך כל מיני האילנות, ויוציאו פירותיהם בריבוי שמנים וטובים, ותברך את הגפנים,

luscious, wholesome grapes; so that the wine produced from them may be available in abundance for all the members of your people Israel; and so that they will be able to perform on Sabbaths and festivals the commandment of sanctifying the wine and the commandment of blessing the wine at the Havdalah service signifying the end of the Sabbath or festival. For us and all our Jewish brothers and sisters, may the following verse from Ecclesiastes (9:7) become a reality: "Go forth, eat your bread with joy and drink your wine with a happy heart, for your actions have found favor in God's eyes."

שיוציאו ענבים הרבה שמנים וטובים, כדי שיהיה היין היוצא מהם מצוי לרוב לכל עמך ישראל, לקיים בו מצות קידוש ומצות הבדלה בשבתות וימים טובים. ויתקיים בנו ובכל ישראל אחינו, מקרא שכתוב (קהלת ט, ז): "לך אכול בשמחה לחמך, ושתה בלב־ טוב יינך, כי כבר רצה האל־ הים את מעשיך".

We see, then, that entirely new prayers were written by completely normative Jews, including great authorities – in this particular case, a prominent leader of Sefardi Jewry – in order to give new meaning to specific days or events. In the case of Tu bi-Shevat, Rabbi Yosef Hayyim felt that there was not enough within the existing liturgy, and composed a new prayer himself. Indeed, this was by no means an innovation; for we encounter this practice in the thirteenth, sixteenth, seventeenth, and eighteenth centuries, when whole books of additional prayers were written to supplement the existing liturgy. To give yet another example, we may point to the now more or less universally accepted *Tefillah Zakah,* which we recite shortly before *Kol Nidrei* on the eve of Yom Kippur. The source of this prayer is the *Hayyei Adam* by Rabbi Abraham Danzig, which was first published in Vilna in 1809, and which contains a discussion about the new prayer in the second edition of 1819. The author (in *Klal* 145) claims as his source the work *Hemdat Yamim* (Izmir: 1731), which was controversial because it was attributed to the Sabbatean Nathan ha-Azati (see A. Yaari, *Taalumat Sefer: Sefer Hemdat Yamim – Mi Hibro?* Jerusalem: 1954). As a consequence, in some subsequent editions of *Hayyei Adam*, the words *Hemdat Yamim* were removed, and in the Zolkiev edition of 1838 (Vilna: 1849, Tchernowitz: 1864), "in the works of the Arizal" has been substituted. It is for this same reason that some authorities advised against reciting this prayer (see Y. Mundshein, *Otzar Minhagei Habad* [Jerusalem: 1995, 200–201]), also claiming that it was newly created and might also lead to improper sexual thoughts (R. G. Zinner, *Nitei Gavriel: Hilchot Yom ha-Kippurim* [Jerusalem: 2001, 185, n. 4]). The Hafetz Hayyim, according to his

son, required printers to change the location of the paragraph granting for-giveness to those who sinned against the worshipper from the middle of the prayer to the beginning (Aryei Leib ha-Cohen, *Michtevei ha-Hafetz Hayyim Zatzal*, second edition. New York: 1953, 21–22; see my *Minhagei Yisrael*, vol. 4, 1995, 274). However, despite its problematic source and the various other doubts that were raised, *Tefillah Zakah* has become almost universally ac-cepted. (See Sperber, *Minhagei Yisrael*, vol. 2, Jerusalem: 1991, 37, n. 10; M. Meir's article in *Kenishta* 2 [2003]: 119–138; Dan Rabinowitz, in his Seforim blog [http://seforim.blogspot.com], article entitled "*Tefillah Zakah*: History of a Controversial Prayer" [http://seforim.blogspot.com/2007/09/teffilah-zakah-history-of-controversial.html]). Therefore, if the text of our liturgy is not really formally and finally crystallized, and since we see that, in all peri-ods, additions, changes, alterations and updatings were made, why can we not continue in this age-old liturgic tradition by adding our own prayers to the "standard" liturgy, together with changes that will suit the contemporary situ-ation? Why can we not add Sarah, Rivkah, Rahel, and Leah to the *berachot*? Why should we not add additional sections in order to make our prayers more responsive to feminist concerns?

8

Talmudic Sources Forbidding Change
in the Liturgy and Maimonides's
Understanding of Them

The problem is that we have texts in the Talmud – in BT *Berachot,* based on the Tosefta *Berachot* – that seem to suggest that we cannot alter the *nusah,* or version, of the liturgy that the rabbis of old instituted; these prayers are referred to as "the coin our sages minted" – מטבע שטבעו חכמים.

Maimonides, in his *Mishneh Torah,* where he presents the laws governing prayer *(Hilchot Berachot* 1:5) writes as follows:

The version of all the benedictions was established by Ezra and his rabbinical court. It is not suitable that we change, add to, or subtract from any of them, and anybody who deviates from the "coin that our sages minted" – that is, from the version of the prayer that our sages instituted – errs, and every *berachah* that does not mention the name of God and his Kingship is no *berachah.*	ונוסח כל הברכות עזרא ובית דינו תקנום. ואין ראוי לשנו־ תן ולא לה־וסיף על אחת מהן ולא לגרוע ממנה. וכ־ל המשנה ממטבע שטבעו חכמים בבר־ כות אינו אלא טועה. וכל ברכה שאין בה הזכרת השם ומלכות אינה ברכה.

In the section on the *keriyat shema* prayer *(Hilchot Keriyat Shema* 1:7), he says much the same thing:

These benedictions that we have mentioned above, in addition to all the other benedictions that all the communities	ברכות אלו עם שא־ר כל הברכות הערוכות בפי כ־ל ישראל, עזרא ובי־ת דינו תקנום. וא־ין אדם רשאי לפחור־ת מהן ולא להוסיף עליהן. מקום שה־תקינו לחתום ב"ברוך" אינו רשאי שלא לחר־תום, ומקום שה־תקינו שלא ל־חתום אינו ר־שאי

of Israel say, were established by Ezra and his rabbinical court and no one may subtract from them or to add to them.

לחתום. מקום שהתקינו שלא לפתוח ב"ברוך" אינו רשאי לפתוח, ומקום שהתקינו לפתוח אינו רשאי שלא לפתוח. כללו של דבר – כל המשנה ממטבע שטבעו חכמים בברכות הרי זה טועה וחוזר ומברך כמטבע.

He then says that our *berachot* have a certain basic structure. They must have a beginning and an end and so on, and we must keep to this general structure:

> Where our sages ruled that we must end the prayer with "Blessed are You, O God," that is how we must end the prayer. Where our sages ruled that we should not end the prayer with "Blessed are You, O God," then we should not. Where our sages ruled that we must begin the prayer with "Blessed are You, O God," that is how we must begin the prayer. Where our sages ruled that we should not begin the prayer with "Blessed are You, O God," then we should not. The rule of thumb is that if we deviate from the "coin that our sages minted" – that is, from the version that our sages instituted – we are committing an error and must repeat the prayer according to the sages' version.

These rulings of Maimonides are based on a passage from BT *Berachot* 40b, where, inter alia, Rabbi Yossi says that if we deviate from the version fixed by the rabbis for the benedictions, then we have not fulfilled our duty with regard to the benedictions. In JT *Berachot* (9 ad init., 12d), we read: "You have no right to add to the formulation fixed by the sages" – "אין לך רשות להוסיף על מטבע שטבעו חכמים" (see n. 2 below). All of this would seem to be completely in contradiction to everything that has been said above. For we have seen that *de facto,* throughout all the generations, in all communities, the greatest of authorities changed, added to, and subtracted from, the "received" version (*matbea shetav'u*). Indeed, as we have seen above, it is difficult to speak of a "received" version when we read all these different ones and see that there are, in fact, numerous versions.

In our own era, we have a *Nusah Ashkenaz,* and a *Nusah Sefarad,* as well as a *Nusah Teman* (Yemenite version), a *Nusah Haleb* (Aleppo version), also called *Eretz (Aram Tzova),* a *Nusach Edot Ha-Mizrah* (Oriental version), and so on. The *nusah* depends to a large extent on the *siddurim* used by the community. When they were printed in Livorno (Leghorn), they followed one version, and when, they were printed in Constantinople (Kushta) they were

printed in another way. What really determined the *nusah,* perhaps more than the rabbis themselves, were the printers and their editions. (See chap. 17, n. 1, last paragraph et seq.).

Maimonides addressed this apparent contradiction between formal *halachah* and factual evidence in several different responsa. In order to understand the halachic situation, we cannot limit ourselves to the brief formulations in the *Mishneh Torah*. We must refer to the expanded discussions in his various responsa.

We have already seen that he has two different formulations. In *Hilchot Berachot*, he says, "ואין ראוי – it is not *suitable*" – and, in *Hilchot Kriyat Shema*, he says, "אין אדם רשאי – one is not *permitted*." These would seem to contradict one another. However, this is not the case. In *Hilchot Kriyat Shema*, he is saying that one cannot alter the structure of the *berachot*, and he explains in detail how the *berachot* have to have a beginning and an end, and mention the name of God and His sovereignty. Unless the *berachot* are structured in this fashion, they are null and void. In the first passage that we read, he refers to a different issue. He says that within the given structure of a prayer or blessing, alterations, additions or omissions are unsuitable, although the prayer or blessing will still remain within the accepted structure. In other words, he interprets the phrase in the Talmud that says that no one may alter *matbea shetavu hachamim* to mean that no one may alter the *structure* of the blessing that the rabbis determined and established.

This is the understanding of R. Yosef Caro in his commentary on the Rambam (*Hilchot Tefillah* 1:5), the *Kesef Mishneh*:

> It is difficult to understand why our master [Rambam] changed the language and wrote that [anyone who changes the format] "is in error." It is also important to examine why he wrote "It is not fitting to change them."
>
> It seems to me that there are two types of "changing." The first is when one says the *nusah* of the blessing established by the *hachamim*, but adds to it or leaves some of it out. In another case, he says something similar to the *nusah* established by the *hachamim*, but in different words which, nevertheless, allude to [the same point as] the *nusah* that the sages established. But since the meaning of his words conveys what the sages decreed, there is no "error," but it is still "not fitting" to do this.

Thus we begin – ברוך אתה ה' א-להינו מלך העולם – *Baruch ata Hashem Eloheinu melech ha-olam"* (Blessed are You, O Lord our God, King of the Universe), and we end with ברוך אתה ה' שומע תפילה – *Baruch ata Hashem shomea tefillah"* (Blessed are You, O God, Who hears prayer). In all those versions which we cited from the *Amidah,* we saw that the general structure was always preserved and was not changed, although many additions and alterations have taken place within that structure. In one of his responsa, Maimonides was asked about the Jews of Alexandria, who insert *piyyutim* that are included in Saadya Gaon's *siddur* into their Friday night prayers. The questioners said that they had heard that he objected to this, and wished to understand his position (ed. Blau, no. 181, 487).

The upshot of his reply is that these *berachot* represent a deviation from the version the rabbis established and that this version may not be changed. According to Maimonides, these *piyyutim* should not be recited instead of the *berachot*. However, he concedes that, if people pray in this fashion with the various additions, then they have certainly carried out what is required of them as far as the benedictions are concerned, (הרי יצא) ידי חובת ברכות, because the original intention of the benediction is still to be found in this expanded version – כי כוונות הברכות שמורות הן. He adds that this point has already been discussed in many other of his responsa.[1]

---

1   ויורנו בדבר מה שנהגו באלכסנדריא בלילות שבת ומוצאי שבתות לומר במעריב ברכות שחיברו המאוחרים אשר מצאנו בסידור רב סעדיה גאון זצ"ל מקויימות והתיר לאומרן.... ושמענו שבמושבו הגדול ירוחם הוא מגנה אותן ומונע לאומרן. לא ידענו הסיבה בזה.... התשובה: אלה הברכות כולן יש בהן שינוי ממטבע בברכות והן מסוג החיזיון המפורסם בכל הארצות, ועיקר זה המנהג שידבק בו הדבק לפי קביעת החזנים, לא לפי קביעת תלמידי החכמים. סוף דבר, אסור לשנות בברכות מן המטבע שטבעו החכמים ולא להחליפן באחד מאותם מאות הפיוטים אשר חיברום המאוחרים. ואם יתפלל המתפלל... הברכות בליל שבת ומוצאי שבת הרי יצא ידי חובת ברכות, כי כוונות הברכות שמורים הן. וכבר התקנו זאת פעמים מספר בתשובות.

On additions of *piyyutim* within *berachot*, see Elbogen ibid., 153–173, 210–265. One may find strong disapproval of the insertion of *piyyutim* within *berachot* in the writings of the geonim of Babylonia and onwards (see Elbogen, ibid., 226, 227, 449, nn. 60–64, 70–74). See Tur *Orah Hayyim*, sec. 68 and Beit Yosef, ibid., *Maaseh Rav* of R. Eliyahu of Vilna, sec. 127, all of whom express their dissatisfaction with the inserted text. However, as Elbogen rightly points out, even these formidable authorities could not undermine the authority of these *piyyutim* and cause them to be removed from the liturgy. See, further, Laurence Hoffman, *The Canonization of the Synagogue Service* (Notre Dame & London: 1979), 68–71, and

Indeed, there are other responsa in which Maimonides discusses the issue of performing what is required concerning the benedictions (הרי יצא חובת ברכות) (e.g., ed. Blau, nos. 254:465–466, and 207:363). In fact, Maimonides talks about this issue in four other responsa. Now, I think that the most

---

78–80 on Saadya's *siddur*; Ginzberg, *Ginzei Schechter*, ibid., 504–573; and the fine comprehensive discussion of Ruth Langer, *To Worship God Properly: Tensions between Liturgical Custom and Halakhah in Judaism* (Cincinnati: 1988). See also Seth Kadish, *Kavvanah: Directing the Heart in Jewish Prayer* (New Jersey–Jerusalem: 1997), 263–265, n. 9, and in general his fine discussion on "fixed prayer" (257 et seq.).

Further on the issue of the insertion of *piyyutim* in the benedictions, see the statement of R. Ephraim of Bonn in ms. Hamburg 152, 446:

מסוד חכמים: כשהחזן מתחיל הקרובה אומר א"ל עליון בונה ברחמיו שמים וארץ מסוד חכמים
ונבונים וכו' אבל לי נראה לסיים את הברכה כך: א"ל עליון גומל חסדים טובים וקונה הכל וזוכר [חסדי]
אבות ומביא גואל לבני בניהם למען שמו באהבה. מסוד חכמים ונבונים וכו'. ... וכן שמעתי מקרובי
אב"ן ישראל שהיה מסיים את כל הברכה של מגן עד חתימתה ואחר כך הוא אומר מסוד חכמים
ונבונים וכו' וכן עיקר, שלא לשנות מן מטבע שטבעו חכמים. כי אפילו מה שמפסיקין את הברכה
ואומרים פיוטים הרבה קשה כאשר כתבתי למעלה, ואף כי מקצרין אותה. ...

We see here that whole sections were inserted into the first benediction of the *Amidah*, *birkat magen*. R. Ephraim expressed dissatisfaction with the practice in light of what he had heard from his relative, R. Eliezer bar Natan (Ravan), who insisted on completing the benediction and only then reciting the *piyyut*, and apparently saw such insertions as "a change in that which the sages coined." (See above for Rambam's view on this subject.) He also makes a distinction between the *Amidah* benedictions and other ones, such as *emet ve-yatziv*, which were altered and shortened in order to receive piyyutic insertions. Indeed, it appears that these piyyutic additions at times even effected a change in the version of the benedictions. This passage is cited by E. E. Urbach in his edition of *Arugat ha-bosem*, vol. 4 (Jerusalem: 1963, 41) and discussed by E. Fleischer in his introduction to *Mahzor Vermaiza* (London: 1996, 48–49), who also points to the changes in the version of the benedictions at times caused by the piyyutic additions. In the same introduction (40–50), Fleischer also shows how there were differences in the version of the standard prayers between Worms and Mainz and even within Worms itself (see also his observations, ibid., 47). See also app. 5.

Regarding differing versions of the *Amidah* benedictions and some reasons for these differences, see N. Wieder's illumination studies in *Hitgabshut*, vol. 1, 65–102. For further examples of the variety of versions of well-known prayers and benedictions, see J. Heinemann, *Prayer in the Talmud* (Berlin, New York: 1977, 37–76), and *Ha-tefillah bi-tekufat ha-tannaim ve-ha-amoraim: tivah u-defusehah* (Prayer during the Tannaitic and the Amoraic period: its nature and pattern). Jerusalem: 1966, 39–41, 48–51.

important part of this discussion is what he says at the very end – if the initial, original intent and meaning of the *berachah* is still being preserved, then, *be-di'avad*, one has fulfilled the duty of saying the *berachah*. Maimonides says as follows: ideally, we should follow the original version – מטבע שטבעו חכמים בברכות. We are certainly not permitted to change the structure – the beginning, the end, the *shem u-malchut* (God's name and sovereignty), and so on.[2]

In fact, Maimonides himself permitted certain additions even in the *avodah* benediction of the *Amidah* (one of the last three), concerning which he stated in *Hilchot Tefillah* 6:3, "One should not make personal requests in the first three or the last three." In a response (no. 184, ed. Blau, Jerusalem: 1960, 336, 339), he was asked regarding this ruling:

> . . . But it is a custom that an individual add in the elective prayer in *avodah*, as an elective prayer (תפילת רשות) the following passage: בהר מרום ישראל שם נעבדך ושם נדרוש את כל אשר ציויתנו. בריח ניחוח תרצה אותנו. תחזינה עינינו – On the lofty hill of Israel [i.e., Mount Moriah, the Temple Mount] we shall worship You, and there shall we seek [to carry out] all that which You commanded us. With the sweet fragrance [of the sacrifices], may You accept us. May our eyes see [Your return to Zion in mercy] . . . .

Maimonides answers:

> This passage, which is added in the *avodah* section, does no harm, nor does it constitute a request for one's needs (שואל צרכיו), but is of the essence of the benediction (אלא זה ענין הברכה).

We see, then, that Maimonides accepts additions "that are of the essence of the benedictions."

Furthermore, in *Hilchot Tefillah* 6: 2–3, he writes:

> He who prays with the community should not lengthen his prayer too much, but in private (בינו לבין עצמו) he may do as he wishes . . . . If he wishes to add in any of the middle benedictions something which is of the nature of the benediction (מעין הברכה), he may. How so? If he knows of a sick person, he may ask mercy for him in the blessing for the sick, according to his personal style (כפי

62

צחות לשונו). If he requires financial support, he adds a request (תחינה ובקשה) in *birkat ha-shanim*, and after this fashion in each one of these [benedictions]. And if he wishes to request all his needs in *birkat shomea tefillah*, he may. But he should not do so in the first three or the last three.

(Cf. ibid., 1:9.) He also agreed to the additions in the Rosh ha-Shanah and Yom Kippur prayers. He writes (ibid., 2:19):

> There are places where, during the Ten Days of Repentance, the custom is to add זכרנו לחיים – "Remember us for life" – in the first benediction, and in the second one מי כמוך אב הרחמים וגו' – "Who is like You, Father of Mercy," and in *hodaah* – the second of the last three benedictions – זכור רחמיך וכתוב לחיים – "Remember Your mercy, and inscribe [us] for life," and they add in the last benediction, ובספר חיים – "And in the Book of Life . . ."

Indeed, in his section on the prayers for the whole year, he writes:

> Most of the nations are accustomed between Rosh ha-Shanah and Yom ha-Kippurim to add in all the prayers of the Ten Days of Repentance: in the first benediction the addition זכרנו לחיים, in the second מי כמוך אב הרחמים, and so on.

Thus, Maimonides too was willing to regard as legitimate, even in the first and last three benedictions, additions that somehow accorded with the benedictions themselves, especially when the various communities accepted them widely.

Under certain circumstances, he also permitted some changes in the wording of a blessing. Thus his disciple, R. Ovadia the Convert, asked him whether he would be permitted to say in his blessings, "Who has separated us," "Who has chosen us," "Who gave our ancestors [The Land of Israel]," "Who took us out of the Land of Egypt," and so on (see *Iggrot ha-Rambam*, vol. 1, edited by Y. Shilat, 333–334, Maaleh Adumim: 1987, 333–334), he replies that the convert may use all these formulations and explains why. However, regarding the statement "Who has taken us out of the Land of Egypt" he writes:

> . . . But "Who took us out of the Land of Egypt," or "Who performed miracles for our ancestors" – if you wish to alter [the formulations] and to say "Who took Israel out of Egypt," and "Who performed miracles for Israel," you may do so. But if you do not alter [the text], there is no loss in this (it is also all right), for once you have come under the wings of the *Shechinah* (become a Jew) . . .

there is no difference between us and you, and all the miracles that took place as it were, both to us and to you . . . etc.

Here, too, for the sake of accuracy and honesty, Maimonides is willing to countenance slight changes in the text of blessings (see Afterword, n. 1).

Hence, if we make additions and changes that do not change the intrinsic meaning of the *berachah* (see responsum no. 254, 465: "However, this does not apply to the *piyyutim*, which introduce new matters and include many things that have nothing to do with the topics of the liturgy" – ואין כמו הפיוטים (אשר הם תוספת עניינים והבאת דברים הרבה שאינם מעניין התפילה), if they add, expand, and relate to a specific situation that may not have existed when the *berachah* was originally composed – then one need not repeat the *berachah* (יצא ידי חובת ברכות).[3]

Indeed, personal additions were permitted in the standard benedictions. Thus, in *Shulhan Aruch Orah Hayyim* 119:1, we read:

> If he wishes to add in any of the intermediate blessings [an addition] that accords with the nature of that blessing, he may. How? If he has a sick person [in mind], he may ask mercy for him in the blessing *refaeinu* (=heal us). If he needs monetary support, he may ask for it in *birkat ha-shanim* . . . and in *shomea tefillah* (who harkens to prayer) he may ask for all his needs because it includes all requests . . . .

This ruling is based on a talmudic passage in BT *Avodah Zarah* 8a, followed by Rambam, *Hilchot Tefillah* 6:3 (however, see Rashi on *Taanit* 14b, where he limited such inserts to *shomea tefillah*). We may further note that the *Zohar* in *Midrash ha-Neelam* Genesis, 1:121a, states that one may even include

---

3   The Raavad holds a similar view, but in a slightly different context. The question raised in BT *Pesahim* 7a–b, and BT *Berachot* 38a–b is whether one formulates certain *birchot ha-mitzvot* (benedictions over performing a mitzvah) with *la'asot, levarech, litol* (lulav) etc., or with *al asiyyat, al birchat, al netilat*. In BT *Berachot*, ibid., the question is raised whether, on eating bread, one should say *ha-motzi* or *motzi*. The issue is which of these formulations suggests a past activity – *al asiyat, motzi* (= *hotzi*) – or a future activity – *la'asot, levarech* etc. Concerning the search for *hametz* before Passover, the question was whether one should say *le-vaer* (in the future tense), or *al biur* (past tense). The Raavad states that if you say *le-vaer*, you have certainly fulfilled the halachic requirement (*yatza*). However, a priori – *mi-lechathila* – you should say *al biur*. See Rabbi David Bagno's recent article, "*Matbea birchot ha-mitzvot (laasot o al ha-asiya)*." *Magal* 15 (2007): 32–33.

birkat ha-derech (the blessing for travelers) in *shomea tefillah* (see M. Spielman, *Tiferet Tzvi*, vol. 2 [Brooklyn: 1988], 327–328.)

Furthermore, Kadish (317–318) has argued convincingly that Rambam did not consider his prayer text in *Mishneh Torah* to be obligatory, nor did he think that it was the original or official text from the time of Ezra. He simply recorded his own customary *nusah* as one valid text among many after making the minor changes necessary to make it halachically and linguistically accurate. This is the most cogent and straightforward explanation of Rambam's prayer text, as Rabbi Nahum Rabinovitch explained in his introductory remarks to the text (*Yad Peshutah* 2/2, Jerusalem: 1984, 1307):

> Prayer books were already numerous and widespread in the days of our Master [Rambam]. Especially well known were *Seder Rav Amram Gaon* and the *siddur* of Rav Saadya Gaon. In addition to this, various customs prevailed throughout the Diaspora, and different communities each kept their own *nusah*. Since most of the differences contain nothing significant that would invalidate [a blessing], our Master did not think it would be correct to incorporate his own *nusah* into his book [*Mishneh Torah*] as an obligatory halakhic ruling. Instead, he put it in a separate section for practical use by the masses. Thus, whoever wanted to continue following one of the accepted *siddurim* that was already in widespread use was permitted to do so. (See Kadish's extended note, ibid., 318–319, note on the various views on this issue.)

9

Limits of Flexibility in Change

We have stated above that Maimonides made a distinction between changing the structure and basic theme of a *berachah* and making additions or changes within the body of the *berachah* that do not alter its basic structure and central theme.

This is the conclusion of the *Kesef Mishneh* (a work by R. Josef Caro, the author of the *Shulhan Aruch*) in his commentary on Rambam, *Hilchot Berachot* 1:6. It answers the question of the Rema (R. Moshe ha-Cohen), who saw a contradiction between two statements of the Rambam (see above). The *Kesef Mishneh* cites further proof for this conclusion from the *sugya* in BT *Berachot* 40b in which Benjamin the shepherd changed the version of the (first paragraph of the) grace after meals, and so on. The Rambam in *Hilchot Berachot* 1:9 states explicitly that in the central blessings of the *Amidah,* one may add or innovate if one is repeating the prayer since it is a *tefillat nedavah* (a non-obligatory, voluntary prayer). (See Ravad and commentators ad loc.)[1]

For a penetrating analysis of Rambam's position on the standardization of liturgical texts, one may refer to G. J. Blidstein's discussion in his *Ha-Tefillah be-Mishnato ha-Hilchatit shel ha-Rambam* (Prayer in Maimonidean Halakha, Jerusalem: 1994, 123–150). There, he concludes that although Rambam's intent was to limit the flexibility and variety in versions of prayers and move toward a more unified prayer book, his rulings on the non-permissibility of change refer mainly to the beginnings and endings of blessings, and not

---

1   See, most recently, the discussions and summary of this issue in M. M. Shiloni's *Shomea u-mashmia* (Jerusalem: 2006), 153, col. 2.

necessarily to the main part (גוף), provided that the main thrust is preserved (124–126). However, regarding the first three and last three benedictions of the *Amidah*, Rambam permits no change whatsoever (*Hilchot Tefillah* 1:9), though Blidstein (128–129) has difficulty in finding a source for this ruling (see, further, Kadish, 276–279, 305–322).

In fact, the same phenomenon that we noted with regard to the intermediate benedictions of the *Amidah* – namely the variety of their versions – also applies to the initial and final blessings. Thus, for example, Luger (55), gives the following variant for the second blessing (*birkat gevurot*) as follows:

אתה גבור משפיל גאים חזק ומדין עריצים חי עולמים מקים מתים משיב הרוח ומוריד הטל מכלכל
חיים מחיה מתים כהרף עין ישועה לנו תצמיח. בא"י מחיה המתים.

Here again, it begins אתה גבור and ends מחיה מתים, but what is between them is very different from that with which we are acquainted. (See Luger's discussion, 56–62.)

This is also true of the third blessing, of *kedushat ha-Shem*. Luger (65) gives us an alternate version (no. 2): קדוש אתה ונורא שמך ואין א-לוה מבלעדך. בא"י
הא-ל הקדוש – which, of course, sounds familiar (see Luger, 66–72).

And perhaps even more so with the final blessing, *hodaah*, where Luger (186) lists the following text as a variant:

מודים אנחנו לך אתה הוא ה' א-לוהינו וא-לוהי אבותינו על כל הטובות החסד והרחמים שגמלתנו
ושעשית עמנו ועם אבותינו מלפנינו ואם אמרנו מטה רגלינו חסדך ה' יסעדינו. בא"י הטוב לך להודות.
(See Luger, 188–195.)

In *sim shalom*, the brief version 2 (Luger, 188) is as follows:

שים שלומך על ישראל עמך ועל עירך ועל נחלתך וברכנו כולנו כאחד. בא"י עושה השלום.
(See Luger, 199–208.)

The above examples are all from the Palestinian rite found in the Genizah. When we study Wieder's findings (16–125), which encompass many other versions, including those of the Babylonian rites (witness on 54–55, eight (!) different versions of the third benediction, or Goldschmidt's listing of *Mahzor Vitry's* readings [69]), we can see the remarkable number of alternative forms of the liturgy. Indeed in our current standard versions, some of the blessings of the *Amidah*, especially the final ones, are not necessarily in accordance with

those that the Rambam gave us in his *Seder Tefillat Rosh ha-Shanah*.² Thus:

שים שלום . . . וברכנו כולנו ממאור פניך נתת לנו ה' א־להינו תורת חיים . . . וכו'.

I believe that Rambam's intent was that one may not add personal or public *requests* in these blessings (see Rabinovitz ibid.), rather than that no changes at all may be made. This is based on BT *Berachot* 34a:

R. Yehudah said: A person should not make his personal requests either in the first three benedictions [of the *Amidah*] and not in the last three, for R. Haninah said: The first ones are like unto a servant who orders his praises before his master; the middle ones are like unto a servant who asks for a reward from his master; the last ones are like unto a servant who receives a reward from his master, takes his leave of him and goes off on his way.	א"ר יהודה לעולם אל ישאל אדם צרכיו לא בג' ראשונות ולא בג' אחרונות אלא באמצעיות, דאמר ר' חנינא: ראשונות־דומה לעבד שמסדר שבח לפני רבו; אמצעיות־דומה לעבד שמבקש פרס מרבו; אחרונות – דומה לעבד שקבל פרס מרבו ונפטר והולך לו.

(Cf. Rambam's *Hilchot Tefillah* 1:4.) Indeed Pirkoi ben Baboi (a student of R. Yehudai Gaon) writes (*Ginzei Schechter – Genizah Studies,* vol. 2, edited by L. Ginzberg, New York: 1929, 546):

From here you learn that it is forbidden to add even a single letter in praise of [God] that has not been instituted by the Sages, and how much more so that a person is forbidden to make his personal requests in the first three and the last three [benedictions]	מכאן אתה למד שאסור להוסיף אפילו אות אחרת בשבחו של [הקב"ה] מה שלא תקנו חכז"ל, וכל שכן שאסור לשאול אדם צרכיו בשלש ראשונות ובשלש אחרונות . . . .³

(It should be noted that there are established places for additional *personal requests* in the eighth [*refaeinu*] and sixteenth [*shema kolenu*] blessings

---

2   See further, *Siddur Otzar ha-Tefillot*, 315–373; *Siddur Tzelota de-Avraham*, vol. 1, 272–324, and see N. E. Rabinovitz, *Yad peshutah* (*A comprehensive commentary* [*upon Rambam's Mishneh Torah*], Ahavah, Jerusalem: 1984), on *Hilchot Tefillah* 2:19, 172–174, for a discussion of whether one may make additions in the initial and final benedictions of the *Amidah*.

3   See further *Sefer Halachot Gedolot*, vol. 1 (edited by A. Hildesheimer, 33. Jerusalem: 1971), and editor's note ad loc.; and Ruth Langer's discussion, in her book *To Worship God Properly*, 118–123. See also *Hagahot Maimoniyot* on *Hilchot Tefillah* 6.3, n. 3, which limits forbidding requests only to personal ones, while those of the public are permitted.

[see chap. 6, near n. 2]. There are changes and additions – seasonal ones that are recited on specific occasions – in other benedictions of the *Amidah*.)

It would also appear that Rav Saadya Gaon's position on this issue of standardization was very similar to that of Rambam.[4] He says so in the introduction to his *Siddur* (1):

I saw fit to collect in this *siddur* the prayers, praises and benedictions, which are essential, in their primary characteristics as they were in their formulations before the exile and after it, and to place them in the *siddur*. And I have made the additions or omissions to them that I heard about, such as [were added or omitted] in accordance with the will of such who acted on their own initiative, villagers or city-dwellers, or [people] from a district or a land. I have also forbidden the recitation of anything that annuls (or conflicts with) the primary intent (of the prayer or blessing). Regarding that which does not, I have nonetheless noted that in any case, it is not part of the basic tradition . . . .

וראיתי לאסוף בספר זה את התפילות והתשבחות והברכות שיש להן עיקר, בדתכונתן הקדומה כפי שהיו צורותיהן לפני הגלות ואחרי כן, ולשימן לסידור. וא וסיף להן מה ששמעתי שנוסף בהן או נשמט מהן לפי ראות עיני אחדים העושים על דעת עצמם, אנשי כפר או עיר או פלך או ארץ. ומה שמבטל את הכונה היסודית אסרתי לומר, ומה שאינו מבטל אותה העירותי בכל זאת שאין בו עיקר מהמסורה. . . .

We see, then, that Saadya did not forbid additions that did not conflict with the theme of the prayer or blessing. He merely noted that they were not part of the original tradition. (See Wieder, *Hitgabshut* 157; Liebrich, HUCA 34 [1963]: 151.)

---

4   See Y. Heinemann, *Iyyunei Tefillah* (edited by A. Shinan, 110–112. Jerusalem: 1981) and Kadish, 264.

    See Y. Shilat's penetrating discussion in his *Rosh Devarecha* (Maaleh Adummim: 1996, 223–230). He further points out (ibid., 227–232) that the Rashba, R. Shlomo ben Aderet, is of the opinion that one may initially (*le-chathilah*) add or substract within the body of a benediction, unlike Rambam who sees this as valid only after the fact (*be-di-avad*).

69

10

The Dynamic Process of Change in Our Liturgy

The position that I have presented on the constant dynamic process of change in prayers is summarized by Y. Heinemann in his classic essay in *Ha-Tefillah ha-Yehudit* (Prayer in Judaism: Continuity and Change, edited by G. H. Cohen, Jerusalem: 1978, 79–82). Because of its importance, I shall quote sections from it in translation:

> [79–80] Furthermore, when the mandatory and fixed prayers were formulated (תפילות חובה וקבע), they [the sages] did not determine their exact formulations (unlike what is accepted in popular books on prayer). The sages established a framework: the number of blessings in each kind of prayer, such as eighteen in the weekly *Amidah*, seven in those of Sabbaths and festivals, and so on. They also established the basic content of each blessing, such as a request for the rebuilding of Jerusalem or the ingathering of the exiles. But they did not determine, or wish to determine, the literal formulations of any blessing or prayer since, generally speaking, this is in the hands of the worshipper – or, more exactly, the *shaliah tzibbur* (prayer leader) (81). So we learn that a great deal of time after the mandatory and fixed prayers were established in the Yavne generation, the actual formulation (נוסח) still remained free and flexible, not merely because there were no written prayer-books, but because this is what the creators of the liturgy wanted; for at no time did they consider doing away with or limiting the element of dynamism and vitality in the versions of our prayer.
>
> Even after the versions began to be crystallized and became familiar to the worshippers of most communities, dynamic creativity continued in the formulation of the mandatory prayers. It was approximately then that the *piyyut* was

born, first in the Land of Israel and later on in many other countries. It served to bring variety into what was becoming standardized, to exchange one fixed version for many other alternatives. The early *piyyut* was not merely an *addition* to the fixed prayers, but eventually took their place .... (82). By means of the *piyyut,* the element of dynamism was reintroduced into the prayer book, which underwent continuous change ....

Rabbi Samuel David Luzzato (1800–1865, an important Italian Jewish scholar known by his acronym "Shadal"), had stated much the same opinion in the previous century:

> Our predecessors of blessed memory set the format of blessings for us to thank God and pray to Him. But they did not mean by their decree that the text of our prayers should be entirely fixed like a nail that cannot be moved, that one may neither add [to prayer] nor subtract from it!
>
> Rather, the purpose of their decree was to set the matters about which we must thank God and pray to Him for all of Israel, and to fix the general order of blessings .... This was so that the major part of prayer and the theme of each blessing and their openings and closings would be the same for all Jews, wherever they may be.
>
> But our predecessors of blessed memory never wrote the blessings and prayers in a book .... Instead, they let each individual or *shaliah tzibbur* lengthen or shorten them according to his understanding. That is why they instituted the silent *shemoneh esreh* – so that the *shaliah tzibbur* could rehearse his prayer to himself before reciting it for the congregation.
>
> Rabbi Eliezer said, "One who makes his prayer *keva* – his prayer is not *tahanunim*" (*Berachot* 4:4). His colleague, Rabbi Shimon ben Netanel, often said, "Do not make your prayer *keva*. Instead, make it *rahamim* and *tahanunim* before God" (*Avot* 2:13). The meaning of *keva* is that one prays with fixed words and says nothing new, as Rabba and Rav Yosef explained (*Berachot* 29b). And Rashi said that the term *keva* means "Just like today – it was the same yesterday and it will be the same tomorrow!"

(Introduction to his edition of the Italian version of the *siddur "Mavo le-Mahzor Benei Roma."* In *Mahzor kol ha-shanah kefi minhag Italiani* (Livorno: 1858) [reprinted in a critical edition by Daniel Goldschmidt. Tel Aviv: Devir, 1966]. See Kadish, 260–261.) Also, see Appendix 5 below ad fin.

The Main Reasons for Change

Indeed, R. David Yitzhaki, in his introduction to R. Yaakov Emden's *Luah Erez* (Toronto: 2001, 47–48), lists nine main reasons for changes in the versions of prayers and benedictions, giving numerous types of examples for each type. His list runs as follows:

- Corrections for halachic reasons (see Appendix 1 below for an example)
- Additions of psalms, *piyyutim* and *tehinot* [1]
- Bringing prayer and *piyyut* into accord with differing and changing situations
- Abbreviating because of lack of time [in the synagogue] [2]
- Additions and changes under the influence of the Kabbalists [3]

---

1 See chap. 1, n. 3 and Berliner, 25–33, and app. 5.
2 See Berliner, 52; Zunz, *Ritus*, 141–155. In fact, Maimonides shortened the service by ruling that the cantor's repetition of the *Amidah (hazarat ha-shatz)* was unnecessary. See his responsum no. 256 (vol. 2, edited by Blau, 469–476. Jerusalem: 1960) and the responsum of the Radbaz (R. David ben Zimra, sixteenth century) (vol. 4, no. 94 [1165]). It is well known that Maimonides did away with the cantor's repetition of the *Amidah* because he believed people could not concentrate so long and paid little attention to the cantor. Rather, he said, "They turn away to chatter with their friends in worthless gossip, and turn their back to the east, and spit ... and when his friend who is not acquainted [with the liturgy] sees this, he too acts thus ...." (Responsum 35; cited by Wieder, *Hitgabshut*, vol. 2, 681; see the whole section on 680–682, first published in his book *Hashpaot Islamiyyot al ha-pulhan ha-Yehudi [Islamic Influences on Jewish Ritual*, Oxford: 1947, 26–28]. See also A. M. Haberman, *Al ha-tefillah* (edited by Zvi Malachi, 72–73. Lod: 1987).
3 Also see the discussion in Tzuberi, *Kenesset ha-Gedolah*, vol. 3, 326–328. See also his discussion (ibid., 314 et seq.) on why, in Yemen, there were not two *tefillot* for

◆ Changes made out of fear of the censor[4]

---

mussaf of Rosh ha-Shanah and only one recitation on the part of a *sheliah tzibur*, who recited the prayer by heart. He explains that the *mussaf Amidah* of Rosh ha-Shanah is very long and the community, which had few prayer books, did not know it by heart and therefore could not recite it on their own. Hence, they relied on the principle of *shomea ke-oneh* (hearing is tantamount to responding) when listening to the leader of the congregation. In effect, this also shortened the *mussaf* service. Tzuberi shows the sources for this practice in the Rambam and other authorities. Further on (ibid., 328–340), he discusses the custom found already among some of the geonim that within a quorum, one says nine benedictions in the *Amidah* of *mussaf* Rosh ha-Shanah, but a single individual praying on his own says only seven, or that in the *tefillah shel lahash*, the silent prayer of the individual in the congregation one says only seven, while in the cantor's repetition there are nine. This abbreviation, which was strongly contested by some, was the result of people's inability to remember all these long benedictions given the absence of prayer books, and the need for recitation by heart.

A further possible example may be the fact the *U-Va le-Tziyyon* seems to have been moved from *mussaf* to *minhah*. This according to geonic sources and *Sefer ha-ittim* (281), who explain that in the former custom there was extensive study by scholars after the *mussaf* service (on Shabbat), but this study and the recitations of *kedushah de-sidra (U-Va le-Tziyyon)* had to be given up, or moved to *minhah* owing to economic reasons so that the worshippers would not be detained too long when they had to go to work (Maan, HUCA 4 [1927]: 269–270; but see his whole discussion [ibid., 267–275, and cf. ibid., 2 (1925): 217], where his interpretation is somewhat different).

See also the Afterword, note 4, below.

See Berliner, 33–39; A. I. Schechter, *Lectures on Jewish Liturgy* (Philadelphia: 1933, 39–60); and n. 36 below.

4 Zunz, *Ritus* 147, 222; idem *Synagogale Poesie*, 437; Berliner, 47–52, and Berliner, *Censur* and *Confiscation hebräischer Bucher im Kirchenstaate*, 1891.

The whole issue of censorship in general, and its effect upon prayer books in particular, requires additional study, though much has already been written about the subject. See, for example, M. Benayahu, *Haskamah u-reshut be-defusei Veneziah* (Copyright, Authorization and Imprimatur for Hebrew Books Printed in Venice), Jerusalem: 1971, 158 et seq.; Amnon Raz-Krakotzin, *Ha-Zensor, ha-Orech ve-ha-Text: ha-Zenzurah ha-Katolit ve-ha-Defus ha-Ivri be-Meah ha-Shesh-esreh* (Censorship, Editing and the Text: Catholic Censorship and Hebrew Literature in the Sixteenth Century) (Jerusalem: 2005), pass.; W. Popper, *The Censorship of Hebrew Books* (New York: 1899) (reprinted New York 1968), pass., especially 112; D. Kahn, *Avraham Yagel Yitzhak Yeranen* (Brooklyn, NY: 2000, 91–121), especially 103, where we are told of a censor who changed from שומר גוי קדוש to שומר עכו"ם קדוש, and from ואני ערל שפתיים (Exod. 6:12) to אני עכו"ם שפתיים, and other amusing examples of ignorance, and also 96. (This is a reworking of his *Ha-akov le-mishor* [Jerusalem–Brooklyn,

NY: 1993, 1–41], but with changes and additions.) On changes in the *Alenu* prayer, see Wieder's fascinating study in *Hitgabshut*, vol. 2, 453–468, and his article on "*Be-fe amo*" in *Baruch she-Amar*, instead of the grammatically correct "*be-fi amo*" (ibid., 469–491), both of which demonstrate how changes were made for fear of the Christian Church; and ibid., 453–468, on changes in the *Aleinu* prayer, where, for example, the phrase שהם משתחוים להבל וריק was excised because וריק ("to nothingness") has the same *gematria* (numerical value) as ישו (Jesus) (=316). Similarly, ומושב יקרו was changed to וכסא כבודות ומושב תפארתו, ומושב כבודו, ומושב הדרו , etc., because יקרו ("His grandeur") = 316 (ישו). See also *Tiferet Tzvi*, vol. 2 (Brooklyn: 1993, 482). Note that the *Aleinu* prayer was forbidden to be recited in Prussia by edict into the mid-eighteenth century. (See *Encyclopaedia Judaica* [Jerusalem: 1971], vol. 2, 557–558.)

One should further take into account what Zunz, in *Ritus* (224), wrote:

> In fear of persecution, falsified explanations were written for falsified passages (of the prayer book) – if only in order not to sacrifice more to the scissors .... Already the Roman *Mahzor* of 1587 had such glosses of pacification ("*Friedens-Anmerkungen*") ... The Sefaradi prayer book printed in Vilna, in 1840, moves in the same grooves. Wherever mention is made of "yoke" or "enemies," it is explained in terms of the inclination to do evil. גוי becomes כותי, and is explained as referring to ancient star worshipers . . . תתיר צרורה is sin – that is, the sin of this edition against beauty and *Wissenschaft*, against history, right and truth.

Petuchowski finds these characteristics evident in the *Siddur Hegyon Lev*, published by Hirsch Edelmann, in Königsberg (1845), which included a commentary with marginal glosses entitled *Mekor Berachah*, by Eliezer Landshuth. In this *siddur*, which was not strictly Orthodox, Edelmann permitted himself some liberties with the wording of some prayers. Thus in the Hannukah prayer *Al ha-Nissim*, מלכות יוון becomes מלכות אנטיוכוס, יוונים becomes יהירים, and in the prayer recited after reading the Megillah on Purim, אשר הניא עצת גוים becomes עצת המן. This apologetic *tendenz* is spelled out in great detail in a four-page dissertation by Edelmann, which follows the introduction. In addition to this introduction, there are numerous footnotes and marginalia to underscore this *tendenz*, which may be summed up as follows:

– Rejection of any invidious comparisons between Jews and non-Jews.
– Denial of the existence of Jewish suffering at the present time.
– Profession of patriotism and absolute loyalty to the government.
– "Spiritualization" of the messianic hope.

This *siddur* must, therefore, be seen within the tradition of *censorship prevention*. Petuchowski explains that:

> Edelmann's apparatus of "*Friedens-Anmerkungen*" and his occasional tampering with the prayer texts themselves can, therefore, be accounted for in terms of the censorship laws prevailing in Russia in 1845 and in terms of Edelmann's desire to export his liturgical publications which were printed close to the Russian

בְּטְחוּ בַ֡ עֲדֵי עַד בִּי בְּיָהּ יְ֒ צוּר עוֹלָמִים

וְיִבְטְחוּ בְךָ יוֹדְעֵי שְׁמֶךָ כִּי לֹא עֲזַבְתָ ד

דֹרְשֶׁיךָ יְ֒ · יְ֒ חָפֵץ לְמַעַן צִדְקוֹ יַגְדִּיל

תּוֹרָה וְיָאְדִּיר ו

עָלֵינוּ לְשַׁבֵּחַ לַאֲרוֹן הַכֹּל לָתֵת
גְּדֻלָה לְיוֹצֵר בְּרֵאשִׁית שֶׁלֹּא
עָשָׂנוּ כְּגוֹיֵי הָאֲרָצוֹת וְלֹא שָׂמֵנוּ כְּמִ
שְׁפְּחוֹת הָאֲדָמָה · שֶׁלֹּא שָׂם חֶלְקֵנוּ
בָּהֶם וְגוֹרָלֵנוּ כְּכָל הֲמוֹנָם · שֶׁהֵם מִ
שְׁתַּחֲוִים לְהֶבֶל וָרִיק וּמִתְפַּלְלִים אֶל אֵ
לֹא יוֹשִׁיעַ · וַאֲנַחְנוּ כּוֹרְעִים וּמִשְׁתַּחֲוִים
וּמוֹדִים לִפְנֵי מֶלֶךְ מַלְכֵי הַמְּלָכִים ה
הַקָּדוֹשׁ בָּרוּךְ הוּא · שֶׁהוּא נוֹטֶה שָׁמַיִם
וְיֹסֵד אָרֶץ וּכְסֵא כְבוֹדוֹ בַּשָּׁמַיִם מִמַּעַל
וּשְׁכִינַת עֻזוֹ בְּגָבְהֵי מְרוֹמִים · הוּא אֱלֹהֵינוּ
אֵין עוֹד · אֱמֶת מַלְכֵּנוּ וְאֶפֶס זוּלָתוֹ ·

Prague Siddur 1519: Non-censored "Alenu"

דאנו כורעים ומשתחוים ומודים לפני מלך מלכי
המלכים הקב״ה שהוא נוטה שמים ויוסד ארץ ומושב
יקרו בשמים ממעל ושכינת עזו בגבהי מרומים הוא
אלהינו ואין אחר אמת מלכנו ואפס זולתו ככתוב ב
בתורתו וידעת היום והשבות אל לבבך כי ״ הוא האלהים
בשמים ממעל ועל הארץ מתחת אין עוד : על כן
נקוה לך ״ אלהינו לראות מהרה בתפארת עזך להעביר
גלולים מן הארץ והאלילים כרות יכרתון לתקן עולם
במלכות שדי וכל בני בשר יקראו בשמך להפנות אליך
כל רשעי ארץ יכירו וידעו כל יושבי תבל כי לך תכרע
כל ברך תשבע כל לשון לפניך ״ אלהינו יכרעו ויפלו
ולכבוד שמך יקר יתנו ויקבלו כלם את עול מלכותך
ותמלוך עליהם מהרה לעולם ועד כי המלכות שלך היא
ולעולמי עד תמלוך בכבוד : ככתוב בתורתך
״ ימלוך לעולם ועד :

תפלה   ערבית

והוא רחום וכפר עון ולא
ישחית והרבה להשיב
אפו ולא יעיר כל חמתו ״ ה' הושיעה
המלך יעננו ביום קראנו :
ברוך אתה ״ המבורך ברוך ״
המבורך לעולם ועד ׳

Siddur Torino (Turin) 1525. The "Alenu" text is censored and has
no reference to Christianity. But the notes on the bottom (right) in
cursive script have a reference to the "fuller" text, by saying that one
should read ואנחנו and not אבל אנחנו, "and we" as opposed to "but
we," i.e. they prostrate themselves to … but we ….

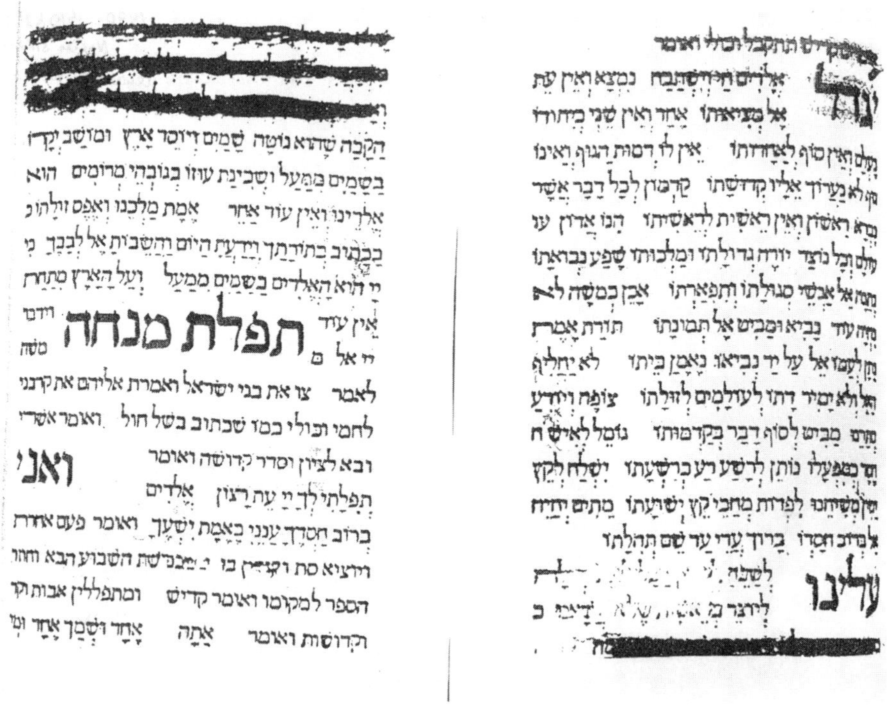

...מקבל ומתקבל וכל ואמר

יגדל אלהים חי וישתבח נמצא ואין עת

אל מציאתו אחד ואין שני כיחודו

נעלם וגם אין סוף לאחדותו אין לו דמות הגוף ואינו

גוף לא נעריך אליו קדושתו קדמון לכל דבר אשר

נברא ראשון ואין ראשית לראשיתו הנו אדון עו[לם]

לכל נוצר יורה גדולתו ומלכותו שפע נבואתו

נתנו אל אנשי סגולתו ותפארתו אבן כמשה לא

קם עוד נביא ומביט אל תמונתו תורת אמת

נתן לעמו אל על יד נביאו נאמן ביתו לא יחליף

האל ולא ימיר דתו לעולמים לזולתו צופה ויודע

סתרים מביט לסוף דבר בקדמותו גומל לאיש ח[סד]

כמפעלו נותן לרשע רע כרשעתו ישלח לקץ

ימין משיחנו לפדות מחכי קץ ישועתו מתים יחיה

אל ברב חסדו ברוך עדי עד שם תהלתו

עלינו לשבח ...

ליוצר ...

הקבה שהוא נוטה שמים ויוסד ארץ ומושב יקרו

בשמים ממעל ושכינת עזו בגובהי מרומים הוא

אלהינו ואין עוד אחר אמת מלכנו ואפס זולתו

ככתוב בתורתך וידעת היום והשבות אל לבבך כי

יי הוא האלהים בשמים ממעל ועל הארץ מתחת

אין עוד

תפלת מנחה

לאמר צו את בני ישראל ואמרת אליהם את קרבני

לחמי ותולי כמו שכתוב בשל חול ואומר אשרי

ובא לציון וסדר קדושה ואומר ואני

תפלתי לך יי עת רצון אלהים

ברוך חסדך עונני באמת ישעך ואומר פעם אחרת

ויוציא סת וקצין בו יי מברכשת השבוע הבא וחזר

הספר למקומו ואומר קדיש ומתפללין אבותיך

קדושות ואומר אתה אחד ושמך אחד ומ[י]

Siddur Napoli (Naples) 1490, censored "Alenu." Note censored lines. Note also the version ואין עוד אחר, "אחר" being a reference to Jesus. (See Wieder, *Hitgabshut*, pp. 426–429.)

שֹרֹחֹנוּ בֹּמֹלֹכוּתֹך שוֹמֹיֹרֹ • שֹׁבֹת וְקֹרֹאֹי •
עוֹנֹג עֹד מֹקֹרֹאֹי שׁבֹיֹעֹי כֹּלֹם יֹשֹבֹעוּן
וֹיֹתֹעֹנֹגוּ מֹטֹוּבֹך וֹבֹשֹבֹיֹעֹי רֹצֹיֹתֹ בֹי
וֹקֹרֹשֹתוּ חֹמֹרֹתֹ יֹמֹיֹם אֹוֹתֹו קֹרֹאֹתֹ רֹ
זֹמֹי לֹמֹעֹטֹה בֹרֹמֹטֹיֹתֹ

עֹלֹיֹנוּ לֹשֹׁבֹח לַאֹרֹוֹן הַכֹּל לֹתֹת גֹרֹלֹ
לֹיֹוֹצֹר בֹרֹאֹשֹיֹתֹ שֹׁלֹא עֹשֹׂוֹמוּ כֹּגוֹיֹ לֹ
הֹאֹרֹץ וֹלֹא שֹׂמֹנוּ כֹּמֹשֹׁפֹחֹוֹתֹ הֹאֹדֹמֹתֹ
שֹׁלֹא שֹׂם חֹלֹקֹנוּ כֹּהֹם עֹרֹלֹנוּ כֹּכֹל הֹם
הֹמוֹנֹם • שֹׁהֹם מֹשֹׁתֹחֹוֹיֹם לֹהֹבֹל וֹרֹיֹק
וֹכֹוּכֹפֹלֹיֹם אֹל אֹל לֹא יֹכֹסֹיֹעֹ • וֹאֹנֹתֹן כֹוֹרֹעֹיֹם
וּמֹיֹשֹׁתֹחֹוֹיֹם לֹפֹגֹ מֹלֹך מֹלֹכֹי הֹמֹלֹכֹיֹם •
הַקֹדֹשֹׁ בֹרוּךֹ הֹוּא שֹׁהוּא נֹוֹטֹה שֹׁמֹיֹם וֹיֹוֹסֹר אֹרֹץ וֹמֹסֹ
כֹבֹוֹדֹן בֹּשֹׁמֹיֹם מֹמֹעֹל וֹשֹׁכֹיֹנֹתֹ בֹגֹן בֹ
בֹגֹוֹבֹהֹי מֹרֹוֹמֹיֹם • הוּא אֹלֹהֹינוּ אֹיֹן עֹוֹד
כֹּדֹכֹתֹוּב וְזֹמֹה נֹמֹיֹן וֹלֹדֹכֹוּ וֹמֹיֹן זֹוֹלֹתֹן כֹּכֹתֹוּב

◆ Changes supported by arguments relating to grammar and language[5]

border, in Königsberg and in Danzig.

See his detailed study entitled "From Censorship Prevention to Theological Reform: A Study in the Modern Jewish Prayerbook" (HUCA 40–41 [1969–1970]: 299–324), reprinted in his *Studies in Modern Theology and Prayer* (edited E. R. Petuchowski and A. M. Petuchowski, 193–219. Philadelphia and Jerusalem: 1998; and most recently in Judith Bleich's article, "Liturgical Innovation and Spirituality: Trends and Trendiness" (in *Jewish Spirituality and Divine Law*, edited by A. Mintz and L. Schiffman, 388–398. New York: 2005 [on "Fundamental Beliefs"]).

5 The importance of correct grammar and accurate vocalization, and consequently pronunciation in prayer, has been stressed frequently by authorities both early and late. Thus, for example, we read in *Zohar Hadash, Aharei Mot*, 49:

> He who reads each word of *Keriyat Shema* correctly influences the heavenly spheres with each of his limbs. But if he does not read it correctly day and night, each of his limbs will be filled with an evil spirit (*ruah ra*) and all kinds of subversive elements (*mar'in bishin*).

In R. Alexander Ziskind's *Yesod ve-shoresh ha-avodah* (Horodna [=Grodna]: 1795, sec. 5, chap. 3), we are told:

> It is found written in a book thus: A certain hasid gave witness that once he saw Elijah the Prophet in his cave, and he asked him why he delays his arrival [i.e., to announce the redemption]. And he replied: "Because they [i.e., the Children of Israel] do not know to take care in the reading of the words and vocalization of their prayers."

See further the introduction to *Maaneh lashon* by R. Eliyahu Gamliel (Rishon le-Tziyyon: 2008, 19–23), for additional references.

See, for example, Yitzhak Satanov, *Siah Yitzhak* (Berlin: 1797, Vienna: 1814, the whole of which is devoted to grammatical corrections [and see below in this note]); so too Klatzki, 61 et seq. See app. 4. In addition to the references that Yitzhaki gives, I would like to call attention to one particular example. R. Hayyim Krauss wrote a series of articles and books arguing that all should read (i.e., both in *Nusah Ashkenaz* and in *Nusah Sefarad*) *mashiv ha-ruah u-morid ha-geshem* (and not *gashem*), as in *Nusah Ashkenaz*. He claimed that this was the original version and that it had been changed in the late eighteenth century by Isaac Satanov (1792–1804), who edited a prayer book in accordance with his notion of correct Hebrew grammar. Rabbi Krauss demanded further that the original version be restored in all communities and succeeded in getting many major rabbinic authorities to support his demand. This triggered a widespread controversy in which the "traditionalists" responded with counter-pamphlets. The arguments back and forth touched upon the core issue of deviating from an accepted tradition and bringing about changes in the accepted version of a given community. See his *Birkot ha-Hayyim*, first published in *Otzrot Yerushalayim* 284 (1979): 530–544; ibid., 238; 1979, 594–608; ibid., 240, 1979,

- Changes in accordance with other versions
- Correction of verses in the liturgy on the basis of the *Minhat Shai*, etc.

We may add a tenth reason: various kinds of printers' errors.[6]

626–640; ibid., 248; 1979, 654–668; ibid., 249; 1970, 770–784; ibid., 265; 1970, 1026–1040. He returned to this issue in a volume entitled *Mechalkel hayyim be-hesed* (Jerusalem: 1982, 17–96), a polemic study rebutting his opponents, and again in his *Imrei Habad* (Bnei Brak: 1983), in a section entitled "*Birkot Hayyim Tinyana*," 115–132, 156–173, 183–188 (on Satanov), and yet again in his *Kuntres Hayyim ve-Hesed* (Bnei Brak: 1985, 1–24). Satanov published his *Tefillah mi-Kol ha-Shanah al pi Kellalei ha-Dikduk* (Berlin: 1785) and his *Va-Yeetar Yitzhak* (Berlin: 1784). (On this problematic personality, see the *Encyclopaedia Judaica*, vol. 14 [Jerusalem: 1971, 905–906].) Among the vehement attacks on Krauss is the pamphlet *Kuntres meshiv ha-ruah* by R. Moshe Hayyim Marzel (Jerusalem: 1981). (The title itself is a subtle rejoinder.)

6 See further the very detailed discussion on whether in the *birkat ha-zimmun* for ten people, one should say נברך לא־להינו or נברך א־להינו in Yehiel Avraham Zilber, *Birur Halachah: Orah Hayyim*, vol. 2 (Bnei Brak: 1976, 148–149). *Shulhan Aruch Orah Hayyim* 192:1 rules clearly not to say לא־להינו against the Mishnah, the Rambam and several other early testimonia. He follows several other authorities, many of whom argue that לא־להינו is grammatically incorrect. Thus, the Meiri, on *Berachot* 49b, writes: מדרש הדקדוק כתבו רבים שאין לומר ברך לא־להינו – from a point of view of grammar many wrote that one should not say נברך לא־להינו. So too the *Michtam* (ibid.) wrote: מצאתי כתוב אע"ג דלישנא דמתניתין הוא נברך לא־להינו, אמרו המדקדקים שאין לומר לא־להינו בלמ"ד, משום דלשון שירה מצאנו בלמ"ד, כמו שירה לה', אשירה לה', אבל לשון ברכה אינו נקשר בלמ"ד ... In other words he follows the "grammarians" against the reading of the Mishnah. And so too the Rosh (*Berachot* sec. 25), Tosafot Rosh (*Berachot* ibid.), Rabbenu Yonah (ibid. as the Rif 36b) etc. Here, then, we see the power of the "grammarians" (המדקדקים) in changing the early (Mishnaic) version of a liturgical text.

See further the article of Hayyim A. Cohen, "*Yitgadal ve-Yitkadash*" (*Masoret* 8 [1984]: 59–69, who demonstrates that the original vocalization was *yitgadel ve-yitkadash*, and only later this was in some communities changed to *yitgadal ve-yitkadesh*. He traces this development and explains it in detail. See also below app. 3.

But on whether one should emend "incorrect" vocalization, or should leave it as it is in accordance with ancient traditions even though it seems to be grammatically faulty, see Responsa *Rav Poalim* of R. Yosef Hayyim, vol. 3, *Orah Hayyim*, sec. 3, question 4, and in vol. 2, sect. 25, question 2, who strongly inveighs against any such "emendations." Earlier, the Hidah, in his *Yosef Ometz*, sec. 10, wrote against those who make textual changes in accordance with the rules of grammar and even in vocalization. He writes:

Those who make innovations and belittle myriads of Jews (i.e., who had the original tradition)
and one should invalidate their views and force
them to respect God and his Torah and to respect
the Great ones of Israel, both early authorities
and later ones, so many and so mighty [in learn-
ing] ... the smallest of his disciples' disciple is far
greater than these "alterers." ... And I weep over
this, this orphan generation that relinquishes the
important and seizes upon the insignificant, and
who think that they know better than their fore-
bears, and that the whole of the House of Israel
errs, and [only] they know the truth. As for me,
my heart burns with fire .... Whosoever has a
heart, and has a good soul should act in accordance [with the tradition] of all Israel, and not
remove himself from the collective.

עושי חדשות מזלזלים לאלפי
רבבות ישראל, ויש לבטל
דעתם ולכופם לכבוד ה'
ותורתו וכבוד גדולי ישראל
ראשונים ואחרונים רבים
ועצומים. ... אשר קטנם
של תלמידי תלמידיהם עבה
ממתניהם של אלה המשנים
... ועל אלה אני בוכיה, על דור
יתום שמניחין העיקר ולוקחים
הטפל, ובכפיהם ירצו שהם
ידעו מה שלא ידעו הקדמונים,
וכל בית ישראל טועים, והם
ידעו האמת. ולבי בוער באש
... מי שיש לו לב אם בעל
נפש הוא ינהג בכל ישראל, ואל
יוציא עצמו מן הכלל.

(See also R. Yaakov Moshe Hillel's remarks, in his journal *Mekabtziel* 21 (1956):
238, who cites these sources.)

However, the same Hidah, in his *Tov Ayin* (Jerusalem: 1961), sec. 7, writes differently. Thus (13a):

ולעניין מה שנהגו לשנות לשנות תיבות זה מכח הדקדוק וזה בא מכח הבנת העניין וחיבור הדברים וכיוצא. ויש
יוצא לטעון מכח חכמת האמת. דע דאין קפידא בזה דכל אחד יאמר שהנסחא עיקרית כדבריו ונפל
טעות בספרי הדפוס, והרוצה לשנות יכול לשנות. ...

And again at the end of first section (13b):

ומשם באר"ה שהמשנים תיבה או תיבות בתפילה וטוענים מצד הדקדוק או מצד יפוי הלשון הרשות
בידם, שאינו דבר איסור והיתר.

In other words, here he says that one may make changes for grammatical reasons
or for literary aesthetic ones (יפוי הלשון), for there is no prohibition in this regard.
However, it should be noted that *Tov Ayin* appeared (with Sefer *Vaad le-Hachamim*)
in Livorno in 1786, while *Yosef Ometz* appeared there in 1798. So perhaps the Hidah's
view changed in the interim period, or, alternatively, his later statement was directed against uncontrolled and ill-conceived grammatical emendations.

Sometimes, the variation in the vocalization of a single letter can make all the
difference, and hence be a subject of controversy. That, for example, is the situation
in the case of קדושה/קדושה – *kedoshah/kedushah* in the *Yotzer or* prayer of *shaharit*. Thus, some read בשפה ברורה ובנעימה קדושה, "in pure speech and sacred melody,"
while others read: בשפה ברורה ובנעימה. קדושה כולם כאחד עונים ואומרים ..., "in pure speech
and with melody. They all together answer and declaim [the] *kedushah* ..." We see
here that the change in vocalization also causes a change in the punctuation. The

former reading is prevalent in Sefaradi prayer books, while the latter in Ashkenazic ones. The matter is copiously discussed in the *Baer Siddur*, 79, who prefers the former reading and brings a variety of early testimonia to support his claim; similarly in *Kenesset ha-Gedolah* of Tzuberi, vol. 1, 77–78. On the other hand, *Tzelota de-Avraham*, vol. 1, 251–252, prefers the latter version, demonstrating that this was the reading of Rashi (Isaiah 6:3), Tosafot *Hagigah* 13b, and the *siddurim* of the Rema, etc., "Who then in these communities can change [the reading]?!" This was also the reading that the Ari, R. Hayyim Vital, the Hidah, and others accepted. This difference also has halachic implications, as we see from a passage in *Seder Rav Amram Gaon*, etc. Goldschmidt, 13–14 (sec. 20), citing *Toratam shel rishonim*, vol. 1 (edited by C. N. Horowitz, 52, Frankfurt a.M.: 1881, sec. 21).

בסדר רב עמרם: ושישאלתם יחיד המתפלל בינו לבין עצמו בשחרית יכול לומר "בורא קדושים" עד
"כולם עונין באימה ואומרים ביראה". או דילמא כיון דקדושה היא יחיד אינו אומרים כל עיקר? כן
המנהג: יחיד המתפלל, אם אמר "עונים באימה ואומרין ביראה", צריך לומר קקק [קדוש קדוש קדוש],
אבל אין לו רשות לומר "קדושה כולן כאחד עונין" וכו', אלא אומר "בורא קדושים", וכשיגיע עד "שפה
ברורה ובנעימה", מדלג ואומר "לא-ל ברוך" וכו'.

We see that according to his reading – the latter one – an individual worshipper had to omit part of this passage as it was considered *Kedushah*, which is recited only in a *minyan* (quorum of ten). (Goldschmidt suggests that this passage might well be part of the original *Seder Rav Amram Gaon*.)

The issue remained one of uncertainty for many authorities. Thus R. Hayyim Benvenisti, in his *Shiyarei Kenesset ha-Gedolah* on *Beit Yosef* (sec. 59) writes:

Even though in my youth my custom was like that of Rashi, and I used to read: קדושה כולם עונים, I read: ובנעימה קדושה בדלת בחולם, i.e., *Kedoshah* ....

While we are relating to the word *kedoshah*, we might also call attention to the passage in *rahem* of the Grace after Meals, where we find two readings: כי אם לידך המלאה הפתוחה הקדושה והרחבה – "but only upon Your full, open, *holy* and generous hand..." or: המלאה הפתוחה והגדושה – "Full, open and *brimming*" *Tzelota de-Avraham* (vol. 2, 520–521), finds the first reading unlikely. Why, he asks, should "holy" be between "open" and "generous"? He notes that in Sefardi *siddurim*, the reading is only: וידך המלאה והרחבה, "Your full and generous hand." He then states that in a certain book, the holy R. Yisrael Baal Shem Tov wrote in the margin of his *siddur* הגדושה, "brimming," and this is very much the correct reading, and it is the language of the Mishnah *Tamid* 5 [:4] "full and brimming." There are, however, a variety of different readings of the passages, e.g.:

Or Zarua:	לידך הקדושה והמלאה והרחבה
Sefaradim:	לידך המלאה והרחבה העשירה והפתוחה
Leket Yosher:	לידך המלאה הרחבה הקדושה והפתוחה
Italian:	המלאה הרחבה והפתוחה והשבעה והטובה

In some versions, all this latter section of *rahem* is completely omitted. See

Kenesset ha-Gedolah, vol. 1, 649.

I shall give yet another example of what at first I thought to be an error, this time due to the misinterpretations of an abbreviation, that I first heard from the late Chief Rabbi of Jerusalem, R. Yitzhak Kolitz. In the *Kedushah* of Shabbat *shaharit*, we read: אז בקול רעש גדול אדיר וחזק משמיעים קול, "Then in a great noise, *awesome and strong*, they give voice . . . ." He pointed out to me that the phrase אדיר וחזק – "awesome and strong" never appears in biblical literature, and is, in fact, unique to this locus, and is unnecessary for the meaning of the verse, which would read perfectly well without it. He therefore suggested that this is a mistaken interpretation of the abbreviation או"ח, which was actually an abbreviation of אופנים וחיות [הקדש], and the *Ofanim* and the [holy] *Hayyot*" (Holy Beasts, types of angels), in the *Shabbat shaharit kedushah de-sidra*. If we now compare the two *kedushot*, we see how convincing this suggestion is:

אז בקול רעש גדול אופנים וחיות	והאופנים וחיות הקדש ברעש גדול
משמעים קול מתנשאים לעומת	מתנשאים לעומת שרפים לעומתם
שרפים לעומתם משבחים ואומרים	משבחים ואומרים

Subsequently, I heard this from others, but so far have not found it in any of the commentaries on the *Siddur*. However, I note that on page 37 of *Seder Saadya Gaon*, we read: ברעש גדול אדיר וחזק and again on page 38 in the *Kedushah* of *Shaharit*, which surely points to this being a genuine reading and not the result of an error. Perhaps even more decisive to the fact that אדיר וחזק is already found in ancient Genizah manuscripts, such as ms. Cambridge T-S 8 H21/1, fol. 1a (Fleischer, *Tarbiz* 69 [2000]: plate opposite 330 and 332; and see further his remarks in *Tarbiz* 62 [1993]: 219, n. 152).

Most recently I found that R. Pinhas Wiliger of Montreal made this suggestion in *Or Yisrael* 30, 2003, 241, and it was outright rejected by R. Yoshua Mundshine, in the following issue (31 [2003]: 231), but not with any really convincing argument. Nonetheless, I believe the rejection to be correct.

Since we have mentioned the *Ofanim* and the *Hayyot*, we may note the part they play in the controversy between the Hasidim and the *Mitnaggedim*. To this end we shall cite Moshe Idel's *Hasidism: Between Ecstasy and Magic* (New York: 1995, 168, with references on 351, nn. 130 and 131).

The voice is the primal element that can influence supernal processes – here involving the divine Althought that exerts its influence on the Supernal Voice. In the previous passage the blowing of the *shofar* is supposed to arouse divine compassion. Mental prayer is thus not the most powerful means for Israel, but rather the blowing of the *shofar*, which is viewed as superior to speech and replete with theurgical qualities. The Besht himself is reported to have prayed "with a great cry" that was unbearable for the Great Maggid, who had to leave the room. According to R. Alexander of Shklov, the *Mitnaggedim* claim that we must pray as they do, and pray hurriedly and without any bodily movements or

raising of the voice just like those angels . . . . But this is only said of the highest rank of angels known as *Seraphim*, and it does not apply to the other ranks,
as it is said, "And the *Ophanim* and the Holy Beasts with a great noise of great
rushing." Even of the *Seraphim* it is written, "A noise of tumult like the noise of
a host (Ezek. 1:24).

To add a further element of complexity to this issue, we should note that there
are three differing versions at the end of the *El Adon* prayer in *shaharit* of Shabbat:

שרפים ואופנים וחיות הקודש

חיות ואופנים ושרפים

שרפים וחיות ואופני הקודש

The first is in accordance with *Zohar* 2, 132b, and this is the reading in the
Abudarhim, who rejects the third one. However, in *Tikkunei ha-Zohar* (*Tikun* 69)
107a, the order is שרפים חיות אופנים, and R. Avraham ha-Levi, in his *Gan ha-Melech*
(sec. 52, found as an appendix to his *Ginat Veradim*, ed. P. Ovadia, vol. 1, Jerusalem:
1991, 8), decides on this reading, which was the preferred reading of the Arizal
(*Shaar ha-kavvanot* 51d). This is the reading in *Tikkun Tefillah* (Bavel: 1870, 7b).
(See additional bibliography in Moshe Hallamish, *Hanhagot Kabbaliyyot be-Shab-
bat* [*Kabbalistic customs of Shabbat*, Jerusalem: 2006, 398, nn. 1590–1591].) The
question at issue is which is the more important category, *Ofanim* or *Hayyot*, and
this appears to be a subject of controversy (see Tosafot *Hullin* 92a as opposed to
Tosafot *Hagigah* 13b). In *Hilchot yesodei ha-Torah* 2.7, Rambam states that *hayyot*
are the highest grade, over and above *ofanim, erelim, hashmalim* and *seraphim*, and
if the order in our prayer is of ascending holiness, they should surely come last
(version 1). Furthermore, it is they, the *Hayyot*, who are called *kodesh* (holy), not
the *Ofanim*, according to the Rambam (ibid.). This discussion is also the subject
of a responsum in R. Meir Margaliot (*Meir Netivim*, Jerusalem: 1960, sec. 6), who
was a disciple of the Baal Shem Tov. He adds a third possible order: (2) חיות אופנים
ושרפים, but finally decides on version 1, adding that one should not connect the
other readings, because they are also correct. R Yaakov Verdiger, examines this
passage in considerable detail, and with rich bibliographic reference, in *Tzelota
de-Avraham* (vol. 3, Jerusalem: 1953, 419–424), preferring the Ari's reading (see
above). However, our comments earlier in the note suggest the order אופנים וחיות,
i.e., version 1.

Examples of this kind, which are commonplace, may be found on almost every
page of our *siddurim*.

Thus, for example in the twelfth benediction of the *Amidah* (את צמח דוד), some
siddurim include the phrase ומצפים לישועה – "and we are awaiting salvation." However,
originally this was a directive to the worshipper that at this stage of the benediction
he should turn his thoughts to awaiting salvation as he recites the words כי לישועתך
קוינו כל היום – "for we have hoped for your salvation all day long" (see *Eshel Avraham*

on *Shulhan Aruch Orah Hayyim*, sec. 118, citing *Mishnat hasidim* by the Kabbalist R. Rephael Immanuel Hai Riki (Amsterdam: 1717). "However, the printer of *Siddur Zolkiew* [1744?] erred and printed these words, ומצפים לישועה, in large letters in the blessing itself, as if it were a part of it" (*Tzelota de-Avraham*, vol. 1, 288; S. Tal, *Ha-Siddur be-Hishtalsheluto*, 55; Shapira, *Maamar Nusah ha-Tefillah*, 169).

12

Examples of Internal Censorship

Furthermore, we find many examples of what we may call "internal censor-ship," changing the text for fear that it might be interpreted incorrectly. Thus, Weider (in *Hitgabshut*, vol. 1, 65–84, 186–188) demonstrated that the original reading in *birkat magen Avraham* (the first benediction of the *Amidah* prayers) was א־ל עליון קונה שמים וארץ – "God the Most High, Possessor of heaven and earth," a phrase based on Genesis 14:20, which existed in both the Babylonian and the Palestinian rites. But this was changed in a complex process to the current א־ל עליון גומל חסדים וקונה הכל. "God the Most High, Who bestows acts of lovingkindness and possesses all." Why, he asks, was "Possessor of heaven and earth," which came from the Bible, changed to "Who possesses all"? His answer is that the rabbis of the Midrash interpreted the biblical phrase "Possessor of heaven and earth" as referring to Abraham, "who became as a partner to God in the creation of the world" (*Genesis Rabbah* 43.7, 421), "to whom God gave (הקנה לו) heaven and earth . . . and placed him as ruler over his world" (*Numbers Rabbah* 12.11; *Seder Eliyahu Rabbah* chapter 6, 29; *Midrash Proverbs* 19, *Tanhuma Buber, Be-Har* sec. 1, etc.), "and He gave him dominion over the upper and the lower worlds (עליונים ותחתונים)" (*Tanhuma Buber* ibid., sec. 3). Since the first benediction of the *Amidah* is named after the patriarch Abraham, there was a fear that the phrase "Possessor of heaven and earth" might be taken as referring to Abraham rather than to God Himself. The al-teration to "Who possesses all" and its separation from "God the Most High" obviated the change, and this was the reason for the change in formulation. Wieder also showed that there were intermediate stages and even composite formulations found in Genizah fragments such as: א־ל עליון קונה שמים וארץ גומל

חסדים טובים (ו)קונה הכל... – "God the Most High, *Possessor of heaven and earth*, Who bestows acts of lovingkindness (and) *possesses all*." Interestingly enough, the biblical phrase "survived" in the Friday night prayer after the *Amidah* (*me-ein sheva*): האל הגדול הגבור והנורא א-ל עליון קונה שמים וארץ – "the great, mighty and awesome God, God the Most High, possessor of heaven and earth." In this prayer, there was no danger of identifying the phrase as a sobriquet for Abraham.

In this context we should also recall the extensive discussion as to the correct version in *birkat yotzer* (*ha-me'ir la-aretz*):

They (the angels) are all beloved, pure, mighty and holy, and all of them perform, in awe and reverence, the will of their Maker.	כולם אהובים כולם ברורים כ=ולם גבורים כולם קדושים וכ=ולם עושים באימה ויראה רצון (קונם) [קונהם] [קוניהם].

קוניהם (*konehem*), which is plural, might be taken to mean "their Makers." קונם (*konam*), which is singular, can be understood only as a single Maker. קונהם (*konham*) without the *yod* may be viewed as singular (cf. Lev. 25:50; Isaiah 1:3: קנהו, "his owner"). It is clear that in all the early versions, the reading is קוניהם. See, for example, *Perush ha-Tefillot ve-ha-Berachot le-Rabbi Yehudah b. R. Yakar* (Nahmanides's teacher) (25): כולם עושים באימה ובירא*ה רצון קוניהם. (Cf. *Genesis Rabbah* 10:9 ad fin.: שהיו ידי קוניהם משמשין בהם .... And so, too, ibid., 102, in *El Adon*: עושים באימה רצון קוניהם. So too, R. Amram Gaon and R. Alfasi in chapter *Tefillot ha-Shahar* ad fin., and Rambam *Hilchot Berachot* 10:16, etc., have קוניהם. The basis of such testimonies, R. Abraham Landau in his *Emek ha-Berachah* (apud *Tzlota de-Avraham*, vol. 1, 250), wrote:

> In any case, it is true that all the early versions had קוניהם, and only in the new *siddurim* was קונם printed, on the basis of a grammarian (שלא מדקדק) who was not careful in his grammar (שלא דקדק), for this is the language of the Bible . . . .

R. Shabtai Sofer (57) also held that it is a mistake to alter the text from קוניהם to קונם.

In the Baer *siddur*, on the other hand (78), he insists on the reading קונם lest one suspect a belief in two authorities, "and even though in the Bible and among *Hazal* we find קוניהם referring to God . . . nevertheless, in our prayers we must use only such formulations that are clear and unambiguous" (see

below, Afterword, n. 1). Indeed, in *birkat ha-levanah*, as found in early sources (BT *Sanhedrin* 42a, etc.), we find: שׂשׂים ושׂמחים לעשׂות רצון קונם, and this is brought as proof that so one should also read in *birkat yotzer*. And this was the version chosen by Satanov in his *Va-Yeetar Yitzhak*. However, this argument was rejected by R. Avraham di Boton in his Responsa *Lehem Rav*, Izmir 1660, sec. 11, arguing "...Who are we to alter an ancient readings attested by scholars and books, elders and youths?" See the *Pri Hadash* on *Orah Hayyim* 426, who would have קוניהם in *birkat ha-levanah* too. Thus, the original version, קוניהם, which survives in many Ashkenazic *siddurim*, for internal censorship reasons, was altered to קונם, and appear in many Sefardi *siddurim*. The version קונהם is a compromise suggested by the *Ateret Zekenim* on *Orah Hayyim* 49. (See, further, M. Spielman, *Tiferet Zvi*, vol. 6 [Brooklyn: 2003], 110–112, 206–209; R. Amar, *Libi Er* [Jerusalem: 1998], 160–161. On the basic question of whether our liturgy reflects biblical or rabbinic grammatical usage, see the polemic discussion in *Va-Yaan Shmuel* [3 (2000): 293–340], [by "Ish Matzliah," Rav Mazuz]; and *Li-Gedor Peretz* [Anon.: 2004, 30–31], citing *Luah Erez*, 593, and Appendix 3 below).

Additional examples may be found in Tzuberi, *Kenesset ha-Gedolah*, vol. 3 (349–354). We shall describe them very briefly.

In the two great yeshivot of Babylonia it was the custom to recite, in the *mussaf* services of Rosh ha-Shanah and Yom Kippur: ותתן לנו, ה' א־להינו, באהבה, מועדים לשׂמחה חגים וזמנים לשׂשׂון, את יום הזכרון הזה, או את יום הכפורים הזה – "And You, Lord our God, have, in love, given us festivals for rejoicing, holy days and seasons for joy, this day of remembrance, or this Yom ha-Kippurim day," just as was said in the three pilgrimage festivals. This wording is present in Rav Amram Gaon, Rav Shalom Gaon, Rav Paltoi and Rav Shmuel ben Hofni. However, in Ashkenaz, in Sefarad and among the Yemenites, the words מועדים לשׂמחה, חגים וזמנים לשׂשׂון – "festivals for rejoicing, holy days and reasons for joy," were deleted from the Rosh ha-Shanah and Yom Kippur prayers on the grounds that such rejoicing is only relevant on the pilgrimage festivals (Ramban, cited in *Tur Orah Hayyim*, sec. 582; Rashi, *Sefer ha-Pardes*, sec. 166; *Shibolei ha-Leket*, sec. 286, etc., relying on Rav Hai Gaon and Rav Saadya Gaon in his *Siddur*, 219, etc.).

Similarly, the early geonic custom was to recite והשׂיאנו – "Bestow upon us," in the *mussaf* of the Days of Awe, just as is recited during the three

pilgrimage festivals, as is found in Rav Amram Gaon, Rashi (*Pardes,* sec. 166), stating clearly that this was the practice in the academies of Babylonia and Eretz Yisrael. In some communities it was recited on Rosh ha-Shanah, but not on Yom Kippur (*Abudarhim, Shibbolei ha-Leket,* sec. 286, etc.). However, many early authorities rejected these views and omitted this prayer completely from the *mussaf* of the Days of Awe. Among them were the Rosh (end of Tractate *Rosh ha-Shanah; Orhot Hayyim, Rosh ha-Shanah* sec. 4; *Kolbo,* sec. 64, Rashi, *Pardes,* sec. 168), stating that "R. Yitzhak ha-Levi did away with this prayer in Vermaiza, because a person could say את ברכת מועדיך – 'the blessing of Your festivals . . .' other than on the three pilgrimage festivals," and so too stated R. Eliezer of Germaiza (*Rokeah,* sec. 204) in the name of R. Yitzhak ha-Levi, and so too in *Sefer ha-Ittur* (104a), etc.

In a far later period, some, such as the *Noda bi-Yehudah,* wished to omit the *berich shmei* passage, taken from the *Zohar Va-yakhel* (206b). Others wished to alter the words בר א־להין (son of God) to מלאכיא עילאי (celestial angels), for various obvious reasons, as was actually done in *Siddur Derech Yesharah* (Frankfurt on Oder: 1703), and again in *Siddur ha-Shlah,* called *Shaar ha-Shamayim* (Amsterdam: 1717), where we find מלכא דשמיא, surely an error for מלאכא דשמיא (angels of heaven), which is the reading in *Kitzur ha-Shlah.* See Mordechai Spielman, *Tiferet Zvi,* vol. 1 (Brooklyn: 2003, 221) in note, with additional bibliography, and Rabbi Yitzhak Fraenkel's discussion in *Yeshurun* (2 [1997]: 577–578). Incidentally, in the modern edition of *Siddur ha-Shlah ha-Shalem* (Jerusalem: 1998), the reading is: (מלאכא) בר א־להין).

We see, then, that great authorities were willing to delete from their prayer books passages, and even whole prayers, which they felt were unsuitable for one reason or other. Such examples could be greatly multiplied, but these should suffice to demonstrate this point.

On occasion, changes were made out of fear that a liturgical passage might be interpreted as supporting heterodox ideology. Wieder (*Hitgabshut,* 80, n. 59) gives a revealing example of this phenomenon. Solomon Geiger, in his *Divrei Kohelet* (Frankfurt am Main: 1862, 64), reports that in Frankfurt "they rebuked anyone who said in the Sabbath prayer of the *shaharit Amidah* וינוחו בה ישראל מקדשי שמך, which halachically is very suitable since it accords with the *hatimah* מקדש השבת, and was therefore recommended by R. Isaac Tyrnau in his *Minhag Book,* as opposed to the earlier ואוהבי שמך, because the

numerical value (*gematria*) was the same as that of Shabbetai Zvi, "the evil one who reduced and led astray many people of Israel to believe he is the Messiah."

At other times, it would appear that changes were made for literary-aesthetic reasons, and/or with some additional associative reason. Consider, for example, the following passage as it appears in most Ashkenazic *siddurim* in the Sabbath *shaharit* liturgy, at the end of *nishmat:*

תתהלל	ישרים	בפי
תתרומם,	חסידים	ובלשון
תתברך,	צדיקים	ובדברי
תתקדש.	קדושים	ובקרב

The *yod* of *yesharim,* the *tzadi* of *tzaddikim,* the *het* of *hasidim* and the *kof* of *kedoshim* comprise the name *Yitzhak* (the biblical patriarch). And in many *siddurim* these letters are emphasized graphically to show up the name; (e.g., the Baer *Siddur,* 209). The *Kol Bo* (ed. David Avraham, vol. 2, Jerusalem: 1990, 214, n. 28 and 238, n. 33), explains the relationship of this passage to Isaac referring to a Midrash in *Yalkut Shimoni,* Psalms, sec. 720. The *Kol Bo* himself had a slightly different version (ibid., 214):

תתהלל	ישרים	בפי
תתברך,	צדיקים	ובדברי
תתרומם,	חסידים	ובלשון
תתקדש.	קדושים	ובקרב

However, in most of the Sefardi *siddurim* we find the following:

תתרומם	ישרים	בפי
תתברך,	צדיקים	ובשפתי
תתקדש,	חסידים	ובלשון
תתהלל.	קדושים	ובקרב

In this version, the *resh* in *titromam,* and the *bet* in *titbarach,* and the *kof* in *titkadash* and the *heh* in *tithalal* make up the name Rivkah, Yitzhak's wife.

The *Kol Bo,* after citing his own version, comments as follows:

So it is written in the old *mahzorim.* But the new ones twisted the straight [text] (עקבו את המישור), for when they saw Yitzhak inscribed (חתום) at the beginning of the lines (בראשי השטות, perhaps read: השורות), they wished to inscribe Rivkah at the end of the lines (בסוף השורות).

R. Simhah of Vitry, in his *Mahzor Vitry* (ed. Horowitz, 152), ascribes this version to R. Yaakov b. R. Shimshon of Falaise (a French disciple of Rashi), who apparently compiled a *mahzor* similar to that of R. Simhah of Vitry, but he adds:

but [the names] Yitzhak and Rivkah have no place here, אבל אין עניין יצחק ורבקה
and one cannot possibly interpret it [i.e., the text] thus. לכאן ולא יתכן לפרש כן.

So, too, R. Elazar of Worms (cited in *Arugot ha-Bosem*, vol. 4 [edited by E. E. Urbach, 103 Jerusalem: 1963], for manuscripts) writes:

בפי ישרים תתהלל, כדכתיב "לישרים נאוה תהילה" (תהלים לג א), הרי בפה הישרים שייך הילול.
ויש מהפכין ואומרים "תתרוממ", ואומרים יצחק ורבקה תקנוהו . . . אבל אני לא קבלתי כן . . . .

We see, then, that he, too, did not accept what he saw to be a change in the original version (ויש מהפכין ואומרים). Indeed, it would appear that the original version (מחזורים זקנים of the *Kol Bo*) did only indicate Yitzhak, and later on, through a simple transposition of certain words Rivkah was included. This constituted both an associative as well as an attractive literary textual alteration.

I suspect that this is also the reason for the variant reading in the *tikanta* prayer of the Shabbat *mussaf* service. As is well known, it is written with the initial letters of each word in the reverse alphabetical order תקנת שבת :תשרק רצית קרבנותיה, etc., ending with the word אז, *alef* being the first letter of the Hebrew alphabet. The continuation in most *siddurim* and early testimonia according to the *Baer Siddur* (239) is: אז – מסיני נצטוו עליה, but there is a variant in a *siddur* from 1719 (Baer, ibid.) which contains אז מסיני נצטוו צווי פעליה כראוי. The initial letters of the words in the variant version are מנצפ"ך, the Hebrew letters of the alphabet that have a final form. It would therefore seem that someone wished to complete the alphabetical structure by adding these special letters to the reverse alphabet.

Thus, there were multiple reasons for changes in the *nusah ha-tefillah*.

Now, returning to Maimonides: when we demonstrate that there have been changes, modifications, additions, subtractions, and expansions of *berachot* throughout all the generations, and that new *tefillot* that related to specific situations were composed, according to Maimonides this is legitimate as long as we do not change the structure of the *berachah,* or alter or obscure the

original intent of that *berachah* and its primary meaning. Thus, when we recite a *berachah* about God accepting our prayers, we must preserve the element of שומע תפלה "*shomea tefillah*" (hears our prayers), שמע קולנו "*shema koleinu*" (O hear our voices) and מברך השנים "*mevarech ha-shanim*" (blesses the years). Similarly, if we are talking about *la-malshinim* (regarding the informers), we may add or change the term to *notzrim* (Christians) because this also accords with the same basic concept, and we may end with *machnia zedim* (forces villains to surrender), etc. Here, again, we have not changed the blessing's original intent.

13

The Talmudic Sources Revisited

Let us look a little further and a little more searchingly into this issue. The Tosefta on Tractate *Berachot* (4.4–5; with parallels in BT *Berachot* 40b and JT *Berachot* 6.2) reports the following controversy:

> Rabbi Meir says: "Even you see a loaf of bread and say, 'Blessed is He who created this loaf! How beautiful it is' – that is its blessing (i.e., that is a legitimate blessing). If you see figs and say: 'Blessed is He who created these figs! How beautiful they are' – that is their blessing. Rabbi Yossi says, "Anyone who changes the formulations that the sages determined has not fulfilled the obligation of saying the required blessing" (לא יצא).[1]

Apparently Rabbi Meir permits, *de facto* (*be-di-avad*), a completely new formulation, while Rabbi Yossi rejects any change in existing blessings.

The Jerusalem Talmud (ibid.) continues:

> Rabbi Jacob, son of Aha, said, quoting Samuel: "The *halachah* [correct view of this Jewish law] is in accordance with the view of Rabbi Meir." That, too, is the opinion of Rav. [We learn this from the following story:] "Once a certain Persian came to Rav [and said], 'When I eat my bread – not knowing how to

---

1 The passage in JT *Berachot* 9.1, 12d, seems to be in accordance with R. Yossi's view. The passage runs as follows:

> R. Yohanan and R. Yonatan went to mediate between villages in the south. They came to one of them and heard the cantor saying: הא־ל הגדול הגבור והנורא והאביר והאמיץ, and they silenced him. They said to him: You have no right to add to the version coined by the sages with regard to benedictions.

recite the blessing – I say, "Blessed be He who created this piece of bread." Have I fulfilled my obligation?' He [Rav] said to him, 'Yes.'"

(Compare the story in BT *Berachot* 40b.)

Rabbi Hai Gaon (cited in *Sefer Ha-Eshkol*, part 1, 72) follows Rabbi Meir's ruling, as does the view found in Maimonides (*Hilchot ha-Yerushalmi*, 40), Tosafot of Rabbi Judah on the Babylonian Talmud, BT *Berachot* ibid., etc.

Since the Jerusalem Talmud rules in accordance with the view of Rabbi Meir and since the Babylonian Talmud has no clear ruling on the subject, most *poskim* follow the Jerusalem Talmud, thus permitting changes and new formulations. Even those few who reject this view are willing to overlook small changes. Indeed, the *Tashbetz* (Rabbi Shimon Ben Zemah Ibn Duran, cited in *Responsa Teshuva me-Ahavah*, by Rabbi Eliezer Flekeles, 90) holds that the prohibition against changing formulations refers only to the beginning (פתיחה), the end (חתימה), or the basic kernel of the *berachah* (עיקר הברכה).[2]

---

2 One of three morning blessings (mentioned above) is "Who has not made me a gentile" (*goy* or *nochri*), and this in accordance with Tosefta *Berachot* 6:18 (ed. Lieberman, 38). In the Vilna editions of BT *Menahot* 43b, instead of this formulation, we find "Who has made me an Israelite" – שעשני ישראל. Clearly this version is a "correction" made out of fear of the censor. The testimonia of earlier editions of the Talmud and early authorities clearly have "Who has not made me a gentile." Thus, for example, the Magen Avraham, in *Orah Hayyim* 46:9, writes:

> Who has not made me an idolator (עכו"ם) – so one should say, and "who has made me a Jew (יהודי)" was changed by the printers.

(See *Shulhan Aruch Orah Hayyim*, vol. 1, edited by Machon Yerushalayim, 267. Jerusalem: 1994, nn. 30, 33.) See also *Minhagim de-kehilah kedoshah Vermaiza* (*Wormser Minhagbuch*), vol. 1, by R. Jousep (Juspe) Schammes, edited by B. S. Hamburger and E. Zimmer, 9. Jerusalem: 1988: "Who has not made me a *goy*" – and one does not say: "who has made me an Israelite." (See editor's nn. 3 and 4 ad loc., with copious bibliographic information.) And in R. Juda Löw Kirchheim's *Minhagot Vermaiza* (The Customs of Worms's Jewry, edited by I. M. Peles, 13. Jerusalem: 1987), in n. 8 (in *Hagahot*):

> In the year 1629, there came here the Aluf and Gaon R. Petahiah . . . and commanded us . . . [to say]: "who has not made me a *goy*."

However, it should be noted that in the main text of this work the reading is "who has made me an Israelite." See further *Siddur Hanau* (27–28) for additional material, and Wieder, *Hitgabshut*, vol. 1, 199–218, for a full and detailed examination of these benedictions. There we find additional variants, such as "Who has not

made one a Cuthean (כותי)" (208), "an Israelite and not an Ishmaelite (=Moslem)", (209), "Who has not placed me [as one] of the nations of the world but of your people Israel" (216–217). This later version appears in a Genizah fragment, but, interestingly enough, R. Yosef Zechariah Stern, a great Lithuanian authority of the nineteenth century (1831–1903), made the following innovation: "Who has not made me a *goy* like the *goyim* of the Lands" (שלא עשני גוי כגויי הארצות) (Responsa *Zecher Yehosef,* *Orah Hayyim,* Warsaw: 1899, sec. 13, and similarly R. Hayyim Hezkiah Medini, in his *Sedei Hemed,* New York: 1959, vol. 6, 2623). But this is because in biblical parlance, the Hebrew word *goy* can also refer to Jews (Wieder, ibid.). Therefore, here we also find individual authorities making radical innovations in the liturgy.

See also the curious passage in *Siddur Raschbam* by R. Solomon Schück (Vienna: 1894, 3a–4b), with its strange chronological confusions that seek to explain why these blessings were instituted by R. Meir (!) in whose time "the women of Israel were denied the status of kashrut ... until the Redeemer comes to us," and so on. (See below, app. 8.)

14

The Positions of Geonim and Rishonim

Many early authorities share this opinion, including geonim and rishonim such as Rav Natronai Gaon and Rabbenu Gershon Meor ha-Golah (cited in *Shibolei ha-Leket,* sec. 28 [see Appendix 5], *Mahzor Vitry,* sec. 325, R. Yosef ibn Megas, responsum no. 87, in the name of R. Yitzhak Alfasi, etc. [see Y. Tzuberi, *Kenesset ha-Gedolah,* vol. 4 (Jerusalem: 1996, 394), and cf. vol. 3 (Jerusalem: 1991)], 102).

This too is the position of Rav Saadya Gaon (sec. 4, Heinemann, *Iyyunei Tefillah* [Jerusalem: 1981], 110–123).

And because of the central importance of this point we shall cite the Rashba (R. Shlomo ben Aderet, Spain, c. 1235–1310) in his novellae on BT *Berachot* 11a (Jerusalem: 1984, cols. 38–43, omitting some of the discussions of his proof texts):

> It would appear to me that that which we learned [in the Mishnah, *Berachot* 1:4]: "Where the long [benediction] is prescribed, the short is not permissible; where the short is prescribed, the long is not permissible," does not come to tell [us] that one is not permitted to shorten or lengthen the version of the benediction – that is to say, to add and to subtract to and from its words; for if that were the case, [the sages] should have established the exact text of each and every blessing, with numbered words and clearly known contents, and teach us the precise version of every blessing. But we have not found this anywhere, for they only told us only those words which they insisted upon .... But otherwise, the sages gave us no limit as to which words and how many may be said, [saying that there should be] no less or no more. Nor did they say how many words are considered "long" or "short." Furthermore, they expressly stated (BT *Avodah Zarah* 8b) that "in the eighteen benedictions prayer (=*Amidah*), if one wishes

to add in each blessing something of the nature of the blessing, one may do so,"
even if the addition should be longer than the basic text, even though those
benedictions are [considered] short . . . . Hence, it is clear that there is no strict
limitation as to the expansion or contraction of the text, only that the versions
which the sages established (מטבע שטבעו חכמים) means that there are blessings
which open with *Baruch* and close with *Baruch*, and they are the ones that are
called "long."

In his responsa (vol. 1, no. 473), he writes:

Concerning your question about the order in which you are accustomed to
recite in your prayers and your prayer books, different places do not have identical [versions], and in each place if he did not say [the prayer] thus, it does not
matter (אינו מעכב), and not as those who say that this is called deviating from the
version established by the sages" (משנה ממטבע שטבעו חכמים, BT *Berachot* 40b),
in which case he has not fulfilled his obligation (ולא יצא).

Similarly, in responsum no. 470, he writes:

One should not say that anyone who changes the versions established by the
sages regarding benedictions errs, for this applies only when he changes the
structure of a blessing by saying a short version instead of a long one – i.e., that
he begins it [with *baruch*] but does not end it, or ends it but does not begin
it . . . .

R. Menachem Meiri (Provence, 1249–1316) held the same position in his
novellae on *Berachot* (ibid.). In a lengthy and detailed discussion of the issue,
he states clearly that:

In any event, to add words that conform with the general sense of the benediction, or relating to the occasion in the form of *piyyutim* that constitute praise
to the Lord conforming to the sense of the blessing – one may do so without
concern (אין לחוש). Even in the benedictions of the *Amidah*, a person may add
his personal requests in accordance with the theme of the benediction, as is
clearly stated in *Masechet Sofrim,* chap. 18. And it is on the basis of this view that
the custom is to add *piyyutim* conforming to the theme of the benedictions . . .
And should you say that this is only *ex post facto* (בדיעבד) as some have suggested
. . . others have explained that this is even *ab initio* (לכתחילה) . . . .

This latter distinction between *ex post facto* and *ab initio* is the view of the
Rashba, the Ritba (R. Yom Tov Ishvili, thirteenth–fourteenth century Spain),

on *Berachot* chap. 6, sec. 14, while the Tashbatz (R. Shimon ben Tzemah Duran, Algiers, 1361–1444, vol. 3, no. 247) clearly follows the Rashba's line of thinking. (See also R. Yitzhak Ratzabi's introduction to *Piskei Maharitz* [=R. Yihye Tzalah], *Orah Hayyim*, vol. 2 [Bnei Brak: 1981], sec. 12, 368–372. Indeed his *Kuntres Milei de-Berachot* [ibid., 331–420] is an exhaustive analysis of this whole subject. See ibid., sec. 14–15, 374–385, for the position of the geonim, Saadya and Amram Gaon, and sec. 19–10, 24–25, 394–401, and 412–420.)

We see, then, that all those authorities, and others too, go so far as to encourage additions when they are in accordance with the character of the *petihah* and *hatimah* – additions such as requests or *piyyutim* that offer praise, and that increase worshippers' *kavvanah* in their prayers to God.

This has become the accepted norm, as anyone who examines the liturgy of the pilgrimage festivals, fast days or the Days of Awe will readily see. For within their *amidot* (primarily of the *hazarat ha-shatz*) are interspersed numerous *piyyutim*, many of which we will readily recognize and with which we are well acquainted (see chap. 5, n. 5). In fact, the *Kedushah* – the trishagion – is also an addition in the third of the three initial blessings, although it may be seen as a separate and discrete literary unit (see *Kenesset ha-Gedolah,* vol. 4, 402).

15

Attempts to Fix a Single, Crystallized Version, and Their Failures

It is true that at various times, there have been attempts to establish an absolute, crystallized form of the *berachot*. The geonim had already laid the groundwork for a canonized version of the liturgy (see L. Hoffman, 170–171). However, for fixing an exact text of the liturgy we must turn to thirteenth century Ashkenaz, the period of Hasidei Ashkenaz, when Rabbi Judah the Pious (Yehudah he-Hasid), a great Ashkenazic rabbinical authority in his era, was said to have claimed that he had received a tradition from Moses at Sinai that each of the *berachot* in the *Amidah* and all the other *berachot* that we say all have a specific number of words and even letters, that books and manuals existed that set the number of words required for each blessing, the biblical verses to which they refer and that have the identical number of words and/ or letters, or have the same *gematria*, and so on.[1] This kabbalistic approach was also an attempt to crystallize, standardize, and finalize the *nusah* of the liturgy so that no more radical changes could be made. According to Rabbi Judah, one was limited to the formula of the exact number of words or even the number of letters in each *berachah* (see Appendix 1).

As Talya Fishman wrote in her excellent study (Appendix 1, n. 9):

> R. Yehudah heHasid's focus on the number of letters and words in prayer was essential to the prayerful praxis of recollection, but it also fulfilled another purpose. Just as the enterprise of *masorah*, with its careful tabulations of words,

---

1   See Groner's discussion, ibid., 22–25.

letters, and orthographic anomalies, fixed the precise text of scripture and ensured uniformity of the Torah scrolls, R. Yehudah he-Hasid's *masorah* of prayer fixed a particular version of liturgy – his version – as authoritative.

The Tur mentions that his father, the Rosh (Rabbenu Asher), had such a *kuntres* (book) that listed all the codes needed to understand the number of letters or the number of words in each of the *berachot*, and the Tur cites these "codes."[2] However, in the fourteenth century Rabbi David Abudarhim, one of the dominant authorities in formulating the *Nusah Sefarad*, wrote, "I have read what the Tur says, and I can tell you that I have been in many synagogues and no two synagogues pray in the same fashion and have the same *nusah*. I think it is a waste of time to try to establish the *gematria,* the number of words, or the number of letters in each *berachah* because no two *kehillot* (communities) have the same tradition."[3] Therefore, each Jewish community will have

---

2   See what I wrote in *Minhagei Yisrael* I (Jerusalem: 1991), 18, n. 15, and 122–133; 2, 157–188. See also *Tur Orah Hayyim*, sec. 113; D. Abrams, "From Germany to Spain: Numerology as a Mystical Technique" (*Journal of Jewish Studies* 47 [1996]: 89–101); and see most recently the excellent article by Simhah Immanuel, "*Ha-pulmus shel hasidei Ashkenaz al nusah ha-tefilah*" (*Mehqerei Talmud* III part 2, Talmudic Studies Dedicated to the Memory of Prof. Ephraim E. Urbach, edited by Y. Sussmann & D. Rosenthal, 598–628. Jerusalem: 2005). On kabbalistic elements in our liturgy, see H. Hallamish, *Kabbalah in Liturgy, Halakhah and Customs* (Ramat Gan: 2000) (Hebrew); A. Z. Idelsohn, *Jewish Liturgy and Its Development* (New York: 1992), 47–55, and above n. 27.

3   Cited in the Beit Yosef commentary on *Orah Hayyim*, sec. 113. It would appear that R. Yosef Caro accepted this position. See R. Amar, *Tefillat ha-Arar* (published with his work *Libi Er*) (Jerusalem: 1998, 32). R. Yaakov Emden, in the introduction to his *siddur* (*Kuntres Sulam Beit El*, 15), expresses wonderment at R. Yosef Caro for accepting this position which has no place in his "great house" (*beito ha-gaddol*, referring to the Beit Yosef), (Amar ibid., 34). But R. Yosef Caro is consistent, as may be seen from his responsum in *Avkat Rochel*, sec. 28. Much the same observation, but with the opposite argumentation, may be found in the beginning of *Maamar nusach ha-tefillah*, by R. Hayyim Elazar Shapira of Munkacz, in *Sefer hamishah maamarot* (Beregsas: 1922, reprinted Jerusalem: 1981), 159, who writes as follows:

> Behold, I have seen that the versions of the prayer are in a scandalous state, for the one is not like the other, and the variations between them are so plentiful, so that they amount to hundreds of differences and varying versions in the *Shemoneh Esreh*, not including the rest of the prayers and benedictions . . . .

However, he then goes on to quote the Tur and refers to the numerical calculations of Hasidei Ashkenaz (see app. I below). He points out that "most of these

its own version of the prayers. And, indeed, already the Rashba, R. Shlomo ben Aderet (1285–1310), came to much the same conclusion: that there never was an exact official text for the blessings, as we have noted in extenso in the preceding section.

Kadish (278) calls our attention to another Spanish authority who did not put much stock in the idea of one "correct" text for the various blessings, Rabbi Shimon ben Tzemah Duran (known by his acronym Rashbatz, 1361–1444), in his response (*Teshuvot Rashbatz*, or simply *Tashbatz*, Lemberg 1891). One of the morning blessings praises God for enabling the rooster to distinguish between day and night. A questioner asked Rashbatz whether the proper word for that blessing is *lehavin* (to understand the difference between day and night) or *lehavhin* (to distinguish). In his response (no. 247), he showed that both words make sense in the context of the blessing, and concluded as follows:

> We are used to saying "*lehavin*." But it is wrong to criticize a person who says "*lehavhin*," and it is not considered changing the format [of the blessing]. Because "changing the format" is only forbidden in blessings when one changes the opening – to begin with "*Baruch*" or not to do so when it is against the format created by our rabbis of blessed memory. [It is also forbidden] to change the closure, to add, improperly, the closing formula "*Baruch* ..." or to omit it, or to change those things that are important to the blessing, such as mentioning [God's power over] dew or rain, or asking for rain.
>
> But when it comes to the *nusah* of the blessing in other, less important matters such as "*lehavin*" or "*lehavhin*" – this is not considered "changing the format." The rabbis said (*Avodah Zarah* 8a) that if one has a sick person in his home he should lengthen the blessing for the sick, and if he needs material sustenance he may lengthen the blessing for that. And we add liturgical poems

---

changes and additions come from Sefaradim, and that we Ashkenazim are not permitted to change to the Sefaradi version, but have accepted from the disciples of the Baal Shem Tov that we should pray in accordance with the version of the holy Ari .... We may change only to this one, out of all the other ones ...." (Cf. his responsum in his work *Minhat Elazar*, vol. 1, Munkacz-Pressburg: 1902, sec. 11, and the whole of the *Maamar*, which is replete with valuable information and insights.) See further the extended discussion of R. Amar, ibid., 27–42. See also my comments in my *Darkah shel halachah* (Jerusalem: 2007, 44–45).

in the middle of the blessings and prayers, but it is not considered forbidden as "changing the format" as long as the poems are about the topic of the blessing.

The Rema (Rabbi Moses Isserles), for his part, says, "There are so many entrances (twelve gates) that reach the Throne of Glory and, regardless of your liturgical version, your prayers will go through their respective entrance (*shaar*) and reach the divine seat of God."[4]

---

4   This is an oft-quoted statement the like of which is found, for example, in *Pri Etz Hayyim* (attributed to R. Hayyim Vital), chapter *Inyan ha-Tefillah*. Also the Baal ha-Tanya, R. Shneur Zalman Mi-Liady, cites this statement. See *Ha-Siddur: Mivneh ve-Nusah Sidduro shel ha-Admor ha-Zaken* (edited by G. Oberlander and N. Greenwald, 3–6. Monsey: 2003). This volume, with its collecteana, has the best and fullest discussions to all aspects of this *siddur*, and includes the introductions to R. Avraham David Lawot's *Shaar ha-Kolel*, and R. Avraham Hayyim Naeh's *Piskei ha-Siddur*. On 116–119, there is also a list of changes due to the censor (in Yehoshua Mundshine's chapter), and in R. Baruch Oberlander's chapter (236–243), there is a discussion of R. Zalman's Hanau's grammatical corrections.

16

Nusah ha-Ari and the Hasidic Position

To this end the Ari ha-Kadosh, and later on R. Shneur Zalman of Lyady, the
Baal ha-Tanya and founder of the Habad movement, restructured and reformulated much of the Sefardic version by collating and selecting from various
versions to create a "standard version," to serve an all-inclusive "thirteenth
gate," the "*shaar ha-kollel*," through which all prayers could reach heaven.[1]

---

1   This is a Lurianic notion that originates in the *Zohar* (vol. 2, 251a, *Hechalot Pekudei*):

> The earthly synagogue is paralleled (לקבל) by the celestial one. The celestial one
> has windows just as has the earthly one. The celestial great synagogue has twelve
> windows, so too has the earthly one, and they all [as it were] face one another.

On the basis of this passage R. Yosef Caro ruled in the Shulhan Aruch that a
synagogue should have twelve windows. The Ari developed this concept into the
notion of the special function of each of the twelve windows, now called by him
"gateways" – *shearim*, each of which served one of the twelve tribes, and he could
link this to what we learn from Mishnaic sources (*Shekalim* 6:1, *Middot* 2:6, and BT
Bava Batra 1220) that there were gateways in the Temple (hinted at in Ezekiel 48),
and each Israelite would prostrate himself at the gate of his own tribe, meaning that
this was the entrance, as it were, through which his prayers would pass on their way
to heaven. (See *Shaar ha-kavvanot* by R. Hayyim Vital, Jerusalem: 2002, 50d, and
Pri Etz Hayyim [Dubrovna: 1804, 4d], where this notion is clearly set forth.)

It should further be noted that Polish synagogues, both wooden and masonry
from the seventeenth century onwards even into the twentieth century, followed
this window arrangement of twelve windows in the main hall. Such is the case in
Gwozdziec Synagogue, and indeed over 75 percent of the wooden synagogues recorded in Maria and Kazimierz Piachotka's *Wooden Synagogues in the Territories of
the Polish Kingdom* (Warsaw: 1996). (See Thomas Hubka, *Resplendent Synagogue:
Architecture and Worship in an Eighteenth-Century Polish Community* [Hanover
and New Haven: 2003, 147, 203, n. 64]. See further on the twelve windows in S.

There is, perhaps, a certain parallel in Rav Goren's attempt to institute the

---

Spielman, *Tiferet Zvi* [vol. 6, Brooklyn: 2003, 359–362]).

However, in the Temple there was also a thirteenth gateway, which was understood to be general and all-inclusive – *kollel*. The Baal Shem Tov's disciple, R. Dov Baer of Mezridj, writes (*Likutei amarim – magid devarav le-Yaakov* [Koretz 1781, 25b]) concerning this thirteenth gateway:

> Behold: The holy Ari, who was fully acquainted with the pathways of heaven, taught [us] a way for those who do not know their tribal affiliation to be able to direct their prayers through the all-inclusive gateway – *Shaar ha-kollel* – by formulating an eclectic version of the liturgy (סדר מלוקט מכמה נוסחאות) . . . .

For a full analysis of the stages of development of this concept, see M. Hallamish, *Kabbalah in Liturgy, Halakhah and Customs* (Jerusalem: 2000 [Hebrew], 106–113). This is also clearly set forth in the introduction to R. Avraham Lawot's *Shaar ha-Kollel* (Vilna: 1896, Brooklyn: 1990), who also stresses the fact that *Nusah ha-Ari* is basically an eclectic text and that the *Siddur ha-Rav Baal ha-Tanya* of R. Shneur Zalman mi-Liady, which is based on *Nusah ha-Ari*, is likewise eclectic. (See *Ha-siddur: mivneh ve-nusah sidduro shel ha-Admor ha-Zaken* [11–17, 117–180, 301–308].) Indeed, there is a tradition, in the name of the Zemah Zedek, that he had before him sixty *siddurim* with variant versions, from which he, after careful examination, selected the version for his *siddur* (see *Beit Rabi*, vol. 1, by R. Hayyim Meir Heilprin, Berdichev: 1900. Chap. 27, 84a, n. 1; B. Oberlander, *Ha-Siddur*, 178, 251). In other words, he chose, collected and altered formulations in much the same way as the Ari was said to have done, creating an "all-inclusive portal" – *shaar ha-kollel* – so that everyone would be able to find their opening to that place in heaven where all prayers are received.

See further on *Nusah ha-Ari*, Y. Alfasi, in *Temirin – Texts and Studies in Kabbala and Hasidism*, vol. 1 (edited by M. Weinstock, 287–303. Jerusalem: 1972 [Hebrew]; L. Jacobs, *Hasidic Prayer* [New York: 1978, 38–39]).

We should further note the absolute importance with which the use of the "correct" version was regarded. So, for example, we read in *Hanhagot ha-Ari*, edited by M. Benayahu, 326, sec. 33. Jerusalem: 1967:

> One has to say וכסא דוד עבדך – "and the throne of David Thy servant," and not the Romaniot version. For once a scholar came before my master of blessed memory [the Ari], and he gazed at his forehead and said to him that he had never once in his life prayed as required. And that scholar asked him why. And he said to him that he had not said וכסא דוד עבדך במהרה תכין, "and the throne of David Thy servant may you speedily prepare" in the *tishkon* benediction [the tenth benediction of the *Amidah* according to the Sefaradi version = *ve-li-Yerushalayim* in the Ashkenazic version].

See *Pri-Etz Hayyim, Shaar ha-Amidah*, chap. 19, 58c.

Gwóździec Synagogue.

Window Locations, Gwóździec Synagogue. Aerial diagram.

Window locations, Gwoździec Synagogue. Aerial diagram.
Hubka, 6, 49, 147.

Nusah Ahid (unified version) for the Israel Defence Force (see chap. 19, n. 3).

Moreover, when the Hasidim, followers of the Baal Shem Tov, began to use *Nusah ha-Ari* they were actually rejecting their traditional *Nusah Ashkenaz* and taking upon themselves the newly constituted *Nusah Sefarad*. This sparked off an acrid controversy with harsh criticism on the part of the *mitnaggedim*, opposers of Hasidism. Thus, we find R. Avraham Katzenelbogen, rabbi of Brisk, writing to the great Hasidic master, R. Levi Yitzchak of Berdichev, in 1884:

> Whence do you derive the authority to change the ancient custom of the version of the *tefillah* that has been set out for us by our holy forefathers in [this] land, and to chose for yourselves the versions of the Sefaradim? . . . Moreover, how come you have also adopted customs that were not even practiced by all the Sefaradim?[2]

R. Moshe Sofer, the Hatam Sofer, ruled that the *Kavvanot ha-Ari* (proper liturgical intentions of the Ari) are only for Sefaradim, not for Ashkenazim (*Responsa Hatam Sofer, Orah Hayyim* sect. 15–16).

Of course, this particular attack on the part of the *mitnaggedim* was only a relatively small element in their overall opposition to the hasidic theology of prayer, which appeared to give supremacy to worship over Talmud Torah (Torah learning),[3] believing in the inherent sanctity of each letter. Thus we read in *Tzavaat ha-Rivash* (The Will of R. Yisrael Baal Shem Tov, sec. 34, edited by Yaakov Emanuel Shohat, 10. Kehot Publication Society, Brooklyn: 1975):

---

2   See Y. Alfasi, apud *Temirim* (vol. 1, 288), referring us to S. Dubnov, *Toldot ha-Hasidut* (Tel Aviv: 1930–1931, 152–153); L. Jacobs, *Hasidic Prayer*, (160–161), citing by R. Hayyim Halberstam of Zanz (d. 1876), *Divrei Hayyim*, part 2 (Lemberg: 1875, *Orah Hayyim* no. 8, who justifies the use of the Sefaradi version on the part of Hasidim, and ibid., 40–45).

3   See Norman Lamm, "Study and Prayers: Their Relative Value in Hassidism and Mitnagdism" in *Samuel K. Mirsky Memorial Volume* (New York: 1970, 37–52). See, most recently, the excellent discussion of Alan Nadler in his *The Faith of the Mitnagdim: Rabbinic Responses to Hasidic Rapture* (Baltimore and London: 1999, 55 et seq.). See also *Vikuha Rabba*, Brooklyn 1962, for a polemic discussion of this issue between R. Benyamin Zeev of Slonim, a disciple of the Gaon of Vilna, and R. Yosef of Nemirov, a disciple of R. Levi Yitzchak of Berdichev. See J. Katz, *Tradition and Crisis: Jewish Society at the End of the Middle Ages* (New York: 1977, 244).

Know that every letter [in our prayers] is a complete world in itself (הוא קומה שלמה), and one must exert all one's energy in it. If one does not do so, it is as if one of its limbs were missing.

Compare ibid., sec. 75, 23, and sec. 118, 41, in which it is stated once more that "every letter has in it worlds and souls and godliness (עולמות ונשמות ואלוקות). In a similar vein, *Maggid Devarav le-Yaakov* by Reb Dov Baer, the Maggid of Mezridj (sec. 3, Jerusalem: 1971, 106a) states:

The letters of the prayers represent the divine palaces. You go from palace to palace, and at each palace you will be tested to see whether you are worthy to enter . . . .

(Translation in J. Dan, *The Teachings of Hasidism* [New York: 1983, 111])

17

The Response of the *Mitnaggedim*

Perhaps the most expressive formulations of the deep antagonism of *mitnaggedim* to *hasidim* may be found in the Brody Proclamations of 1772, banning the budding Hasidic movement (emphasis mine):[1]

---

1 See also the fierce condemnation of the use of Lurianic *kavvanot* in prayer by R. Yaakov Emden, a vehement adversary of Hasidism (*Mitpahat Soferim*, Lvov: 1871, 112, cited from Idel, *Hasidism: Between Ecstasy and Magic*, 150):

> I did not read the book *Mishnat Hasidim* at all, since, in my view, the author collected it from the writings of the Ari. However, I tell and command my sons and my descendants, my lovers and friends, and whomever is obeying my orders: I decree and prohibit praying according to *Mishnat Hasidim*, or [to use] a manuscript named "Prayer according to Luria's writings," by R. M[eir] Poppers, since it has not been compiled either by Luria or R. Hayyim Vital, his student. Even the book *Kavvanot* by the Ari was not composed for the purpose of using the *kavvanot* de facto, but only to study them. And even if Luria, and likewise his students, could use the *kavvanot* during prayer, in the way he taught them, in any case nowadays the understanding of people is limited, and whoever will use the *kavvanot*, his understanding will doubtless be confused and he will certainly lose more than he intended to profit. Therefore I warn and admonish the people who are listening to my voice not to attempt to achieve grand and marvelous things, surpassing them; would that they be able to use the more general *kavvanot*, which I have arranged in a clear fashion in my prayer book. Do not think that I defame Luria's works, God forbid; our generation is not worthy of that [i.e., the *kavvanot*], until the [Divine] Spirit descends from above; now, because of our sins, we are not worthy. Therefore, let no one say, "I shall multiply the use of *kavvanot* and will not turn aside," since he will deceive himself, because all of the works of Luria were falsified, and all copies contain a multitude of errors and scribal mistakes. I have seen with my [own] eyes a prayer of Luria in the hands of a quasi-Hasid, and it is full of errors that are serious and not small, but

A public Proclamation made here at our Glorious Community of Brody, may God protect it, on the twentieth of Sivan 5532 [=1771], during the fair when all congregate.

Listen, O holy community. With your permission, the honored notables, rulers, leaders, together with the well-known selectmen of the county, have unanimously ordered that the following be proclaimed:

Whereas it has been reported throughout the camp of the Hebrews that by reason of our great sins the [sinful practice] has been rekindled, in the midst of our people, of sects and groups detaching themselves from the unified and just community, adopting new practices and evil laws. They throw off the yoke of Torah and prefer license. [...]

They build themselves [separate] altars to set themselves apart from the holy community, making their own special *minyanim,* not praying with the community in the synagogues or study halls appointed for the public. *They also alter the phrases coined by the sages, the great codifiers [who determined] the entire liturgical order in these lands.* They also blaspheme and mock the messengers of God [i.e., the recognized scholars], and let pass the [prescribed] time for the recital of the *shema* and for prayer, *deliberately altering the formulas that are*

---

he does not realize it. Therefore, intelligent men, hear me and do not desire to ascend and fly to heaven without wings, since you will surely fall .... It is better [to have] a bit of fear of God, [since] He prefers the intention of the heart. Let Him be your hope.

Idel states, "In Emden's eyes the versions of Luria's writings are so complex that any use of them is dangerous, and simple prayer, with good intentions, is preferable to Lurianic *kavvanot.* Emden's testimony, as well as his recommendation, is corroborated by a passage in R. Shmuel ben Eliezer of Kalvaria's *Darkhei Noam,* a work written in approximately 1760 (Königsberg: 1764, vol. 98a; Idel, 151, and 333, n. 12). Describing the prayer of unspecified kabbalists, he asserts that their prayer books are manuscripts and they were copied from one copy to another, and the *Kabbalah* or the [Divine] Names written above a word change their place from one word to another, and those of one word are transposed upon another and vice versa, and God's glory is despised. And they [the prayerbooks] are full of mistakes, almost at each word, and their owners are not able to correct their faults, since they are ignorant and cannot distinguish between good and bad which they prepared [namely the prayerbooks], and it would be better for them not to pray at all, like the gentiles around them, than to pray from the prayerbooks before their eyes."

See *Zmir Aritzim,* in M. Wilensky, *Hasidim and Mitnaggedim* (Jerusalem: 1970 [Hebrew], vol. 1, 44–49); this translation is taken from *The Jewish Political Tradition* (vol. 1; *Authority,* edited by M. Walzer, M. Loberbaum, N. J. Zohar and J. Loberbaum, 358–360. New Haven and London: 2000).

customary in these lands, having been established by the great ones of old, from which there is no way to depart, whether right or left. It has now been discovered that these criminals in their very persons – their evil is immeasurable – remove the yoke and abandon eternal life: [they gather] in groups and gangs, chanting all day long. They deride the entire oral Torah, saying: learn only Kabbalah. *They pray out of the prayer book of the holy man of God, the Ari of blessed memory, thereby surely "cutting the branches"* [misuse of mystical knowledge, cf. BT *Hagigah* 14b].

For some time now these evildoers have been around . . . . And there is room for concern lest . . . God forbid, the divine name become desecrated amongst the nations; lest [the gentiles] say that our Torah is, God forbid, like two Torahs; so that we become, God forbid, a laughingstock amongst the nations. How long shall these people be a snare to the House of Israel? Arise in righteousness to the aid of the Lord among the warriors! Anyone who has the fear of God in his heart should wholeheartedly take the initiative in this matter, to act zealously for the Lord of Hosts, for the honor of His great and awesome name . . . . [And act] to secure the breach, to repulse these evil men in any location where they or their influence prevails, for certainly there is some trace of heresy and apostasy [among them]. How much longer shall this wicked community [persist], which contrives . . . new practices unknown to our fathers? . . .

Therefore the holy community has decreed by the great and awesome *herem* . . . by all the sanctions and curses written in the Torah . . . that from this day onward, it is strictly forbidden for any one of the synagogues or fixed minyanim in our community . . . to alter – God forbid – anything of our customary formula of Ashkenazic prayer. Certainly, none may dare pray out of the prayer book of the godly Ari of blessed memory, or of the other kabbalists, whose secrets were never attained by these sinful men. Also it is forbidden for any individual to pray other than according to the Ashkenazic liturgy, which we received from the ancient great of the world – except for the remnants named by God, those who pray within the first *shtibl* by the side of the *kloyz* of our congregation. With regard to them, it is crystal clear that these persons . . . are full of the exoteric Torah – Talmud and codes – and are also established scholars of the esoteric Kabbalah. They have for years been praying out of the prayer book of Ari of blessed memory, which practice they have followed in the presence of rabbis advanced in age, the . . . great ones of our community, who never protested against this. For these [individuals], from a young age, were well known in [their] piety, and their main studies concerned the exoteric Torah, Talmud, and codes. They know their Master and have true intentions. [They] are permitted to pray, as

has been their practice, out of the prayer book of God's holy one, the Ari of blessed memory – and none besides them. And outside of the *shtibl*, it cannot even be suggested that any minyan alter the formula of Ashkenazic prayer by even one letter, they have no business whatever with esoteric matters, nor [may they adopt] Sephardi customs, but rather [must adhere to] the customs of this land alone. Any alteration from the custom of our fathers is strictly forbidden. (The exception mentioned above applies only to men over thirty years of age, but those less than thirty are strictly forbidden from joining the . . . *shtibl*) . . . .

There is a stern admonition upon all members of our community and those under our authority: . . . They are strictly forbidden from deviating from anything said above, on pain of incurring the punishments of the great and awesome bans . . . .

Now, it is true that our community lacks power to enact a decree upon other communities of Israel . . . . We only make a plea, for the honor of the blessed God, the Holy One of Israel, that all communities act zealously for the Lord; we are all alike sons of one father, the living God . . . .

But this ban, like subsequent ones,[2] was ineffective. The *hasidim* developed *Nusah Sefarad* on the basis of the *Nusah ha-Ari*, and then the various Hasidic courts (*hatzerot*) adjusted the version in accordance with their own specific ideology, so that almost every Hasidic sect. has its own *siddur* with its own version.

Therefore, when I am asked questions such as "To what extent may we add elements in our prayers?" "What method can be used for incorporating additional prayers?" "Can we add new elements to existing prayers?" "Can we mention the *imahot* (foremothers) in addition to the *avot* (forefathers)?" I see the answer as very simple: It is all completely permissible. Adding completely new prayers where one is not changing *matbea shetavu hachamim* – because that would amount to a new creation, a new composition – is certainly permitted. Adding words or phrases to an established *berachah* is less acceptable, according to Maimonides, but if the basic content is not changed, one who recites such a *berachah* does not have to repeat it in its previous form. Thus,

---

2   See further the subsequent bans of Vilna: in 1781 (Wilensky 102–105), Grodno (ibid., 112–113), Pinsk (ibid., 114–115), Slutzk (ibid., 118–121), all from the same year (almost each of which includes, among its accusations and rationale for the ban, assertions that the Hasidim change time-honored customs and make alterations in the prayer service).

for example, as we have mentioned above, the words ומצפים לישועה, in the sixteenth benediction of the *Amidah*, was originally a directive to the worshipper that at this juncture he should yearn for redemption, and it was printed as such in brackets or smaller type, or in a separate line as a directive. However, later it was mistakenly inserted into the body of the blessing in identical typeface, thus appearing to become an integral part of it. It appears this way in many *siddurim*, while others have tried to correct this error, as, for example, *Tzelota de-Avraham*, vol. 1 (298). In this case, neither the basic structure nor the content has been changed, so there is no halachic necessity to correct this error. The question might therefore be more a sociological one than a halachic one. How do new prayers or new additions become accepted? Is it because they were written by great authorities like Rabbi Yehudah he-Hasid, R. Elazar of Worms, Rabbi Moses Cordovero, Rabbi Isaac ben Solomon Luria, or the Ben Ish Hai? Surely "*Lecha Dodi*," which we recite on every Friday night in the synagogue, is accepted by everybody, and that was a completely new creation!

Can we nowadays sit down and decide to add to, subtract from, change or formulate new *berachot*, such as *she-asani ishah ve-lo ish* (who has made me a woman and not a man) or *she-lo asani amah* (who has not made me a slave-woman)? Halachically, yes. Sociologically – will it be accepted, and by whom? That is a completely different question that a sociologist, not a halachist, will have to confront. Many of the changes that have come about, or that are coming about, will gradually become accepted in any case without a full awareness of the fact. If you look at modern *siddurim* such as ArtScroll, Rinat Yisrael or Koren,[3] they incorporate many changes of which most people are not fully aware, but which have become completely accepted mainly because they are in a printed edition. The printed book has become the canon.[4] Even

---

3 We may point out that they have eliminated many of the medieval *piyyutim* that appeared in earlier siddurim in much the same way as the Reform movement did in the nineteenth century (see Idelsohn, 269, 278). The appearance of these new Reform prayer books triggered heated opposition on the part of the Orthodox rabbinate, which repeatedly issued prohibitions against their use (Idelsohn, 270, 379, n. 6). In some cases a form of compromise was found by printing the *piyyutim* on a gray background. But we must bear this in mind as a kind of cautionary tale when considering making changes and shortening our liturgical texts.

4 On the effect of printing on liturgical versions and their standardization, see S. C. Reif, *Judaism and Hebrew Prayer: New Perspectives on Jewish Liturgical History*

its mistakes have been canonized. See, for example, the brief introduction by Koren in the *mahzorim* of Rosh Hashanah and Yom Kippur in which the publisher pointed out that he tried to print certain *piyyutim* in a different format in order to eradicate mistakes, errors that entered into earlier *mahzorim*. The truth is that nevertheless, everyone who chants these *piyyutim* from the "corrected" *mahzorim* do so in the wrong fashion because they cannot free themselves from what they are used to.

(Cambridge: 1933): 235–239; *The Hebrew Book: An Historical Survey* (edited by R. Posner and I. Ta-Shma, Jerusalem: 1975); and in greater detail in the excellent introduction of R. David Yitzhaki to R. Yaakov Emden's *Luah Erez* (Toronto: 2001), 46 et seq.; and, in general, see E. L. Eisenstein, *The Printing Press as an Agent of Change* (Cambridge: 1979). Incidentally, an indication of the effect of this change in the halachah may be seen in the *Mishnah Berurah* on *Shulhan Aruch Orah Hayyim* 128:20, sec. 75–76. We should also like to refer to Stefan C. Reif's fine summarizing essay, entitled "From Manuscript to Printed Volume: A Novel Liturgical Tradition?" in *Liturgy in the Synagogue: Studies in the History of Jewish Prayer* (edited by R. Langer and S. Fine, 95–108. Winona Lake, Indiana: 2005). He ends the essay with the following summarizing observation:

> The phenomenon of printing also had its more novel aspects. The production of numerous copies made possible an unprecedented degree of standardization and democratization and removed a significant amount of control from the rabbinic authority to the printer and publisher. The product became more user friendly, and more emphasis came to be laid on its practical use than on its potential as a transmitter of the broader halakhic traditions. Editions were produced for specific purposes, and some rare versions were preserved by the new medium while other, more common ones, were assigned virtually to oblivion. The capacity of the prayer book to make a major impact on Jewish education and on Hebrew knowledge was quickly appreciated, and influenced at least some people who produced and marketed it. This development – as indeed the other innovations just noted – played no small role in the modern history of Judaism and Hebrew literature and may still be identified in current theory and practice.

J. J. Petuchowski makes a similar such comment in his "Some Laws of Jewish Liturgical Development," in *Studies in Modern Theology and Prayer* (edited by E. R. and A. M. Petuchowski, 163–165. Philadelphia & Jerusalem: 1998).

18

The Impact of Printing on the Hebrew Prayer Book

In order to appreciate fully the impact and influence of printing upon the Hebrew prayer book, I shall cite extensively from Stefan Reif's comprehensive essay (referred to in chapter 16, note 4):

> We must remember that the printing press brought about as revolutionary a change in cultural development in its day as the computer has in our own, and this is particularly true in the case of printed Hebrew prayer books. Data collection and preservation became an altogether less haphazard and difficult proposition. As long as one manuscript was available, it could be used by the printer, and a rare item could be given a "greater lease on life" by being produced in numerous copies. While only a very wealthy patron could engage a scribe to transcribe a text for him, multiple copies made it more feasible for merchants to purchase a greater stake in learning and thereby to increase their involvement in decisions about the future of the liturgical wording. The numerous incunables and sixteenth-century editions of the Ashkenazi, Sefardi, and Italian prayer books produced on the Iberian Peninsula and in Italy ensured that the future of such rites was no longer exclusively dependent on the employment of copyists, the memory of the *hazzan* in the synagogue, or the whim of a censor or persecutor. Indeed, the mass destruction of Spanish and Portuguese Jewish communities and their cultural inheritance might have been even more disastrous for the survival of their traditions, had a small proportion of their printed editions not succeeded in escaping destruction.
>
> It should be added that the wide dissemination of printed prayer books in Poland and the surrounding areas was matched by similar activity in Turkey in

the sixteenth century and subsequently in Germany and Holland. The amplification and reinforcement of knowledge was another benefit of the printed volume. Previously, a view or a piece of information was likely to be known in a small circle and only rarely became widespread enough to win universal acceptance or to attract extensive comment. Now the reverse was possible. Whereas the fate of Jewish communal worship had in earlier periods been dependent on personal relevance, theological status, halakhic centralization, or ritual dominance, now it was in large measure subject to the printing press and those who could or would exercise control over it.

As the content of the printed *siddurim* became more sophisticated, writers began to record not only the rites themselves but rubrics about their use, reasons for their suitability, and justifications for their inclusion. The order of topics, the juxtaposition of individual items within the given topics, and the relative print size of all the constituent parts said a great deal about the priorities and values of the various contents, as the compositor saw them, and this undoubtedly left its mark on the user of the edition. Printers of Hebrew liturgies produced a more common set of texts for daily and Sabbath use in larger format for the cantor and of less-imposing size for the individual; with separate volumes for festivals and booklets for special contexts and occasions, such as grace after meals, Passover Haggadah, and fast days. Some of the basic characteristics of the simpler manuscript liturgies were followed, but it was apparently not yet possible to adopt their grander elements. The precise division between the volumes ultimately became a matter of distinction between Sefardi and Ashkenazi prints. Nevertheless, there was at first little to distinguish one part of the prayer book from another; other characteristics were: few headings, rubrics, or incipits; fairly primitive line justification; precious little commentary, and text repetition as seldom as possible.

But there was always a negative as well as a positive side to typographical developments. Control over choice of text fell into the hands of the printers and publishers, and some of their decisions were motivated more by market forces than by scholarly or halakhic considerations. Shoddy editions were sometimes produced, and some of the minorites and liturgical poems were virtually consigned to oblivion for want of a popular edition. Even the new availability of a text to ordinary congregants, who had previously had to rely on the rabbi for theory and the *hazzan* for practice, was not always welcome. Whatever its degree of validity, a text that had been printed in hundreds of copies could soon become the norm, and a community was not easily convinced that what appeared before their eyes in printed form was not necessarily

authentic.[1] Furthermore, while texts were widely available to Jews, they were

---

1　Shapira, in his *Maamar Nusah ha-Tefillah* (158), also notes the state of accuracy of the different *siddurim*. There, he writes:

Behold, I have seen in the matter of the versions of the liturgy that the situation is scandalous in the House of Israel, for no one version is like the other and the differences between them are so great that they add up to many hundreds, both in the *Amidah* as well as other prayers and blessings	הנה ראיתי בזה בסדר נוסחאות התפילה שערוריה בבית ישראל כי אין דומה נוסח של אחד לחבירו והשינויים רבו כל כך ביניהם עד כי עלו למאות חילוקים ושינויים בנוסחאות בשמונה עשרה מלבד בשארי התפילות והברכות.

Later on, he discusses the various causes for these differences – censorship, conflation, printing errors – and seeks to correct them. See also Klatzki, *Erech Tefillah* (15–16); *The Hebrew Book: An Historical Survey* (62–207, 209); S. Reif, *Shabbethai Sofer and His Prayer-Book* (Cambridge: 1979, 15–16, 34–41). (A magnificent, exhaustively annotated edition of this *siddur* was produced by R. Yitzhak Satz in five volumes [Baltimore 1987–2002].) Reif continues to note (ibid., 106–108), that:

A group of Polish rabbis in the sixteenth and seventeenth centuries called printers to task for insufficient effort and liturgical standardization. In assessing the significance of their remarks, it is important for us to note that the "errors" they bewailed were not simply printers' mistakes, of which there are obviously many examples, but also the preservation of linguistic traditions that did not match what they had come to regard as "standard." Nathan ben Samson Spira, Meshulam Faivush of Cracow, Jacob Koppel, and Shabbethai Sofer of Przemysl variously censured the printers for their inadequacies.

Shabbethai makes numerous references to errors that he notes in the texts of printed prayer books. In one case, he complains that the contemporary *siddurim* are wholly inconsistent in their pointing of a particular word and that what they have in common is that they are all totally at sea, erring in both theory and practice. He points out that, in spite of what is (wrongly) printed in some *siddurim*, it is grammatically impossible for a letter to have both a *rafeh* sign and a *dagesh*. He invites all those with authority to express their disapproval of the printers in the various countries of the Ashkenazi dispersion for failing to insert the correct *rafeh* and *dagesh* in their editions of the Pentateuch and the prayer book. This confuses the reader, he says, who is left wondering about the quality of the letters and unable to read them correctly. It is consequently no wonder that the Jewish exile is so prolonged and that their passionate prayers are ineffectual.

Meshullam Faivush in his recommendation for Shabbethai's work refers to the numerous mistakes and the unbelievable errors of all sorts that constantly occur in the prayer books because of the printers' inadequacies. Jacob Koppel describes the prayer books as full of stupid errors in matters of pointing and textual rite and notes how difficult it is to eliminate habits that have become ingrained. The Council of Three Lands complains about the inconsistency of

also open to the critical eye of the non-Jew and the apostate. When a text was erased from a manuscript, the evidence of the erasure remained. Even if an early printer had taken care to leave a space where the censored text had once stood, his later colleagues might take exception to the wasted space and lack of elegance and neatly join the passages that had survived. Alternative texts that were less "offensive" to non-Jews were printed as another way of dealing with the difficulty. Thus, innovations that would hardly have been tolerated for other reasons made their way into the unsuspecting *siddur* . . . .

A greater variety of fonts came to be used, pagination was added, and the precise makeup of each set of prayers was made clear to the worshiper by the use of incipits, headings, helpful layouts, line justification and text repetition. Not only the format of the text but also its precise wording was of major concern to the editor of a new publication: whose version was to be followed, which linguistic conventions were to be adopted, and what the criteria were for such preferences. Once such decisions were made, they obviously had a major impact on the future history of any given text. For years to come, even centuries, the choice of an early printer came to be regarded as the standard edition. There were particular Jewish rites that fell at this first hurdle. Provençal liturgies did not receive

---

the *siddurim* in matters of spelling and pointing and about the tendency of the Jewish public to rely on printers who publish pointed texts that are totally corrupt.

See his references in nn. 36–43 ad loc., and for further elaboration of this last paragraph, see his *Shabbethai* (34, 91). There he writes as follows:

Meshullam Phoebus of Cracow (1547–1617) notes the many unintelligible errors in matters of text and ritual to be found in an temporary prayers-books, and leaves no room for doubt that the responsibility for this state of affairs lies firmly with the printers: "על הסידורים הנמצאים בידינו שיש בהם הרבה טעויות ושגיאות מי יבין הן מצד הנוסחאות הן מצד שאר טעויות הנמצאים ונופלים שם שגיאות המדפיסים".

Jacob Koppel of Przemysl (d. Cracow 1630) laments that his co-religionists are "like blind men groping in the dark," that they are at a loss when reading the prayers, unable to distinguish "between right and left" and that this ignorance has become traditional among them. He points to the additional complication created by corrupt texts of the printed liturgies and to the difficulties of eradicating inveterate errors.

ראה ראיתי הנה ילדי העברים כעוורים ממששים באפילה בדקדוק קריאת דברי התפילה בדגשות ורפיון ונח ונע טעו ונבוכו בין ימין לשמאל לא ידעו ולא יבינו בחשיכה יתהלכו זה דרכם כסל להם מנהג אבותיהם בידיהם מצורף לזה רוב סדורי הברכות והתפילות מלאים שגיאות והוללות הן בנקודות הן בנוסח המלות ושבשתא דינקותא כיון דעל על.

typographical attention until the eighteenth century because of their junior status compared with the "heavyweights," while the geographical and cultural isolation of Yemenite Jewry denied them printed prayer books until a century later than that. No doubt a wide variety of local traditions once followed in hundreds of synagogues of Spain and in their equivalents farther north in Europe simply disappeared for want of a printer's interest or a bookseller's market.

The observations made in this succinct historical description are true not only of the sixteenth and seventeenth centuries but also of our own day, as we have briefly indicated above.

Furthermore, the advent of printing and of the printed *siddur* had halachic implications as well. Thus, R. Yehiel Michel Epstein in his *Aruch ha-Shulhan* (*Orah Hayyim* 110:3), writes:

> It seems to me that [the reason *havinenu* is not recited in situations where there is a lack of familiarity with prayer is] because nowadays the text [of the *Amidah*] is found in all the *siddurim* [and] it is no longer relevant to include one who has difficulty composing one's prayers [among the factors that allow one to recite *havinenu*]. Only in Talmudic times, when prayers were recited by heart, was it relevant to say that prayer does not dwell in one's mouth – not in our time, when we all pray from *siddurim*.

This idea, that printed *siddurim* reduce confusion, is found elsewhere. Thus, the *Magen Avraham* on *Orah Hayyim* 128:31, when discussing the priestly blessing, writes regarding the *Shulhan Aruch's* ruling (ibid., subsec. 20):

> If the cantor is a priest, if there are other priests, he should not bless the people, and even if there is no other priest there he should not do so unless he is certain that he will be able to return to [the regular prayer] without being confused . . . .
> "Certain that he will be able to return" – and for us, who pray from the printed text, we are always certain that the cantor will be able to return to his prayers [without becoming confused] . . . . *Nahlat Zvi* (subsec. 20) wrote that [the current practice] relies on the fact that we now pray from printed texts . . . .

The *Magen Avraham* continues by casting doubts as to the legitimacy of this argument, but nonetheless, it is clear that he is keenly aware of this new technology, even if he is not convinced of its efficacy in this specific halachic context. (See M. J. Broyde, *Innovation in Jewish Law: A Case Study in Chiddush in Havinenu*. Atlanta: 2008, 145.)

Siddur R. Shabtai Sofer,
Amsterdam 1647.

Siddur R. Shabtai Sofer, Prague 1669.

19

The Permissibility of Making Changes

Returning to our basic question, halachically it would seem that although there were many attempts at various times to canonize a specific version of the liturgy, the overwhelming evidence shows it to be quite permissible to make changes as long as one does not alter the overall content and structure of the blessing or prayer.

Let us strengthen our argument further by quoting from one of the leading Ashkenazic authorities of the early fifteenth century, R. Yaakov Moellin (the Maharil, 1355–1427). In his book of customs, *Sefer ha-Maharil – Minhagim*, he expresses himself clearly as one who was generally zealous not to change established local customs or even the local liturgical melodies (see S. J. Spitzer's edition, Jerusalem: 1989, 339, and of ibid., 345). Nevertheless, he was apparently willing to alter "many words" of the accepted service of the High Holidays. We read (ibid., 301 – the whole work was penned by his disciple, R. Zalman from Stuttgart) as follows:

> I the author heard from the pure mouth of Mahari Segal (=Maharil), when we were studying Tractate *Yoma* with him, and that was in the year 1426, a year before he was taken up to heaven, and he said: "If the Lord, blessed be He, will give me life so that I am able to pray on the High Holidays, then I would wish to change many words in the Rosh ha-Shanah and Yom Kippur prayers from that to which we have been accustomed till now." Therefore I returned to find them out and wrote them out between Rosh ha-Shanah and Yom Kippur, as they were heard by R. Zelmelin of Erfurt, who passed them on to me so that I could record them for posterity. And let no one contradict me . . . .

In a gloss in the margin of the Maharil manuscript, we read the following (Spitzer ibid., n. 13:1):

> Anyone who reads my book ... should know for certain that for many years I was very close to my master, Mahari Segal, and I took great care to record changes in the words [of prayer] that I heard from his mouth when he recited the prayers of Rosh ha-Shanah and Yom Kippur, and before he died in the month of Elul 1427, we discussed [them] before him .... But it happened that in that year, 1427, I could not be with the Rabbi in Vermaiza [Worms], and I presented these words [that were altered?] before a dear friend, a righteous and most reliable person, R. Zelmelin of Erfurt, and I asked him to listen carefully to the rabbi's prayer and to pass the changes on to me. I have recorded them in this book, between the prayers of Rosh ha-Shanah and Yom Kippur, exactly as he passed them on to me. Therefore let no one contradict me ....

We see, then, that even the great Maharil, for all his "ultra-conservatism" regarding customs and even liturgical melodies, was willing and even eager to make changes in the service, presumably for halachic, kabbalistic or grammatical reasons, deviating from the traditional version. (See, further, Y. Dinari, *The Rabbis of Germany and Austria at the Close of the Middle Ages: Their Composition and Halacha Writings* [Jerusalem: 1984 (Hebrew)], 54–55.)

It has been argued that while it is clearly true that there was always a multiplicity of concurrently competing liturgical versions, for each individual authority, or community, their version was the correct and unalterable one. Hence, anyone who has a received tradition of the liturgical text, cannot make his own changes in order to bring it up to date or in accordance with contemporary sociological, political or even spiritual trends. I believe that the material we have cited above refutes any such argument, and demonstrates clearly that there were conscious changes made at different times in different places, in response to specific circumstances, and that such changes were over all accepted as legitimate. Traditionally what has happened is that these changes came about either through a great authority, such as, for example, Hasidei Ashkenaz, the Ari ha-Kadosh, and Ben Ish Hai, or because a *kehillah en masse* decided to adopt a certain change. Sometimes these changes come from the "top," i.e., a leading authority,[1] and sometimes they come from the "bottom"

---

1   We may further add that which we read in *Siddur R. Hirz (Trevish) Shatz* (Tihingen:

i.e., the community itself.[2] To bring about such changes is by no means easy.

1560) (edited by Y. Klugmann, vol. 1, 97 Bnei Brak: 2004):

וידעתי שגם זה הבל לסבות שתים, האחת לספרים שאינם מוגהים בנמצא, ואף אותם מפרשים נדים
ונעים ואיבריהם מתפרקים בהעתקתם בלי מבין, ושיבושי טעות סופר עומדים, יקל לקורא במרוצה
למכשול, ושבשתא כיון דעל על. . . .

We see from this passage how he deplores the fact that there are few books available to the public, and especially to the cantors, that have been carefully proofread,
and most of them are full of mistakes and inaccuracies due to copyists who do not
understand the material, etc.

It is also interesting to read the *haskamot* appearing in the *Siddur Tefillah
Derech Siah ha-Sadeh*, by R. Azriel and his son R. Eliyahu of Wilna, published in
Frankfurt am Main (1704, and republished several times, such as the third edition
Wilmersdorf, 1721). For example, R. Gavriel, of Metz writes as follows:

. . . כי כל סידורי תפילות שנדפסו מכמה שני' מימות החסיד המופלא המדקדק הגדול מוהר"ר שבתי
סופר מפרעמשלא אולם לא נאמר בהן כי טוב. ומחד כ"א [כל אחד] בונה במה לעצמו ומוחק וכותב
ומוסיף ושולח יד להגיה לפי שכלו בלי שום קבלה בדברי' העומדים ברומו של עולם שיסדו וסידרו לנו
אנשי כה"ג [כנסת הגדולה] להיות מפתח לפתוח שערי שמים לעלות בית א"ל והמצפה צופי' אמרום
שכחום וחזרו אב ובנו ה"ה [הוא / הם] מוה"ר עזריאל יצ"ו ובני מוה"ר אלי' ויסדום ביתד ותנועה עד
היסוד בה כפי אשר מצאו אחר הטורח והעיון בספרי' ישני' כתוב' ונדפסי' מפי נדיבי עם במחקק
במשעניותם. . . .

Here he decries the state of printed prayer books which are full of errors, lacu-
nae, distortions, since the printers "each one builds himself a high place [*bamah*, al-
luding to an altar of idolatry] for himself, erases, writes, adds and recklessly emends
according to his (limited) understanding not based on tradition," etc.

This after extolling R. Shabtai Sofer's prayer book for its extreme accuracy.
Similarly, R. Shemuel of Frankfurt writes:

אחד ראיתי את שאהבה נפשי, זה שחמד לבי, מיום שעמדתי על דעתי, מתי יבוא לידי ותחת עיני,
לראות סדר תפילות נדפסים בלי טעות ע"פ הדקדוק. לא כראשונים שמלאים טעויות וקמשוני'
והמכשלה הזאת הית' תחת ידינו. לא כאלה חלק יעקב, המייתרים או מחסרים אות אחת או אפילו
נקודה אחת כאלו מחריבים כל העולם כידוע. . . .

He, too, described the sad state of his current prayer book with the errors, additions, subtractions, incorrect grammar, which he believes have such dire cosmic
(!) effects. This, of course, in accordance with their tradition of Hasidei Ashkenaz
that even the loss of a letter, or even, he adds, a vocal point, brings disaster upon
the world.

See *Seder Tefillah Derech Siah ha-Sadeh*, facsimile edition, with notes in the back
(Toronto: 2007, 81, 83, etc; and R. Yaakov Yosef Schechter's remarks in *Yeshurun*
2 [1997]: 531–536).

2   It is interesting to read Aaron Choriner's recantation of what he had earlier written
in *Sefer Nogah ha-Zedek*, ed. Eliezer Liberman, Dessau 1818, in his *Qinath ha-Emeth*,

Nowadays, you will not find many "tops" who are willing to make these types of changes for a variety of reasons that do not need to be spelled out here. On the other hand, the hope or the challenge is that, if numerous congregations are willing to be creative, struggle against the trend and adopt for themselves new modes of prayer, making changes within the parameters that we have pointed out, eventually these changes will be accepted, maybe not across the board, but certainly within a certain sections of the Jewish Orthodox community.[3] Needless to say, the ultra-traditionalists do not, and will not, accept this position. So the conflict will go on well into the future, but so too will changes continue to appear throughout the pages of our prayer books.[4]

---

justifying various changes in the Reform prayer book and service, instituted under the directions of Israel Jacobson in Berlin 1815 onwards. Thus in *Eleh Divrei ha-Brit* published by the Hamburg Bet Din, Altona 1819, he writes (29):

> Now that I have heard that they have also abbreviated the benedictions and the prayers, that they do not pray for the Ingathering of the Exiles – the belief in which is the very foundation of our holy Torah – and that they alter the text of the prayers, I apply to myself the verse (Isaiah 3:6): "And let this ruin be under thy hand." I, therefore, declare in public: All my words in *Qinath ha-Emeth* are null and void, and that I am not entitled to deal with this matter and to reach decisions. *The Sages of Israel, the great scholars of the age, they alone have the* right *to do so; and my own views must be considered as naught and nothing as against theirs.* (emphasis mine – D. S.) (Cited from J. J. Petuchowski, *Prayerbook Reform in Europe*, 93–94.)

He demonstrates that this change of mind came about due to the pressure put upon him by R. Moshe Sofer, the Hatam Sofer (see ibid., 91–92). On Israel Jacobson's Reform worship services, see David Philipson, *The Reform Movement in Judaism* (New York: 1907, 33); S. Bernfeld, *Toldot ha-riformazion ha-datit be-Yisrael* (Cracow: 1900, 240–243); Petuchowski, ibid., 133–134. See also, most recently, the excellent study of Judith Bleich, "Liturgical Innovation and Spirituality: Trends and Trendiness" (in *Jewish Spirituality and Divine Law*, edited by A. Mintz & L. Schiffman, 321–344, 371–376. New York: 2005 [on *piyyutim*]).

3 The Carlebach-style *minyanim* are an example of this. See the thoughtful article of Uri Kreuzer, *Lev she-ba-avodah* (*Deot* 37 [2001]: 20–23).

4 This has already been clearly pointed out by Joseph Heinemann, in his remarks in *Prayers in Judaism: Continuity and Change*, 32:

> In particular, I think of the weekday morning service, to which a person would need to devote at least one hour if he wished to recite it properly and suitably in a quorum, and this hardly any synagogue in the world is prepared for. We can say that this prayer really stultifies itself. Moreover, we ought not to wait for

I think, therefore, that, in the same way as great revolutions have taken place in the last thirty to forty years in *limmud Torah* (Torah study) by women, which at one time was anathema and now is almost universally accepted, and in much the same way that there are more and more *kehillot* that are developing and adopting in varying degrees certain elements of egalitarian prayer, so too, if we begin to make these changes in our different *kehillot*, gradually they will gain acceptance in ever wider circles. It should always be borne in mind that, in any case, there is no standard version of Jewish liturgy.[5] Yemenites pray

---

the Rabbis to come along and give their halachic approval to needful changes. Halachic rulings of that sort will never be given, and they are also not necessary because this is an area where, in large measure, we may do as we see fit, so long as we do not add to, or subtract from the (eighteen) blessings of the *Amidah*. Everything else is really in our own hands, including the reformulation of several of the eighteen blessings themselves if we feel that it is necessary.

It seems to me that this can be done if there is a community prepared to do it. The main problem is that no "ultra-Orthodox" group is prepared to contemplate such an attempt, at least not here in Israel. Even in synagogues made up of thinking, educated people, a great uproar ensues as soon as someone attempts the smallest change, such as omitting *Yekum purkan*, in which we pray for the Exilarch in Babylon!

5 A good example of the complex evolution of a prayer in Amoraic times is to be found in BT *Sotah* 40a:

בזמן ששליח ציבור אומר מודים, העם מה הם אומרים? אמר רב: מודים אנחנו לך ה' א-להינו על שאנו מודים לך. ושמואל אמר: א-להי כל בשר על שאנו מודים לך. רבי סימאי אמר: יוצרינו יוצר בראשית על שאנו מודים לך. נהרדעי אמרי משמיה דרבי סימאי: ברכות והודאות לשמך הגדול על שהחייתנו וקיימתנו על שאנו מודים לך. רב אחא בר יעקב מסיים בה הכי: כן תחיינו ותחננו ותקבצינו ותאסוף גלויותינו לחצרות קדשיך לשמור חוקיך ולעשות רצונך בלבב שלם על שאנו מודים לך. אמר רב פפא: הילכך נמרינהו לכולהו.

We see then that the prayer that we call *Modim de-Rabbanan* is actually a conflation of five different versions suggested respectively by Rav, Samuel, Rabbi Sinai, Nehardai, and Rabbi Aha Bar Yaakov. Rav Papa suggested blending them into one united prayer that would include all these different elements. See what I wrote in *Minhagei Yisrael*, vol. 2 (Jerusalem: 1991), 23–24. In JT *Berachot* 1.5, we find additional versions:

ר' סימאי: מודים אנחנו לך אדון כל הבריות אלוקי התשבחות צור עולמים חי העולם יוצר בראשית... מחיה מתים שהחייתנו וקיימתנו וזכיתנו וסייעתנו וקרבתנו להודות לשמך. בא"י א-ל ההודאות. רבי בא בר זבדי בשם רב: מודים אנחנו לך שאנו חייבים להודות לשמך תרננה שפתי כי אזמרה לך ונפשי אשר פדית. בא"י א-ל ההודאות. רבי שמואל בר מינא בשם ר' אחא: הודייה ושבח לשמך לך גדולה לך גבורה לך תפארת יהי רצון מלפניך ה' אלקינו ואלקי אבותינו שתסמכנו מנפילתנו ותזקפנו מכפיפותנו

differently from Ashkenazim, and Halabim (Syrian Jews) differently from

כי אתה סומך נופלים וזוקף כפופין ומלא רחמים ואין עוד מלבדך. בא"י א"ל ההודאות. בר קפרא אמר:
לך כריעה לך כפיפה לך השתחויה לך כריעה לך תכרע כל ברך תשבע כל לשון לך ה' הגדולה והגבורה
והתפארת והנצח וההוד כי כל בשמים ובארץ לך ה' הממלכה והמתנשא לכל לראש והעושר והכבוד
מלפניך ואתה מושל בכל ובידך כח וגבורה לגדל ולחזק לכל ועתה אלקינו מודים אנחנו לך ומהללים
לשם תפארתך בכל לב ובכל נפש משתחוין כל עצמותי תאמרנה ה' מי כמוך מציל עני מחזק ממנו ועני
ואביון מגוזלו. בא"י א"ל ההודאות. אמר ר' יודן: נהגין רבנן אומרים כולהון. ואית דאמרי: או הדא או
הדא.

Here again we see a number of different versions, with one opinion that all the versions should be read, presumably in a conflated manner, and another, that some say one while others say another (see L. Ginzberg, *A Commentary on the Palestinian Talmud*, vol. 1 [New York, 1941], 186–187. The passage from the Jerusalem Talmud is cited in the Tosafot on BT *Sotah* 40a). For a further analysis of this prayer, see Beni and Yair Gesundheit, "*Modim de-Rabbanan' ba-Bavli u-ba-Yerushalmi*" (*Alon Shvut – Bogrim* 23 [2009]: 35–45).

Rabbi Joseph Caro, in his Beit Yosef commentary on *Tur Orah Hayyim*, 127, writes:

I have found it written that it is called *Modim de-Rabbanan*, because it was formulated on the basis of many sages' [statements] (לפי שהוא תיקון הרבה חכמים).

The above example demonstrates the state of fluidity of this prayer up to the later Amoraic period. See also Petuchowski, ibid., 165–167.

Indeed, the tendency to conflate competing versions and to "twin" them in the same prayer is one of the most commonplace phenomena in liturgical literature. See what I wrote in *Minhagei Yisrael*, vol. 2 (Jerusalem: 1991, 30–31), where I cited two examples. One is an Italian custom from Livorno (Leghorn) that appears in a responsum of R. Yosef (ben R. Immanuel) Irgas (flor. 1685–1730) in his Responsa *Divrei Yosef*, Livorno 1742, sec. 15. There he discusses the local custom during the Ten Days of Repentance to say: זכרנו לחיים מלך חפץ בחיים, כתבנו בספר חיים למענך א-להים חיים א-ל חי.

Further on in that same volume (sec. 5, 15 a–b), he admits that this is not a simple or straightforward custom:

... For in all the cities of Germany and Poland it is their custom to omit א"ל חי, and in all Italian cities they omit the words א-להים חיים, and say only א"ל חי. However, to say both these [celestial] names was the Spanish custom ... and it spread under the influence of R. Yosef Gikatilia (1248–1325). However, after the Ari ha-Kadosh appeared, and his writings became accepted throughout the world, most Sefaradim changed their custom and omitted the words א"ל חי, in accordance with the view of the Ari.

These two competing versions were based on two different biblical verses, the one is Psalm 84:3, לבי ובשרי ירננו אל א"ל חי, and the other in verses such as Deut. 5:53: אשר שמע קול א-להים חיים, (and cf. 1 Samuel 17:26, 36; Jeremiah 10:10, 23, 36). Irgas

rightly points out (ibid.) that "nowhere do we find the combinations א-להים חיים and א-ל חי adjacent to one another, but each one has its own place." Clearly, then, we have here two alternative readings, which were paired in the Livorno custom.

This may appear to be a rather trivial issue. However, in the early eighteenth century it triggered off a raging controversy that spread throughout the great eastern communities of Livorno (Italy), Izmir (Turkey), Haleb (Syria) and Egypt. Irgas repeatedly argued his case through five lengthy responsa (1–5), which ultimately favor the Ari's ruling of א-להים חיים alone, (allowing only eleven words in this passage), but also include some suggestions of compromise, such as is found at the end of the final responsum, namely that "the cantor should not repeat זכרנו, but continue with מלך עוזר . . . so that each person (in the congregation) can say whatever he wants," i.e., with א-ל חי or without. See also Zuberi, *Kenesset ha-Gedolah* (vol. 3, Jerusalem: 1991), 4258, for a detailed and extensive discussion on this subject.

A second example that I brought there related to the ending מלך צור ישראל וגואלו, which is a conflation of מלך ישראל וגואלו (cf. Isaiah 44:6) and צור ישראל וגואלו, based on Psalm 19:5. (See Wieder's discussion in *Sinai* 77 [1971]: 118–119). For further examples see *Minhagei Yisrael* ibid. 31–34, n. 2, such as the *Manhig's* (sec. 32, ed. Raphael, 65): אהבת עולם רבה, which is a conflation of אהבת עולם and אהבה רבה, and the examples are legion. See further Wieder's discussion in *Hitgabshut* (55–56).

A third example is found in the *Torah Temimah's* note to the benedictions over the *haftarah* (Bereshit, 442), note ודבר אחד מדבריך אחור לא ישוב and ודבר אחד מדבריך אחור לא ישוב ריקם. And we have: ודבר אחד מדבריך אחור לא ישוב ריקם. The author of the *Torah Temimah*, R. Baruch Ha-Levi Epstein, used the standard edition of *Masechet Soferim* (13.11). However, see M. Higger's edition (New York: 1937, 246–247), which has our reading, and the apparatus to line 40, where some testimonies do not have the word אחור. Epstein himself expresses discomfort at what he sees as a conflation of two versions.

Here we shall add one more example of obvious conflation, this time in the fourth benediction of the *Amidah*. This benediction is called חונן הדעת in M. *Berachot* 5.2, for its ending (*hatimah*), BT *Megillah* 17b calls it בינה, *Berachot* 33a חכמה, while JT *Berachot* 2.4, 4d calls it דיעה – all these for its content. The variety of versions found in *siddurim* as to the main part of the benediction is as follows:

דעה ובינה	Genizah
חכמה בינה ודעת	Oriental and Sefarad
בינה חכמה והשכל דעה	Saadya, Persia, Haleb, Genizah
בינה, דעה חכמה והשכל	Mahzor Vitry
דעה חכמה בינה והשכל	Rambam

Some *siddurim* have דעה בינה והשכל and חכמה בינה ודעת alongside one another, sometimes in different typefaces suggesting that they are alternative versions, something in different kinds of brackets, with the same intention as above, and sometimes in identical typeface with no clear indication that they are alternative versions. (See Luger, 73–74, 79–80 *Tzelota de-Avraham*, vol. 1, 283.)

R. Elazar Shapira (*Maamar Nusah ha-Tefillah*, 159–160), inveighs heatedly

Moroccans. Indeed, there are *siddurim* in which variant versions of a specific prayer were printed alongside one another in parallel columns (e.g., *Siddur Hanau* 1628, 29 and fol. 3b). Over the past forty years or so, changes and modifications have been made in certain prayers to fit new political situations in the

---

against such conflations. R. Avraham David b. Asher of Buczacz, on the other hand, in his *Daat Kedoshim*, sees this as a positive phenomenon (Shapira ibid.,160, 163). See also J. Mann's seminal essay, "Changes in the Divine Service of the Synagogue due to Religious Persecutions" (*HUCA* 4 [1927]: 244–310 (=J. Mann, *The Collected Essays*, Gedera: 1971, vol. 1, 264–333). Shapira (ibid., 177) also notes that during the Shabbat morning service, some worshippers read וגם במנוחתו לא ישכנו רשעים instead of ערלים. This is due to censorship. Others read לא ישכנו רשעים וערלים, which is a mistaken conflation of the original version and the censored one.

A further example of a conflation of versions is found in the *shema kolenu* benediction in the *Amidah* where many *siddurim* have: תפילת כל פה עמך ישראל ברחמים, which is a conflation of two different versions. Sefarad – תפילת כל פה, and Ashkenaz – תפילת עמך ישראל ברחמים. Shlomo Tal, in his *Ha-Siddur be-Hishtalsheluto*, 55, explains how this hybrid version came about as follows:

> When the Hasidim of the Baal Shem Tov began to pray with the *kavvanot* of the Ari, they had not as yet before them a *siddur* of *Nusah Sefarad*, for in those areas such *siddurim* were not available. And so they all prayed from a *siddur* of *Nusah Ashkenaz*. But since the *kavvanot* of the Ari were in accordance with *Nusah Sefarad* the worshippers wrote in the margins [of their prayer books] the variant: תפילת כל פה. The printers, who wished to supply the Hasidim with a *Nusah Sefarad siddur*, grafted the *Nusah Sefarad* onto the *Nusah Ashkenaz*, and the result was: תפילת כל פה עמך ישראל ברחמים.

Tal adds that in *Siddur Habad*, the Baal ha-Tanya determined that the version should be: תפילת כל פה.

Indeed, many more such examples could be cited, and it could further be demonstrated that such processes continued on into much later generations. However, that would be beyond the scope of this study. See in the meanwhile Reif's discussion, 123–206. See also Petuchowski (ibid., 155–156, Klatzki, *Erech Tefillah* 18–19, 124, no. 58), for additional examples. See also A. Spanier, *"Dubletten in Gebettexten"* (*MGWJ* 83 [1939]: 142, and Weiser, ibid., 38–39).

Very telling is a single example of an addition in the *Kaddish* prayer, discussed by Hallamish, ibid., 619–626, who ends this chapter with a significant quote from S. Y. Agnon's *A Guest for the Night* (95):

> . . . they differ as to the versions of the prayer and quarrel over each custom that a person brings from his city as though it is from Sinai, and make a fight over *"ve-yatzmach purkanei ve-yekarev meshichei,"* and there are those who add *"ve-yekarev ketz meshichei."* Master of the Universe, send us the Messiah so that at least we may be freed of this (i.e., these squabbles).

State of Israel.[6] Therefore we should not, and need not, seek unanimity in our

---

6   See the very illuminating article by Saul Philip Wachs, "*Birkat Nahem*": The Politics
    of Liturgy in Modern Israel" (in *Liturgy in the Life of the Synagogue: Studies in the
    History of Prayer*, edited by R. Langer & S. Fine, 247–258. Winuna Lake, Indiana:
    2005). He shows how Abraham Rosenfeld changed the traditional text of *Nahem*
    after the 1967 war in the (second) 1970 edition of his English translation of the tra-
    ditional *Kinot* (liturgical laments for the Ninth of Av) and by Prof. E. E. Urbach in
    1967. Rosenberg's revision of *Birkat Nahem* no longer appears in his *Sefer Kinot* be-
    cause many congregations retained the original 1965 edition and because the most
    recent editions (from 1989 onwards) have deleted his revised text. Urbach's text,
    which was never widely disseminated, is now used only in a few Orthodox kibbut-
    zim. Paradoxically, or perhaps not so paradoxically, his text was printed in the *siddur*
    of the Israeli Conservative Movement's official *siddur, Siddur Va-ani tefillati* (edited
    by S. Roth, Jerusalem: 1998, 139), the Israeli Reform Movement's *siddur, Avodah she-
    ba-lev* (Jerusalem: 1982), 233, and in a resource book on *Tishah be-Av*, published for
    the *Kibbutz ha-Meuhad* movement (*Yalkut Tet be-Av*, ed. A. Ben Gurion, Tel Aviv:
    1997, 145), and in various booklets prepared in individual Ramah Camps for *Tishah
    be-Av*. Wachs ends his article thus:

    > As the exuberance of these days waned, so did the perceived disjuncture be-
    > tween the traditional and contemporary, and a traditionalist attitude set in
    > among Orthodox Jews that consigned the new version of *Birkat Nahem* to his-
    > torical memory. Only the segment of Judaism most open to liturgical change,
    > the Reform and Conservative movements in Israel, retain a vestige of those
    > optimistic days in their prayers.

    Dr. Yael Levine, in an article in *Tehumin* (21 [2001]: 71–90), cites four addi-
    tional versions, that of Rabbi Shlomo Goren, Chief Rabbi of Israel in 1967, that of
    Rabbi David Chelouche, Chief Rabbi of Netanya, that of Rabbi Menahem Mendel
    Horwitz, and that of Mr. Yosef Ben-Brit of Hibat Tziyyon. She discusses the varied
    reactions of different rabbinic authorities to these "altered" versions, such as that
    of Rabbi Zvi Yehudah Kook, who felt that "the time had not yet come for these
    changes." R. Ovadia Yosef, who strongly objected to any such change, and likewise
    R. Josef Dov Soloveitchik, R. Avraham Shapira, R. Shlomo Min Ha-Har, albeit not
    all for exactly the same reasons. R. David Ha-Levi, who agreed to slight changes,
    such as turning present tense to past tense – "the city that *was* in mourning," as op-
    posed to "that *is* in mourning," "that *dwelled*," as opposed to "that dwells," and so
    too R. Shear Yashuv Cohen, Chief Rabbi of Haifa, and, on the other hand, R. Shaul
    Yisraeli of Yeshivat Mercaz ha-Rav, who permitted individuals to use the modified
    versions in their private prayer, although he forbade such a change in public prayer.
        Here, then, we see the conflict between the traditionalists and those more open
    to changes, and the interplay between halachah and political ideology. In app. 2 we
    cite the various versions of *Nahem*.

liturgy.[7] Let there be yet another *nusah* of *tefillah*, one that will be acceptable within the context of modern-day Orthodox feminist thinking, and which hopefully will gain ever wider legitimacy.

At the same time, we must exercise great care to retain the traditional elements of our prayer book, to preserve its character and structure, to ensure that any additions, deletions, or alterations do not contradict or conflict with normative halachah[8] and, as far as possible, to preserve the style and spiritual

---

7   Rabbi S. Goren introduced a *siddur* with what he called *Nusah Ahid*, a unified *nusah*. The purpose of the *siddur*, which was created for the army, was to address specific needs. See his *Terumat ha-Goren* (Jerusalem: 2004, sec. 20, 54–57), in which he describes the problematic elements inherent in such an attempt. See my remarks on this *siddur* in *Shiur Times* (2008, 12). S. Weiser, in his article in *Ha-Maayan* (12/3 [1972]: 38–39), has a serious critique of R. Goren's *siddur*. He writes:

> It is dubious if this is the way to achieve a unified version [i.e., use of *Nusah Sefarad*], a goal we all aim at, and it is not clear what are the halachic justifications therefore. And, most especially, it is hardly understandable why "*Nusah Sefarad*" as it stands [i.e., a totally inaccurate and hybrid version of *Nusah ha-Ari* that has been repeatedly reprinted in a somewhat irresponsible fashion, see ibid., 35] should have been chosen to serve as the Unified Version – the *Nusah Ahid* .... For this is not the *Nusah ha-Ari* but an unsuccessful compromise between it or *Nusah Ashkenaz*; and how much more so the *mahzor* for the Days of Awe for soldiers, which is like *Nusah Polin* ... and one cannot understand why it should merit being established as the Unified Version ....

8   Thus, for example, is David Einhorn's Reform prayer book entitled *Olath Tamid*, *Gebetbuch für Israelitische Reform-Gemeinden* (Baltimore: 1858), we find revisions such as:

> אתה גבור לעולם ה'. רב להושיע. מכלכל חיים בחסד. פודה נפש עבדיו ממות ברחמים רבים סומך
> נופלים ורופא חולים ומתיר אסורים ומקיים אמונתו לישני עפר: מי כמוך בעל גבורות. ומי דומה לך
> מלך ממית ומחיה ומצמיח ישועה: ונאמן אתה בכל דבריך. בא"ה נוטע בתוכנו חיי עולם!

At a formal halachic level, we see that the traditional *hatimah* has been radically altered, in contradiction to classical halachic ruling. But more significantly, this *hatimah*, and the words that come directly before it eliminate the notion of the resurrection of the dead, the main subject of the traditional version, and a theme to which the Reformers objected. See Eric L. Friedland, *"Were Our Mouths Filled with Song": Studies in Liberal Jewish Liturgy* (Cincinnati: 1997): 36–37.

Similarly, in Manuel Joel's *Seder Tefillah li-Yemot Hol u-le-Shabbatot u-le-Khol Moadey ha-Shanah* (*Israelitisches Gebetbuch für die öffentliche Andacht des ganzenjahres*, Breslau: 1893), the Tenth Benediction of the Amidah has been drastically reworded as follows:

> תקע בשופר גדול לחרותנו וקול דרור וישועה יישמע באהלינו בא"ה משמיע ישועה לשארית ישראל:

ambience of our traditional prayers.[9] Intense thought and study, together with extreme caution, are required before any emendations may be made, for it is easy to destroy but difficult to build constructively.

Here, again, what we see here is not merely a change in wording both in the main part and in the *hatimah* but a complete elimination of the "Zionist" theme of the traditional version, which puts the main emphasis on the Ingathering of the Exiles to the Land of Israel (see Friedland, ibid., 57), and see most recently David Ellenson, *After Emancipation: Jewish Religious Responses to Modernity* (Cincinnati: 2004, 193–236).

Such examples for the Reform and Liberal prayer book can be vastly multiplied, as is patently evident throughout Friedland's volume and that of J. Petuchowski, *Prayerbook Reform in Europe* (New York: 1968).

9 Jacob J. Petuchowski (in *Prayer in Judaism: Continuity and Change*, 28), rightly points out: "If anything new is created to supplement what is already there, it would have to prove itself as something clearly superior to what has clearly been hallowed by tradition." Eliezer Berkovitz (ibid., 32) adds, "Innovations in prayer are lifeless if they are not rooted in our authentic sources."

AFTERWORD

It is well known that prayer must be truthful.[1] One must believe wholeheartedly in what one says. Non-believing prayer is blasphemous. In his work,
Worship of the Heart: Essays on Jewish Prayer,[2] Rabbi Joseph B. Soloveitchik
wrote as follows:

> The *act* (*ma'aseh*) of prayer is formal, the recitation of a known, set text; but the
> *fulfillment* of prayer, its *kiyyum*, is subjective: It is the service of the heart. The

---

1   On the necessity not be appear to be one who is telling an untruth in prayer, see BT
     Berachot 14b ad fin.: "Anyone who says *keriyat shema* without *tefillin*, it is as though
     he is giving false testimony against himself." See *Shulhan Aruch Orah Hayyim* 25:4;
     37:2. Also see ibid., 565:3, and *Ba"h* (*Bayit Hadash*), ibid., 693; and Responsa *Be-Tzel*
     ha-Hochmah (by R. Betzalel Stern, vol. 3, Jerusalem: 1975. sec. 91). See also *Tzelota*
     de-Avraham, vol. 1, 288 (Responsa Maharit, vol. 1, sec. 139; *Zohar* Lech Lecha). See
     also *Tiferet Tzvi*, vol. 2, 333, and cf. *Shulhan Aruch Orah Hayyim* 591:7.
        See also *Tiferet Tzvi*, vol. 4 (New Jersey: 1993, 122–123), where he discusses the
     heated controversy among both early and late authorities as to the use of the words
     קלס and פתה in the liturgy, words which have both positive and negative meaning.
     Kales can mean either "praise" or "curse," and פתה has a negative connotation of "to
     seduce." Hence, the Ritwa and the Rashbatz, in their commentaries to the *Haggadah*
     shel Pesah, advise against using the term ולקלס, while others argue that the context
     (להודות להלל לשבח לפאר לרומם להדר לברך לעלה ולקלס – to thank, praise, laud, glorify, exalt,
     honor, bless, raise high *and acclaim*) makes the meaning clear; and the *Turei Zahav*
     on *Orah Hayyim* 127 ad fin. states clearly that one should not say: מתרצה ברחמים
     ומתפתה בתחנונים, while others, including the kabbalist R. Herz Shatz, in his *Siddur*
     Tihingen (1560), permits it. Those against the use of these words insist that prayer
     formulations must be crystal clear in their meaning and embody no possible am-
     biguities. And see above chapter "Examples of Internal Censorship," on קוניהם, קונם.
2   Ed. Shalom Carmy (Jersey City: 2003, 147–148).

intention (*kavvanah*) required for prayer is not like the *kavvanah* required for other mitzvot.³ In other commandments the intention is not the most important element. It is a secondary element, even if it is required for fulfillment of the mitzvah. Rather it is the act, the concrete action, that is primary, and *kavvanah* simply accompanies the action.⁴ With prayer, however, *kavvanah* is the

---

3   *Hilchot Tefillah* 4:1, 15–16. See *Hiddushei R. Hayyim Ha-Levi* ad. loc.: "There are two types of intention with respect to prayer. One is the intention relating to the meaning of the words, which is grounded in the principle of intention; the second is that he should imagine that he is standing before God."

Regarding the question of whether prayer is *mi-de-Oraita* (mandated biblically) or *mi-de-Rabbanan* (or rabbinically), we shall cite the *Magen Avraham* to *Shulhan Aruch Orah Hayyim* 106 n. 2: The *Shulhan Aruch* there wrote:

> Even though women and slaves are not obligated to say the *shema*, they are obligated to pray because [prayer] is a positive commandment (mitzvah) that is not time-dependent (*shelo ha-zeman gerama*).

Upon this the *Magen Avraham* comments:

> *Mitzvat aseh* (a position commandment): So wrote Rambam (*Hilchot Tefillah* 1.2), who is of the opinion (*Sefer ha-Mitzvot, Aseh* 5) that prayer is a *mitzvat aseh de-Oraita*, as it is written, "and to worship Him with all your heart" (Deut. 11:13) etc. However, *mi-de-Oraita* it is sufficient [to pray] once a day in whatever form one wishes. And therefore most women do not pray regularly, because they say immediately on rising in the morning close to washing their hands some kind of supplication, and biblically this is sufficient, and possibly the rabbis did not obligate them for more than that [see Beit Yosef, sec. 70]. Ramban, [on the other hand,] is of the opinion that prayer is *mi-de Rabbanan*, and this is the view of most of the decisors. See Tosafot on *Berachot* 20b ad init. The *Semak* [*Sefer Mitzvot Katan*, sec. 11, n. 1] wrote that it is a mitzvah to pray in times of need.

On the view of the *Semak*, see the discussion of R. Yehoshua Pollack in his *Hoshvei Mahshevet*. Tel Aviv [1975], 9.

4   Whether it is necessary to have *kavvanah* in order for the mitzvah to be valid is a matter of dispute. According to many Talmudic sages and decisors, intention is a necessary condition of fulfillment. However, according to many other decisors lack of intention does not prevent fulfillment of the mitzvah. But even if intention is required, it is distinct from the action itself. See BT *Rosh ha-Shanah* 28b; *Berachot* 13a; *Pesahim* 114b and parallels, and *Milhamot ha-Shem* and *Sefer ha-Maor* on *Rosh ha-Shanah*.

This is the view of his grandfather, R. Hayyim ha-Levi Soloveitchik, the Brisker Rav, in *Hiddushei R. Hayyim ha-Levi*, to Rambam, *Hilchot Tefillah* 4:1. He reached this conclusion to solve an apparent contradiction between *Hilchot Tefillah* 4:15–16 and 10:1. See also Maimonides's *Guide for the Perplexed* (part 3, sec. 51, translation by M. Friedländer, 2nd. edition, London: 1942, 386–387): However, if we pray with

the motion of our lips and face the wall, but at the same time think of our business
. . . we are then like those to whom Scripture refers, saying, "Thou art near in their
mouth, and far from their reins" (Jeremiah 12:2). R. David Abudarhim cites this
passage (ed. R. M. A. Baron, vol. 1, Jerusalem: 2001, 214), adding that the Hebrew
word *tefillah* has the same numerical value as *be-kavvanat ha-lev*, with the *kavvanah*
of the heart [515].) However, this explanation, with its serious implications, was not
accepted by all. For example, R. Eliezer Menahem Min Shah, in his work *Avi Ezri*,
vol. 1, on Rambam (ibid., Bnei Brak: 1956), sought to refute it. Likewise the Hazon
Ish, in his notes to Rambam ibid., *Hazon Ish al ha-Rambam* (Bnei Brak: 1959, 13).
Furthermore, this is not the view of *Sefer ha-Hinuch*, sec. 703, nor of Tosafot and
the Rosh on BT *Berachot* 30b, etc. R. Ovadia Yosef, in his work *Yabia Omer* (vol.
3:2, Jerusalem: 1986, 20–21, sec. 8:1–2), brought fuller evidence to refute this view,
citing from JT *Berachot* 2:4: "Said R. Hiyya: All my life I never had *kavvanah* with
the exception of one time, etc." See all the additional sources he marshals to support
his argument. He concludes that it is sufficient to have *kavvanah* at the beginning
of the prayer (*Amidah*, in *avot*), וכל התפילה נמשכת על כוונה זו – and the rest of the prayer
draws upon this [initial] *kavvanah*. This is also the view of R. Moshe Sternbuch in
his work *Moadim u-Zemanim* (vol. 1, Jerusalem: 1958, 196). The *Ketzot ha-Hoshen*
by R. Yehudah ha-Cohen, in section *Kuntres ha-Sefekot*, cited in his introduction to
Terumat ha-Keri (Pressburg: 1858), that a person's prayer, even when not carried out
with real *kavvanah*, is not completely rejected. It is set aside, as it were, and when he
prays with real *kavvanah*, all those prayers without it are, so to speak, retrieved and
given fuller value. See the passage in *Shaarei Orah* cited at the end of our Afterword.
This, too, is the view of R. Yonatan Eybeschütz in his *Yaarot Devash* (Karlsruhe:
1779–1782, part 1. lecture 4). See Y. M. Stern, *Siddur Iyyun Tefillah li-Yemot ha-
Hol* (Jerusalem: 2008, 9). R. Zalman Druk, in his *Shaarei Tefillah: Hilchot Tefillah*
(Jerusalem: 1993, 33–34), sums up this discussion succinctly, adding a reference to
Responsa *Eretz Zvi*, sec. 22 (by R. Aryeh Zvi Frumer, Brooklyn: 1964?), who ruled
that one who did not have full *kavvanah* at the beginning but did when he ended
with "Blessed art Thou, O Lord," has also fulfilled the mitzvah, and explained his
ruling that a כוונה כללית, a generic *kavvanah* that one is standing before God, can also
suffice. One can also concentrate on what the *hazzan* says aloud in order to fulfill
the mitzvah. R. Druk concludes:

In this way he has served as a fine advocate	ובזה לימד זכות על הרבה מן ההמון
for the multitude who do not have *kavvanah*	שאין מכוונין באבות, ומכל מקום
in *avot*, and who nonetheless can complete	מותר להם לסיים השמונה עשרה
the *Amidah*, and their prayer is valid.	ושם תפילה עליה . . . .

Indeed, this is clear from the rulings in the *Shulhan Aruch Orah Hayyim* 101:1.

He who prays must have *kavvanah* in all the benedictions. If he cannot concentrate in this manner during all of them, he should at least concentrate during *avot* (the
first benediction of the *Amidah*). If he did not concentrate in *avot*, he must go back
and repeat the whole prayer even though he concentrated during the rest of them.

To which the Rema adds:

> But nowadays, we do not go back and repeat because of lack of concentration, because even if he repeats [the prayer]' it is most likely that he will [again] not concentrate, and so what is the point of the repetition?

The *Mishnah Berurah* ad loc. (sec. 2) explains that *kavvanah* means knowing the meaning of the words. See also the lengthy and detailed discussion of R. Hayyim's view in R. Shlomo Zalman Shemaya's article, "*Be-inyan kavvanah be-tefillah u-verur be-divrei ha Gra"h* [=R. Hayyim]." *Kovetz Beit Aharon ve-Yisrael* 2/32 (1991): 79–99. He cites, inter alia, Rabbenu Manoah (on *Hilchot Tefillah* 10:1). who writes:

> If he concentrated his intent (לבו) in the first benediction (i.e., *avot*) ... since ... this is the first benediction which has in it the mention of His Godliness (זכר א׳לוהותו) ... and he concentrated on the whole of this benediction, even if he became confused afterwards and lost his concentration ... he does not need to go back and repeat the whole prayer.

Clearly, ordinary people are not capable of the degree of concentration throughout their prayer, or even through their recitation of the *Amidah*, that R. Hayyim's understanding of the Rambam requires. (See R. Hayyim Volozin's introduction to *Sifra de-Zeniuta* [Vilna and Horodna: 1820, ad init.]). Indeed , R. Yehiel Michel Epstein, in his *Aruch ha-Shulhan*, *Orah Hayyim* 110:6, writes regarding the *havinenu* prayer: "But nowadays, we are not able to direct our intentions for prayer regardless (as I have written numerous times) – if this is the case, what good is *havinenu*?" (See M. J. Broyde, *Innovation in Jewish Law: A Case Study of Chiddush in Havinenu.* Atlanta: 2008, 120 – D. S.) Still another description of *kavvanah* was formulated by Abraham Joshua Heschel in a booklet entitled *Yearnings: Prayer and Meditation for the Days of Awe*, edited by R. Jules Harlow (see above Introduction, n. 4, 206):

> In prayer there is a danger of relying on the word, of depending upon a text, of forgetting that the word is a challenge to the soul rather than a substitute for the outburst of the heart. Prayer as a way of speaking is a way that leads nowhere. The text must never be more important than inner devotion, *kavvanah*. The life of prayer depends not so much upon loyalty to custom, as upon inner participation, not so much upon the *length* as upon the *depth* of the service. Those who run precipitately through the liturgy, rushing in and out of the prayer text as if the task were to cover a maximum of space in a minimum of time, will derive little from worship. To be able to pray is to know how to stand still and to dwell upon a word. This is how some worshippers of the past would act. They would repeat the same word many times, because they loved it and cherished it so much that they could not part from it. There is a classical principle in regard to prayer. Better is a little with inner devotion than much without it.

Chief Rabbi Sir Jonathan Sacks, in his introduction to the new *Authorised Daily Prayer Book*, fourth edition, London 2006, xxvi–xxvii, elaborates as follows on the

different levels of *kavvanah*.

Kavvanah: Directing the mind

Prayer is more than saying certain words in the right order. It needs concentration, attention, engagement of mind and heart, the left and right hemispheres of the brain. Without devotion, said Rabbi Bachya Ibn Pakuda, prayer is like a body without a soul. The key Hebrew word here is *kavvanah*, meaning mindfulness, intention, focus, direction of the mind. In the context of prayer, it means several different things.

The most basic level is *kavvanah le-shem mitzvah*, which means, having the intention to fulfil a mitzvah. This means that we do what we do, not for social or aesthetic reasons. We pray because we are commanded to pray. In general in Judaism there is a long-standing debate about whether the commandments require *kavvanah*, but certainly prayer does, because it is supremely an act of the mind.

At a second level, *kavvanah* means understanding the words (*perush ha-milim*). At least the most important sections of prayer require *kavvanah* in this sense. Without it, the words we say would be mere sounds. Understanding the words is, of course, made much easier by the existence of translations and commentaries.

A third level relates to context. How do I understand my situation when I pray? Maimonides states this principle as follows: "The mind should be *freed from all extraneous thoughts* and the one who prays *should realize that he is standing before the Divine presence.*" These are essential elements of at least the *Amidah*, the prayer par excellence in which we are conscious of standing before God. That is why we take three steps forward at the beginning, and three back at the end – as if we were entering, then leaving, sacred space.

The fourth level of *kavvanah* is not merely saying the words but meaning them, affirming them. Thus, for example, while saying the first paragraph of the *Shema*, we "accept of the yoke of the kingdom of heaven" – declaring our allegiance to God as the supreme authority in our lives. In the second paragraph, we "accept of the yoke of the commandments." The word *Amen* means roughly, "I affirm what has been said." In prayer we put ourselves into the words. We make a commitment. We declare our faith, our trust, our dependency. We mean what we say.

There are, of course, higher reaches of *kavvanah*. Mystics and philosophers throughout the ages developed elaborate meditative practices before and during prayer. But at its simplest, *kavvanah* is the practiced harmony of word and thought, body and mind. This is how Judah Halevi described it:

The tongue agrees with the thought, and does not overstep its bounds, does not speak in prayer in a mere mechanical way as the starling and the parrot, but every word is uttered thoughtfully and attentively. This moment forms the heart and thought of his time, while the other hours represent the way which leads

essence and substance: prayer without intention is nothing.[5]

Hasidism, which placed so much stress on the spiritual element, the subjectivity in religious life, and which devoted so much attention to the act of prayer and to the individual's coming closer to God through prayer, is also sustained by Rambam's view of *avodah she-ba-lev* as an all-encompassing, all-penetrating experience . . . .

Prayer, which is like a mirror reflecting the image of the person who worships God with heart and soul, is shot through with perplexity, for worship itself is rooted in the human dialectical consciousness. Hence prayer is not marked by monotonous uniformity. It is multi-colored: It contains contradictory themes, expresses a variety of moods, conflicting experiences, and desires oscillating in opposing directions. Religious experience is a multi-directional movement, metaphysically infused. Prayer too does not proceed slowly along one straight path, but leaps and cascades from wondrous heights to terrifying depths, and back.

If prayer is truly to be "a mirror reflecting the image of the person who worships God," and if *kavvanah* is its "essence and substance" without which it is nothing, then the "set text" recited as the formal act (*maaseh*) of prayer must surely be one with which the reciter is in full accord and with which he can fully identify. If not, that basic condition for "the fulfillment of prayer, its *kiyyum*," that subjective "service of the heart" being absent, or at least blemished, causes the prayer to be nothing.

Surely this is what the sages intended to convey when they made that

---

to it. He looks forward to its approach, because while it lasts he resembles the spiritual beings, and is removed from mere animal existence. Those three times of daily prayer are the fruits of his day and night, and the Sabbath is the fruit of the week, because it has been appointed to establish the connection with the Divine spirit and to serve God in joy, not in sadness.

See also J. Tabory, "Prayer and Halakhah" (in *Prayer in Judaism: Continuity and Change*, 60–63). See also S. Kadish, *Kavanna: Directing the Heart in Jewish Prayer* (New Jersey–Jerusalem: 1997, pass.); and, most recently, M. Katz, "*Iyyun ve-Girsah*" (*Daat Lashon* 1 [2007]: 67–84).

5 [See BT *Berachot* 29b: R. Eliezer said: He who makes his prayer a matter of routine (his prayer is not a supplication). What does "routine" imply? Said R. Yaakov bar Idi [in the name of] R. Oshaya: Anyone whose prayer is seen as a burden upon him, [his prayer is not a supplication – i.e., will not be accepted – D. S.].

famous statement in JT *Berachot* 4.1 and its parallels:[6]

It is written, "To love the Lord and to serve (literally: to labor for) him with all your heart and with
all your soul" (Deut. 11:13). And is there "labor of
the heart"? What can that be? It is prayer.

כתיב, "לאהבה את ה' ולעבדו בכל
לבבכם ובכל נפשכם" (דברים יא
יג). וכי יש עבודה בלב? ואיזו? זו
תפילה.

Indeed, the Rambam cites this (slightly reformulated) statement[7] as the
introductory passage to his rulings on prayer (*Hilchot Tefillah* 1:1).

Surely, then, it is obvious that in order for us to fulfill this mitzvah, our
prayers must be relevant, and the "set text" must be in harmony with the contemporary situation and with the worshipper's subjective needs.[8]

---

6 Parallels in BT *Taanit* 2a, *Midrash Psalms* 67, 157a, *Midrash Samuel* 2:10, 25a. The
primary source is *Sifrei Deut.* sec. 41 (ed. Finkelstein, 88). Additional bibliographic
references apud Finkelstein ibid., note to line 1.

7 Incidentally, although this passage is found in BT *Taanit* ibid., it is not found in
the manuscript versions of this tractate, nor is it cited from there by many early
authorities (*Rishonim*), who knew it from the Yerushalmi and the Sifrei. See also
Ginzberg's comments in *Perushim ve-Hiddushim ba-Yerushalmi* (vol. 3, New York:
1941, 3–4). He further notes that "liturgy" derives from the Greek (λειτουργία),
meaning "public work or service" (from λεῖτο<ς> "public" and ἔργον "work"; see
W. W. Skeat, *An Etymological Dictionary of the English Language*, Oxford 1989, 344b,
s.v.), and bears the meaning of prayer in many European languages. But this Greek
word is never used in rabbinic literature for prayer because its semantic meaning in
that linguistic context is "hard work" (e.g., *Tanhuma* Buber, Exod. 4). See S. Krauss,
Griechische und Lateinische Lehnwörter im Talmud, Midrasch und Targum (vol. 2,
Berlin: 1899, reprinted Hildesheim: 1964, 313a, s.v. לטרוגיה – "And clearly prayer may
not be regarded as 'hard work' or a burden." See above n. 4).
   On the various meanings of the Greek word for "public service," "service to
God," and so on – λειτουργία – see F. W. Danker and W. Bauer, *A Greek–English
Lexicon of the New Testament and Early Christian Literature* (Chicago and London:
2000, 591 s.v.). For meanings closer to the rabbinic connotation, see J. H. Moulton
and G. Milligan, *The Vocabulary of the Greek Testament* (Glasgow: 1930, reprinted
New York: 1972, 373 s.v.), where the meaning is "public burden." For further bib-
liography on this Greek word, see *Repertorio Bibliografico de la Lexicografia Griega*
(Madrid: 1998, 356a s.v.).

8 Surely this is the real meaning of the statement in BT *Berachot* 29b, in the name
of Rav Yosef, that in order for prayer to be acceptable as supplication (תחנונים),
it must not be seen as routine (above preceding note), but must have some personal innovation: כל שאינו יכול לחדש בדבר. As Rabbi Abraham Kon expressed it in
his *Prayer* (London, Jerusalem, and New York: 1971, 9): "The Sages permitted and
even encouraged innovation in the service of prayers, although only to prayers of

That is not to say that each person at each stage of his spiritual development can alter the text of the prayers in accordance with his current state of mind.[9] Of course, this is not feasible, nor is it our intended message. We are speaking only of changes mandated by communal needs, major histori-

---

supplication." This he limits by excluding its application to prayers of praise and exultation, referring to BT *Berachot* 33b. He continues to note: "Obviously, since the Sages justified additions to the set and established prayers, they certainly did not object to modifications in the individual pleas and entreaties that were purely private and unconnected with services for congregations, or established prayers." He refers us to *Deuteronomy Rabbah* 2.1 (and parallels).

One should note that there are clear cases of changes and omissions that were made in order to accord with the contemporary situation. Thus, for example, we find that in *Mahzor Roma* (ms. Parma 887, fifteenth century), the benediction "Who has not made me a slave" is absent, as it is in other sources. Wieder (*Hitgabshut*, 214–215) convincingly surmises that this is because there was no slavery in those areas. He further shows (ibid.) that the geonim did away with the benediction עוטר ישראל בתפארה, "Who crowns Israel with glory," which according to BT *Berachot* 60b is related to the wearing of a headscarf, "since wearing headscarves is not the custom in our area" (*Shibolei ha-Leket*, sec. 4, ed. Mirsky, 137). In a similar vein, Tosafot on BT *Menahot* 44a explain their custom not to make the benediction "Who has not made me an ignoramus" (בור), because in their society such a phenomenon, of one who is ignorant "of Bible, Mishnah and *derech eretz* (proper manners)" (M. *Kiddushin* 1 ad fin.) was extremely rare. (See, further, *Hitgabshut*, 210, n. 53.)

One may also call attention to what Rabbenu Yaakov ben Asher wrote in *Tur Orah Hayyim*, sec. 188, concerning *Birkat Boneh Yerushalayim* in the Grace after Meals:

> We do not follow the version established by [Kings] David and Solomon, for we request the return of Kingship and to rebuild the Temple, while they requested that there be continuity in the peace of the Land, the Kingship and the Temple.

It appears, then, that throughout our history there were updates in the liturgy in accordance with changing situations.

9   This apparently is what is intended in the most recent Reform prayer book, *Mishkan T'filah: A Reform Siddur*, published very recently. As the reviewer, William Kolbrener, writes in his review in *Commentary* (January 2008, 58):

> "For those who choose" is in fact an ever-present locution in *Mishkan T'filah*, a token of its emphasis on the needs and desires of the individual worshipper. Since, as [Rabbi Elyse] Frishman [the editor] asserts, "performance of prayer matters more than fixed words," prayer leaders are instructed to select only one prayer per "page spread," allowing individual congregants to make their own spontaneous choices from the offerings before them.

He continues (59):

cal events or broad sociological changes. Again, we must use a great deal of caution. As the sages said (BT *Megillah* 31b): סתירת זקנים בנין, בנין נערים סתירה – "The tearing down by the old is building; the building of the young is tearing down," meaning that the deconstruction of the wise, mature and experienced is constructive,[10] while the so-called construction of the young and immature

---

> And then there is the matter of navigating the manifold choices presented in this *siddur* .... On offer, for example, are four different versions of *Aleinu*, the proclamation of fealty to the One God that traditionally ends a prayer service; each of the four manifests a distinct attitude toward non-Jews and to the related matter of the election of Israel. Elsewhere, variant versions either do or do not mention the resurrection of the dead. And so forth. A liturgy that requires "real time" decisions about such complex theological issues – how does one make a split-second evaluation of belief in the eternality of body and soul? – hardly sounds like an experience in either informed choice or deep spiritual engagement.

This is an interesting experiment, which the reviewer has grave doubt will work effectively, but it is certainly not what we would propose. See also above introduction (n. 4), and the whole of Harlow's essay (ibid., 199–213).

The *siddurim* of the Conservative movement, on the other hand, have been made more cautious and traditional. See, for example, the introduction to *Siddur Sim Shalom* (New York: 1989), by Rabbi Jules Harlow (xx–xxi):

> The modifications, additions, and deletions which distinguish this prayerbook affect a small portion of the classical texts of Jewish prayer. A Jew of ancient or medieval times familiar with Jewish prayer would be at home with the overwhelming majority of the Hebrew texts in this volume. We are linked to Jews of centuries past who have used these same liturgical formulations in addressing our Creator, confronting challenges of faith and expressing gratitude and praise. The Jew in prayer does not stand alone before God. The first person plural form of almost all Jewish prayer reflects the fact that we in our time stand in prayer together with Jews of all places and all times in our distinctive history. We hope that this will bind us to future generations as well.

For a brief history of the liturgy of the Conservative movement, see ibid., xx–xxiii, and see Robert Gordis's article, "A Jewish Prayer Book for the Modern Age," in *Conservative Judaism* 2/1 (1995): 1–20.

10 Note, for example, the sensitivity and caution reflected in Adena K. Berkowitz and Rivka Haut in *Shaarei-Simcha – Gates of Joy: Traditional Prayers, Songs and Modern Inclusive Rituals* (Jersey City, NJ, 108), where, in the Grace after Meals, after the phrase "*avoteinu Avraham, Yitzak ve-Yaakov*," the following note appears: "Some have in mind "*ve-imotainu Sarah, Rivkah, Rachel ve-Leah*" [with a different transliteration than I have given], or on 108: "Merciful One, may You bless me (and my wife) (and my husband [*ishi* and not *baali*!]) (my dear one) – and all that is mine." The

can only be destructive.[11]

The rich tapestry of our liturgy with its many themes can satisfy the variety of conflicting experiences to which Rabbi Soloveitchik refers. Indeed, just as "prayer does not proceed slowly along one straight path," so, too, our liturgy has leapt in a variety of directions creating that multicolored mosaic that is our prayer book.

⸰⸰

I should like to end by quoting a beautiful passage from the work *Shaarei Orah*, which was written by the Spanish fourteenth century kabbalist R. Yosef

---

added word "*ve-yakiri*" – "and my dear one" – is both subtle and reveals sensitivity, as the editors write in their introduction (xvi):

> Although there are many scholarly and graphically sophisticated *birkonim* within the traditional halachic community, women's spiritual needs have largely been neglected or included as afterthoughts. This *birkon* offers increased liturgical options, enabling women to feel included in the rituals themselves and not marginalized.

Similarly, on page 99, concerning the phrase "*ve-al britcha she-hatamta bi-ves-areinu*" – "and for your covenant that You have sealed in our flesh," a phrase not really pertinent to women, who are not circumcised, there is a note: "Some have in mind: *ve-al mitzvotecha she-hatamta be-libeinu*" – and for the mitzvoth that You have sealed in our hearts." This suggestion is discussed in detail on page xviii.

The editors summarize their editorial approach as follows (xvii):

> The challenge of including women in the liturgy which, at the same time, maintaining the integrity of the traditional text manifests itself most profoundly in the text of *Birkat ha-Mazon*. We have constantly been mindful of the injunction not to depart from "*matbea shetavu Hachamim*," from the formulaic language that the sages created. With this in mind, we have provided throughout *Birkat ha-Mazon* language that is grammatically appropriate for women, and which does not affect the halachic integrity of the text.

Though my proposal is even more radical, I commend the guidelines followed by these wise and thoughtful editors.

11 In the words of John D. Loike and Moshe D. Tendler, in a totally different context – that of stem cell research (*Tradition* 40:4 [2007]: 42): "Application of a new technology is not a simple matter and not all technology should be introduced to society. Technology that can lead to social upheaval and destruction should not be pursued." On the other hand, it is well to be remembered that overcautiousness is also a fault, and can also do much damage.

Gikatilla (1248–1325) (in Gateway, second edition, Bornstein, Jerusalem: 2005, 271–273 (based on Zohar, 2:245b):

ואחר שעוררנוך על אלו העיקרים הגדולים, יש לנו להודיעך כי המידה הנקראת א"ל ח"י היא כדמיון מצרף ומבחן לקבל התפילות מיד אדנ"י, ובהיכל זה עומדים כמה שומרים וכמה חיילות לבחון ולצרוף כל התפילות מתפלל, נכנסה תפילתו דרך היכל אדנ"י ובודקים אותה במקום הזה, ואם היא ראויה להיכנס דרך מידת א"ל ח"י, אז שומרי הפתחים מקבלים אותה תפילה, ומכניסין אותה עד הגיעה לפניה יהו"ה יתברך. ואם ח"ו התפילה שאדם מתפלל אינה הגונה, קורין לאותה תפילה מלמעלה תפילה פסול"ה, וקורין כל דברי אותה תפילה "פסילים", והכרוז קורא, אל תיכנס אותה תפילה לפניה יהו"ה יתברך, והקול מכריז, אני י"י הוא שמי וכבודי לאחר לא אתן ותחלתי לפסילי"ם (ישעיה מב ח). ומיד מוציאין אותה תפילה בנזיפה, ודוחין אותה לחוץ, ואינה נכנסת, וננעלים השערים בפניה, וזהו שאמר.... פנה אל תפלת הערע"ר (תהלים קב יח), כי במקום זה פונים ובודקים כל תפילה שאדם יחיד מתפלל ומערערים עליה.

ואם תאמר נמצאו רוב בתפילות שמתפלל רוב התפילות היחיד נפסדות ואבדות, כי אחת מני אלף לא יוכל להתכוין בתפילת יחיד בענין שתהא ראויה להתקבל. דע שאין הדבר כן, אלא כל אותן התפילות הפסולות הנקראות פסילים, כשדוחין אותן לחוץ ואינן נכנסות, י"י יתברך נתן להם מקום להיכנס בו, שהשם יתברך ברא רקיע ומסר עליו ממונים ושומרים, וכל אותן התפילות הפסולות הנדחות, מכניסין אותן באותו רקיע, ועומדות שם, ואם חזר זה היחיד שהתפלל תפילות פסולות שעומדות בזה הרקיע החיצון, ועמד והתפלל תפילה אחת בכוונה גדולה, ותפילתו זו הגונה ושלימה, אז אותה התפילה הכשרה מסתלקת והולכת ונכנסת באותו היכל החיצון שהתפילות הפסולות שהתפלל מקודם עומדות שם, ומוציאה משם כל אותן התפילות הפסולות שהתפלל, ועולות כולן עם אותה התפילה הכשרה שהתפלל, וכולן נכנסות עמה באגודה אחת לפני ה' יתברך, ונמצא שלא יפול דבר אחד מכל התפילות שהיחיד מתפלל.

I shall translate sections of this longish passage:

There is a chamber guarded by many guards and soldiers who examine all prayers.... If they are worthy to enter ... the gatekeepers accept those prayers and take them in until they reach [a place] before the Lord, may He be blessed. But if ... the prayer ... is not suitable, it is called a disqualified (or unfit) prayer ... and it is immediately removed with reprimand and pushed outside ... and the gates are locked before it ....

And should you say: If so, most of the prayers that an individual prays are worthless and lost, for not even one out of a thousand can really have *kavvanah* in his individual prayers, so that they be acceptable. Know, that this is not the case. For all those disqualified prayers ... the Lord gave them a special place for them to enter, for the Lord created a firmament, and placed over it sentinels and guardians, and all those disqualified and rejected prayers are held in waiting in that firmament. And if the individual who prayed those disqualified

prayers, comes to pray with great *kavvanah*, and his prayer is deemed worthy and perfect, then that worthy prayer . . . goes and enters the exterior chamber of disqualified prayers, and retrieves all those earlier blemished ones, and all of them rise together and enter as one before the Lord, so that not one single element of those prayers is lost.[12]

Let us pray, then, that our prayers and supplications be found fit and acceptable to enter the right chamber, so that they find their way before the heavenly seat, the Seat of Mercy, *Kisei ha-Rahamim.*

---

12 This notion was taken over, and even quoted directly with only very slight changes, in a variety of later works such as Meir ibn Gabbai, *Tolaat Yaakov,* "*Hechal Rishon Yotzer Or*" (Jerusalem: 1996, 39); Y. Yudlov, *Tefillah le-David* (*Yeshurun* 2 [1997]: 521–522); R. Yaakov Emden, *Siddur Shaarei Shamayim* (vol. 1, Jerusalem: 1993, 53), etc. A rich host of additional references will be found in Eliezer Yehudah Brodt, *Bein Kesseh le-Asor* (Jerusalem: 2008, 15–17, especially nn. 22 and 25). He also cites (ibid.) R. Yehonatan Eybeschütz, who in his *Yaarot Devash* (vol. 1, Bnei Brak: 1983, 32d), writes as follows:

> The sin that goes forth from a man's or woman's mouth daily, and most especially, is idle talk in the synagogue, and has much more so during prayer time. All this goes up into a thick cloud which prevents the prayer from ascending. But if afterwards a person prays with true intention and with weeping and tears, all those prayers which had collected together over a period of years and had remained in limbo (*be-rifyon*) without ascending, will now all rise up to the house of God through [this true] prayer.

He further notes (ibid., n. 31) that R. Shmuel Rabin, in his *Bigdei Aharon* (sec. 6, Bnei Brak: 1997, 133) wrote as follows:

> Even though it is written in the books that if a person is able to pray one prayer with the required intention, all the other prayers which were prayed hitherto without [real] intention and till then were cast aside, will ascend with it. It seems likely that this is the case if he prayed each word perfectly, but only the intention was lacking, and the prayer was as if it was dead (or perhaps: inert) thus it could be granted life through the living prayer. However, if the prayer was lacking letters, it is as if it was lacking a limb. Is it possible to make up a missing limb?

Here we recognize his requirement for the exact version of the crystallized form of prayer.

On the Liturgical Theories
of Hasidei Ashkenaz

Above, we pointed to the importance of the element of mystical numerology in the *nusah ha-tefillah* of Hasidei Ashkenaz. Although this was only a part of the theory of prayer, it had the effect of seeking to establish a single, unified, "correct" *nusah* for both prayers and blessings. At times, this position even conflicted with what appeared to be halachic requirements, and was therefore strenuously rejected by the French Tosafists, and a conflict based on the clash of ideologies developed and expressed itself in intense polemic arguments. By way of illustration, I shall give an example of such a debate.

In *Minhagei Yisrael* 1 (Jerusalem: 1991),[1] I discussed the acrimonious debate between the scholars of France and those of Germany as to the correct reading of the Rosh ha-Shanah prayer, "*Ha-yom harat olam*," and most specifically its ending: ותוציא לאור משפטינו היום, איום, קדוש, and here I return to this subject as it exemplifies the issue with which we have been dealing.

The version in our current *mahzorim*[2] usually runs as follows: עד שתחננו ותוציא כאור משפטינו היום (נ"א איום) קדוש, "until You show us mercy, [clear and pure] as the light, and issue our verdict today, Holy One."

The Provençal version of the *mahzor*, recorded in *Sefer ha-Manhig*

---

1   See also my work *Why Jews Do What They Do* (Hoboken, NJ: 1999, 141–149). See also what I wrote on this subject in *Minhagei Yisrael*, vol. 2 (Jerusalem: 1991, 95–98, with further examples of similar such debates).

2   See, for example, *Mahzor le-Yamim Noraim, Rosh ha-Shanah* (ed. D. Goldschmidt, 244, line 5. Jerusalem: 5730) and editor's notes there.

(*Hilchot Rosh ha-Shanah*, sec. 23, edited by Raphael, 327), contains the following:

ותוציא לאור משפטינו קדוש.
והאומר "ותוציא לאור משפטינו
היום" לֹ"א כיוון יפה־־, שאין בדין
להחזיק את עצמינו כצדיקים
גמורים שנכתבים לאלתר לחיים,
כי אם כבינונים, שתלויין ועומדין
עד יום הכיפורים. כך קבלתי
בצרפת.

ותוציא – and whoever says לאור משפטינו קדוש לאור משפטינו היום has not arranged his prayers properly, for we should not be seen to consider ourselves to be like the totally righteous[3] whose names are immediately recorded in the Book of Life, but rather like those in between, whose judgments are pending until Yom Kippur. This is [the tradition] received in France.

---

3   Much the same argument may be found with regard the Rosh ha-Shanah *piyyut* "Ha-yom teamtzenu." For in the version found in *Seder Rav Amram Gaon* (ed. Goldschmidt, 137) we read: היום תכתבנו לחיים – "Today write us down for life." (And see *Mahzor* Goldschmidt for Rosh ha-Shanah 275, in the apparatus to line 6: תכתבנו בספר חיים, according to ms. Bibl. Nats. Paris 641, a manuscript of *Mahzor Roma*, Goldschmidt ibid., 55.) R. Yosef Tzuberi (in his *Kenesset ha-Gedolah*, vol. 4, Jerusalem: 1996, 406) cites the great Yemenite authority, R. Yihye Tzalah (Mahari"tz) as saying that one should not recite this whole *piyyut*, also citing the *Peri Hadash* as stating that "it is not right to regard ourselves as completely righteous people who are written and signed immediately for life (שנכתבים ונחתמים לאלתר לחיים). However, argues R. Tzuberi, this reading which is found not only in *Seder Rav Amram Gaon*, but also in R. David Abudarhim and R. Yehudah Khalatz cannot be so easily done away with. He then offers a different interpretation of this phrase to justify this reading. It is however interesting that in this alphabetical *piyyut*, the phrase representing the letter *kaf* has several alternative readings: תכתבנו בכתר שם טוב, תכבדנו תכלה פשעינו (Goldschmidt ibid.), which avoid this possible theological pitfall. Similar sentiment can be found in other areas of our liturgy. Thus, for example, in the nineteenth benediction of the *Amidah* (*shema kolenu*), many readings have:

כי א־ל שומע תפילות ותחנונים אתה – For you are a God who hears prayers and supplications.

However, in *Seder Rav Amram Gaon* (ed. Goldschmidt, Jerusalem 1931, 25), the reading is: תפילותינו ותחנונינו "*our* prayers and *our* supplications," which reading is also found in the *Abudarhim* (ed. M. A. Baron, Jerusalem: 2001, vol. 1, 230). But he comments on this thus:

So the majority read. And there are those who read: תפילות ותחנונים "prayers and supplications." And that is the correct [reading], for one cannot claim oneself to be so righteous as to be able to say that "He hears our prayers at all times."

This, indeed, is the reading in the *Mahzor Vitry* (67), etc. See *Tzelota de-Avraham*, vol. 1, 299, and Tzuberi, *Kenesset ha-Gedolah*, vol. 1, 140.

It seems that this version, without the word היום, "today," is the version of Rashi's school (see *Siddur Rashi* sec. 181, 83–84):

עד שרתחנונו ורתוציא לראור ... | עד שתחננו ותוציא לאור משפטינו קדוש. :The word היום

משפטינו קדרוש: לרא הימנו לרומר | should not be said, since we cannot be sure that

משפטינו דריום, דרהן היום לרא יצא | our verdict will be issued before Yom Kippur,

לאור, שכך הדבר תלרוי בתשובה עד | since the whole matter depends on [our] repen-

העשור. ואם תאמר: והלא צדיקים | tance. Should you say, "But are not the righteous

נחתמים לאלרתר לחיים? וכי תעלה | sealed immediately for life?" – do you truly

על דעתך שנחזיק עצמינו צדריקים | think that we should consider ourselves totally

בתפילה, וכו'. | righteous?

The same sentiments are expressed in *Mahzor Vitry,* sec. 335, 372:

עד שתחנונו ורתוציא לאור משפטינו קדוש. ורדאומר "היום | and he who says היום לאור is

לאור" טועה הוא וכו': | mistaken.

Thus we see that the sages of France were prepared to change the word-ing of this *piyyut,* eliminating or adding a word in order to make the *tefillah* conform to halachic sources.

On the other hand, the sages of Germany, particularly those under the influence of the Hasidei Ashkenaz, the circle of R. Yehudah he-Hasid, could not permit themselves such changes,[4] since they held that the words and let-

---

See also what I wrote on the *nusah* of the Friday night *Kiddush* in *Minhagei Yisrael* (vol. 2, Jerusalem: 1991, 158–167).

4 This position continues to be found in various circles even up to modern times. A good example of this may be found in the writings of R. Yitschak Yehudah Yehiel Safrin, of Komarna, in his *Shulhan ha-Tahor,* ed. A. A. Ziss, vol. 1 (Tel Aviv: 1963; vol. 2, Tel Aviv: 1965), with Ziss's commentary, entitled *Zer Zahav.* Thus, in *Zer Zahav* (sec. 41) we read that one may not alter the benedictions from "our Ashkenazic rite ... because it was fixed by divine inspiration (or insight – *ruah ha-kodesh*) ... for all our customs and the order of the service were established by those who were invested with divine inspiration who descended in the chariot (*yordei ha-merkavah,* with mystical insight), Rabbenu Shimon ha-Gaddol, the Tosafists, R. Shmuel ha-Navi and his son R. Yehudah ha-Hasid, and R. Eliezer, the author of the *Rokeah,* and the holy Maharil (R. Yaakov ha-Levi Moellin), the smallest of whom could bring the dead to life and create heaven and earth. And they counted all the letters in the order of the service in accordance with celestial secrets. Why, then, should we make changes in the rite of our holy forefathers, the Ashkenazic sages ...." And similarly ibid., sec. 66:6: "One may not make any change in the Ashkenazic rite .... For you should know that the Ashkenazic rite was fixed letter by letter in accordance

ters of the prayers were carefully counted in accordance with mystical

with celestial secrets. And R. Shimon ha-Gaddol prayed according to this rite . . .
and Rashi and all his children . . . each of whom individually had knowledge of the
letters with which heaven and earth were created and who [could] create worlds
and change [the laws of] nature . . . ." He then justifies the slight changes made by
the Baal Shem Tov (R. Yisrael b. Eliezer) under the influence of the Ari ha-Kadosh
(R. Yitzhak Luria), and those appear to be the limit to which he would accept any
alterations in the Ashkenazic rite. See also ibid., sec. 117:2, *Shulhan ha-Tahor*, sec.
118:5, 189:1. The material had been conveniently cited in *Siddur Hechal ha-Berachah,
Komarna*. Jerusalem: 1990, 49–50. And in this same context it is interesting to note
the remarks on *birkat ve-la-malshinim* (discussed above). *Siddur Komarna* has *ve-
la-minim* as its opening word, and in the notes (226–228, based mainly on *Shulhan
ha-Tahor* sec. 118:4–6, 126:2.), there is a lengthy discussion on what should be the
correct reading of this benediction. Then we read: "*Birkat ha-minim* has, due to
our sinfulness, been corrupted . . . so much so that it has almost become a different
blessing, and so also in the Talmud and in many [other] books . . . . A cantor who
changes *birkat ha-minim* and does not recite it in accordance with what we have
received [as the correct version], but uses the corrupt version, which has penetrated
into our prayer books by cause of the censor, we immediately dismiss him . . . . It was
the censor who changed it from *birkat ha-minim* [i.e., Christian non-believers] to
ve-la-malshinim [slanderers, i.e., Jewish informers], and because of pressure and op-
pression . . . . R. Zvi Elimelech ruled to say *ve-la-meshumadim* [and to the apostate
Jews]. (But see what we cited above.) But why should we concoct a (new) version,
when surely the (authentic) version determined by the Men of the Great Assembly
is in our hands in the writings of the Rambam in old printed editions . . . . And whosoever deviates from this (version) and omits all mention of the *minim*, we dismiss
him and his benediction was valueless (*le-vatalah*)," etc.

There are similar such comments throughout this *siddur* that merit close examination. (My thanks to my son-in-law, R. Natan Yisrael, for calling my attention to
this *siddur* and its special character and approach.)

A similar formulation to that cited above in the name of R. Zvi Elimelech in
Seder Rav Amram Gaon (edited by D. Goldschmidt, 32. Jerusalem: 1971) in the name
of Rav Natronai Gaon:

They who have amongst themselves those who appear to be pedantic and delete or add and make changes, their behaviour is out of order, for they are deviating from the custom of the two *yeshivot*. Our custom is that we make no changes from that which *the Sages of the Talmud recorded*, both on Sabbaths and on festivals. And if we come to a place and the cantor says that which does not correspond to [our custom], we remove him	ואלו שיש ביניהם שנראים כמדקדקים וגורעים ומוסיפים ומשנין, לא יפה הם עושים שמשנים ממנהג שתי ישיבות. ומנהג שלנו אין אנו משנים ממה שאמרו חכמים בתלמוד בין בשבתות בין בימים טובים, ואי מתקלעינן למקום ואמר חזן מאי דלא דמי מסלקינן ליה . . . .

considerations. Any change might have catastrophic consequences in terms of the hidden intentions hinted at by these numbers.[5] We find sharp words directed against these practices in R. Yehudah he-Hasid's commentary on the *mahzor* of Rosh ha-Shanah, cited in *Siddur R. Shlomoh b. R. Shimshon of Worms* (ed. R. M. Hershler, sec. 99, 221. Jerusalem: 1972) immediately after the commentary on *Ha-yom harat olam*:

| The *tefillah* of Rosh ha-Shanah is composed in order and we may not add or subtract even one word, for it is as copied from the son of R. Elazar ha-Gaddol, R. Yehudah he-Hasid's own copy of his commentary.... Whoever adds or subtracts *even one letter*, his prayer is not heard [on high], for all | תפילה של ר"ה כתובה על הסדר, ועליה אין להוסיף ואין לגרוע אפילו תיבה אחת, כי הועתקה מפירוש כתב ידו של ר' יהודה החסיד ... בן רבינו אלעזר הגדול. והמוסיף והגורע בדה, אפילו אות אחת |

5 The vehemence with which these polemic statements were formulated expresses itself in a number of additional passages from this same circle. Joseph Dan, in *Jewish Mysticism in the Middle Ages* (Northvale, New Jersey and Jerusalem: 1998, 227), cites the following (from ms. Jerusalem, JNUL 8/3, 296, fol. 7r):

> Give heed, you inhabitants of France and the Islands of the Sea [England], who err utterly and completely, for you invent lies and add several words in your prayers, of which the early sages who formulated the prayers never dreamed, when they commanded us to say the prayers in place of the sacrifices in the Temple. Every benediction which they formulated is measured exactly in its number of words and letters, for if it were not so, our prayer would be like the song of the uncircumcised non-Jews. Therefore, take heed and repent, and do not go on doing this evil thing, adding and omitting letters and words from the prayers.

He explains the extremity of the language used as follows (ibid., 227–228):

> Similar statements concerning many of the basic benedictions abound in this treatise, thus making it impossible to assume that the fury of Rabbi Judah and of his disciple is directed toward people who distort the meaning of a certain ancient text because of some ideological or theological consideration. In order to understand this religious phenomenon, we have to take the basic contention of this treatise exactly as it is stated: Every addition or omission of a word, or even of a single letter, from the sacred text of the prayers destroys the religious meaning of the prayer as a whole and is to be regarded as a grave sin, a sin that could result in eternal exile for those who commit it.

These passages, and many others in this vein, constitute prime testimony, if any is needed, as to the variety of competitive variations in the liturgical text. See further *Minhagei Yisrael* (vol. 2, 95–98).

of it is carefully weighed and measured *by word and letter*, with many secrets involved [in these calculations]. Whoever fears God must not subtract or add, *and one should not listen to the French* or to the inhabitants of the coast, who add several words, for the sages are not pleased with [such activities, or with the people who engage in them], and the reasons for the [wording of] the prayers and the secrets [involved in them] were not handed down to them. For the early Hasidim would hide away the secrets and reasons, until our holy teacher, Rabbenu Yehudah he-Hasid *z"l*, handed them down to the men of his family, the Hasidim, in writing and orally.

Rabbenu Yehudah he-Hasid *z"l*, wrote: He who adds one single letter to the prayer – concerning such a one it is said, "It has cried out against me; therefore I have hated it" (Jeremiah 12:8).

תפילתו אינה נשמעת, כי כולה במדה ובמשקל **באותיות ובתיבות** וסודרות הרבה דיוצאין ממנד. וכל ירא ה' יזהר בה מלפחות ומלהוסיף, **ולא ישמע אל הצרפתים** ואנשי איי הים שמוסיפים כמה וכמה תיבות, כי אין רוח וחכמה נוח בהם. כי לא נמסרו להם טעמי תפילה והסודות, כי חסידים הראשונים היו גונזים הסודות והטעמים, עד שבא רבינו הקדוש, רבינו יהודה חסיד ז"ל, והוא מסרם לאנשי משפחתו החסידים בכתב ובעל פה. . . . .

וכתב רבינו דהחסיד ז"ל: המוסיף בתפילה **אות אחת** עליו, ועל כיוצא בו, נאמר: "נתנה עלי קולה, על כן שנאתיה". (ירמיה יב ח).

However, this debate goes far beyond a difference as to the particular text, and because of the importance of fully understanding this Ashkenazic attempt to crystallize the liturgical texts, I shall quote extensively from E. E. Urbach's introduction to R. Avraham b. R. Ezriel's *Arugat ha-Bosem*, vol. 4 (Jerusalem: 1963, 74–96, omitting many sections):

ר' אלעזר קיבל את סודות התפילה מר' יהודה החסיד בן ר' שמואל וגם מאביו ר' יהודה בר' קלונימוס אף הוא מבני אותה משפחה. במשך כל הדורות נמסרו הסודות רק מפה אל פה. אבל ר' אלעזר סטה מדרך זו והוא אומר "ואכתוב סוד התפלות למען ידע כל אדם מה סוד בברכות ויכוין לבו לעבוד להק' ביראה ואשריו. והנה עדי וסהדי במרומים שלא דבר' בדברים האלו לא לכבודי ולא לכבוד בית אבותי אלא שלא יחלוק עלינו החוטא בנפשו, **כי החולק על זה כחולק על דברי תורה שניתנה מסיני**, כי סוד התפילות קיבלנו רב מרב עד נביאים וזקנים וחסידים ואנשי כנסת הגדולה שתקנוה. והמוסיף והמגרע אות אחת או תיבה אחת אוי לו בזה ולבא, כי אין להוסיף ואין לגרוע, כי לא יסדו בחנם תיבה אחת ואפי' אות אחת, כאשר נבאר בעזרת הבורא המלמד לאנוש בינה. . . .

[עמ' 84 ואילך] . . . "כך פירש הר' אלעזר בן רבי' יב"ק משמו של רבינו שמואל חסיד בר' קלונימוס, (בכ"י קויפמן 393 ל"ג ע"ב–ל"ד ע"א) . . .

"צור ישראל, י"ד תיבות תמצא בברכה זו כנגד י"ד בניסן שנגאלו ישר' ממצרי'. גם בזה שגו צרפתים הרבה מאד, ששמעתי שמוסיפים בצור ישר' ואומ' גאלנו ה' צבאות שמו קדוש ישר'. וסמך שלהם על מה שנמצא כתוב שר' מאיר שליח ציבור שר' זצ"ל היה אומרו וטעות הוא בידם כי

חלילה שעלה על ליבו של אותו צדיק מעולם לאומרו כי בקי היה בר' מאיר שליח ציבור זצ"ל בסודות
ובמדרשים וטעמים, שהרי בצור ישראל י"ד תיבות ושושים אותיות כנגד ששים רבוא שנגאלו
ממצרים בי"ד בניסן וכן תמצא י"ד אזכרות ביושע וכן י"ד אזכרות באנכי לומר שלא נגאלו ממצרים
אלא שיאמרו שירה בי"ד אזכרות ויקבלו את התורה בעשרת הדברות שיש בה י"ד אזכרות וכל תרי"ג
מצוות כלולים בעשרת הדברות ורבינו סעדיה גאון פירשם באזהרות⁶ שלו שיסד כל דיבור ודיבור
מצווה התלויות בו. וכנגדן תמצא י"ד אלהי ישר' בספר ירמיה לומר שאמר להם ירמיה למה בגדתם
באלהיכם ותשליכו את דבריו אחרי גיוכם. דעו לכם שלא הייתם כדי ליגאל ממצרים בי"ד בניסן
כי אם בזכותו של ישר' סבא לקיים הבטחתו שהבטיחו הקב"ה, וזהו וירא ישראל את היד הגדולה,
ואמרו רבותינו ישר' סבא.⁷ נחלקו בו חכמי ישר', יש מהם אומרים ישר' סבא זה אברהם אבינו, ויש
מהם אומרי' יעקב אבינו.⁸ וכן תמצא י"ד אלקים בי"ט פסוקים בחומש שיש בהם ג' אבות יחד,
לומר שבזכות האבות נגאלו ממצרים. וכיון שראה שלמה המלך כוחן וחיבתן של אבות העולם כיון
בתפילתו וקבע י"ד שם שמו לשם זה בדברי הימים. וכן בספר יהושע תמצא י"ד ה' אלהי ישר',
אמ' להם יהושע, דעו לכם שלא הייתם כדי ליגאל ממצרים וליכנס לארץ ישר' אלא בזכות שתקבלו
מלכותו עליכם. וזהו לשם ויאמר יהושע אל כל העם, "כה אמר ה' אלהי ישר' בעבר הנהר ישבו
אבותיכם" וגו' (יהושע כד ב), ועוד האריך רבינו החסיד הרבה מאד אבל אין פנאי להאריך כאן. . . .

[עמ' 92 ואילך] בדוגמאות שהוזכרו לעיל אגב כבר ראינו שרוגזו של ר' יהודה החסיד
יצא על מה שמכונה בפיו "מנהגי הצרפתים", אבל כפי שיתברר לנו אין המדובר תמיד במנהג צרפת
אלא בנוסחאות כפי שהיו שגורים גם באשכנז ויסודם בתקופת הגאונים. דברי פולמוס אלה יבואו
כאן לפי סדר התפילות:

"נהגו אנשי צרפת לומר אשרי תמימי דרך, וכתב רבינו החסיד זצ"ל דטעות גדול, כי מן יהי
כבוד עד תהלה לדוד תמצא י"ט אזכרות ועוד מונה כל י"ט מחוברים יחד בקרסים ובלולאות ויש
בהם טעמים וסודות הרבה מחזיקים יותר מח' קונטרסים גדולים, על כן כל ירא ה' לא ישמע על דברי
הצרפתים אשר מוסיפים פסוק אשרי תמימי דרך, כי לפי טעותם תמצא כ' אזכרות וזהו טעות גדול.
. . . ועוד לדבריהם תמצא ד' אשרי וזהו טעות וטעות ושקר גדול" (כ"י בריט. מוז. 534). . . .

. . . בפירוש ל"אהבה רבה": "הצרפתים מוסיפים בו תחוננו ותלמדנו גם בזה אין רוח חכמים
נוחה מהם שהרי נפל (ה) (ה) [א] מעיניהם וטחו עיניהם מראות מה שכתב החסיד שברכת אהבה רבה
יש בה ד' מיני לימוד ואלו הן ותלמדם א', ללמוד ב', וללמד ג' [ותלמוד ד'] וכנגדן ד' למדין באלפא
ביתא במלוי". בכ"י אחר אין הגורסים "ותלמדנו" צרפתים אלא שוטים בעלמא, וזה לשונו: אהבה
רבה אהבתנו יש אומרים שר' שמעון יסדו ויש בה מאה תיבות ויש בה כנגד מאה ברכות, ויש בה
ארבע לשונות לימוד ואילו הן, ותלמדם, ללמוד, וללמד, תלמוד כנגד ארבעה למדין שבאלפא ביתא
במלוי, ואילו הן, אלף, גימל, דלת, למד. ויש שוטים שמוסיפים ותלמדנו אב' ומדלגין כן תחוננו כדי
להשלים בו מאה תיבות וטעות הוא בידם. כך שמעתי מר' יהודה בר' יעקב זצ"ל ושוב מצאתי סמך
בסודות של הרב ר' אלעזר בר' י"ב'ק.

הדוגמאות שהבאנו די בהן כדי להראות באיזו מידה נטל לעצמו ר' יהודה החסיד את הסמכות

---

6   See *Siddur R. Saadya Gaon* (edited by J. Davidson, S. Assaf, B. I. Joel, 184, 191.
     Jerusalem: 1941 and cf. ibid.).

7   See editors' note 77, ibid.

8   See editors' note 78, ibid.

להכריע בין המנהגים והנוסחאות ולבחור מתוכם נוסח אחד ולקבעו כנוסח היחיד המוסמך....

[שם עמ' 96] בעוד שר' יהודה החסיד נאלץ ונחלץ להגן על דעותיו ועל נוסח התפילה שלו, הרי תלמידיו העלו אותם לכלל נורמה, שאחריה אין להרהר ואותה אין לערער. ואמנם נוסח חסידי אשכנז נעשה בהשפעתם לנוסח אשכנז, אבל הם לא אמרו די בכך, אלא ביקשו להחדיר את תורת רבם גם בארצות אחרות, בעיקר בצרפת ובאנגליה הנתונה להשפעתה. בכתבי יד אחדים נשאר מעין כרוז שבו פנו תלמידי החסיד ל"אנשי צרפת ואיי הים" בעניין נוסח התפילה וזה לשונו: "רפאנו ה' ונרפא. שימו על לב אנשי צרפת ואיי הים, ששקר בימינכם ובשמאלכם, שאתם בודים מלבבכם ומוסיפים כמה תיבות בתפילתכם אשר לא עלתה על לבם של חסידים הראשונים אשר תיקנו לנו התפלות במקום הקרבנות וכל ברכה ותפילה שתקנו, **היא כמו במדה ובמשקל באותיות ובתיבות,** שאם לא כן, אז היה תפילתנו חס ושלום כמו זמר של הגוים הערלים, על כן שימו לבבכם ואל תוסיפו לעשות עוד כדבר הרע הזה להוסיף ולגרוע תיבות ואותיות בתפילתכם, כי שמעתי אומרים שאתם מוסיפים תיבות הרבה בברכה זו. יש מכם אומרים רפאנו ה' אלוהינו וזהו טעות גמור, שהרי פסוק מלא הוא בירמיה (יז יד), רפאני ה' וארפא, ועוד יש מכם אומרים והעלה רפואה שלמה לכל מכותינו ולכל תחלואינו גם בזה נצנצה רוח עועים לפי שמצאתם בפסוק "הסולח לכל עוניכי הרופא לכל תחלואיכי" (תהלים קג ג) על כן הוספתם זה, גם זה הבל ורעה רבה, שהרי רבינו החסיד זצ"ל, שאין בברכת רפאינו כי אם כ"ו תיבות וק"ו אותיות, כ"ו תיבות כנגד כ"ז תיבות בפסוק ויאמר אם שמוע תשמע (שמות טו כו) עד כי אני ה' רופאך, וכנגד כ"ז אותיות באלפ"א בית"א עם הכפולים, לומר לך, אם תשמור התורה שניתנה בכ"ז אותיות, אז אני ה' רופאך. י'ה'ו'ה' שם המיוחד הוא מוצא ואינו שם אחר שהוא כ"ו אותיות ובו ריפא אלישע את המים ואף משה ריפא בו את מי המרה, על כן סמך למי מרה כי אני ה' רופאך. י'ה'ו'ה' שם המיוחד הוא מוצא ואינו שם אחר שהוא כ"ו אותיות ובו ריפא אלישע את המים ואף משה ריפא בו את מי המרה על כן סמך למי מרה כי אני ה' רופאך. וכ"ז אותיות בפסוק הרופא לכל תחלואיכי, וכן נמצא כ"ז סמכי"ן בהלל, וכן תמצא כ"ז י' בפרשת ציצית, וכן תמצא כ"ז י' בפרשת קדושים תהיו, וכן תמצא כ"ז חקים במשנה תורה, וכן תמצא כ"ז קו"ף מבראשית עד ברא אלהים לעשות, וכן תמצא כ"ז נו"ן בקריאת שמע, וכן תמצא כ"ז תוי"ן בתהלה לדוד, וכן תמצא בחומש כ"ז פסוקים, שסופם ה' אלהים, וכן תמצא כ"ז דורות מבריאת עולם עד שנכנסו לארץ וכן תמצא כ"ז אלהי ישראל בתורה ובנביאים".

To give the reader a feel for the style and character of the kind of thinking and exposition of the Hasidei Ashkenaz, I shall translate a small portion of the above:

R. Elazar received the secrets of the liturgy from R. Yehudah ha-Hasid, the son of R. Shmuel, and also from his father, R. Yehudah son of R. Kalonimos, and he too was of that same family. Throughout all the generations, the secrets were passed down by word of mouth. But R. Elazar strayed from that path, saying: "I will commit to writing the secrets of the liturgy so that every person may know the secret of the benedictions and direct his heart to worship the Holy One, blessed be He, with reverence. And behold, I bear witness by God that I have not said these words for my own honor or for the honor of my forefathers, but

only that he who sins in his soul shall not differ from me, for whosoever differs from this it is as if he differed from the words of the Torah given at Sinai. We have received the secrets of the liturgy from sage to sage [going back] to the Prophets and the Elders and the Hasidim and the Men of the Great Synod who established it. Woe to him who adds or subtracts a single letter or word, for one may not add or subtract, for not a single word or letter was established in vain, as we shall explain with the help of the Creator Who gives man his understanding....

[84 et seq.] Thus explained R. Elazar son of R. YBK in the name of R. Shemuel Hasid son of R. Kalonimos (ms. Kaufman 393, 336–340).... "Rock of Israel" – You will find that this benediction contains fourteen words, corresponding to the fourteenth of Nisan, when Israel was redeemed from Egypt. Here, too, the French made a great mistake, for I heard that they add in "Rock of Israel": "The Lord of Hosts has saved us, He who is called The Holy One of Israel," and they based themselves on what is found written in the name of R. Meir Shaliah Tzibbur, may his memory be blessed, that he said this. But they are mistaken, for [God] forbid that that righteous man should ever have thought to say this. R. Meir Shaliah Tzibbur was wholly conversant with the secrets, *midrashim* and inner meanings [of this benediction, knowing that] "Rock of Israel" has fourteen words and sixty letters, corresponding to the sixty [times] ten thousand [Israelites] who were redeemed from Egypt on the fourteenth of Nisan .... So, too, you will find fourteen names of God in "Thus the Lord saved ..." (Exod. 14:30 et seq.), and fourteen names of God in "I am the Lord thy God ..." (Exod. 20:2 et seq.). This means that they were not redeemed from Egypt for any other purpose than to recite the Song [of Moses (Exod. 15:1 et seq.)] with its fourteen names of God and receive the Torah through the Ten Commandments, which have fourteen names of God, and in which are contained all the six hundred and thirteen commandments, as Rabbenu Saadya Gaon expounded in his *Azharot*, in which he determined which commandments are dependent on each [of the Ten] Commandments.

From the above it is clear that it was R. Elazar's intent to warn against the school of Rashi, the "French," who, because of their lack of knowledge of the secrets and mysteries of *tefillah*, would change the wording, ruining the hidden *kavvanot* (esoteric meanings) implicit in the number of words and letters, and, of course, leading also to the creation of a multiplicity of versions.

As we study this issue further, we find the following (ibid., 223):

I have heard that R. Yaakov [=Rabbenu Tam] would *eliminate the word* היום *from mahzorim*, but he would say ותוציא לאור משפטינו קדוש, because the verdict of the wicked is not complete on Rosh ha-Shanah, but rather is pending until Yom Kippur. It may be that he said this, but he must not have known that there are thirty-two words in *Ha-yom harat olam*, corresponding to the thirty-two ways in which the world was created .... There are also thirty-two words from "Let us make man" until "male and female He created them," as well as many other [correspondences] which my teacher, Rabbenu he-Hasid z"l, laid down, giving a reason and a secret for each one .... Therefore, one who fears God should be careful not to add or subtract.

שמעתי בשם ר' יעקב (=ר' תם) שהיה **מוחק במחזורים**⁹ ומוחר מלומר "היום", אך דהיה אומר "ותוציא לאור משפטינו קדוש", לפי שאין גזר דינם של רשעים נגמר בר"ה, אלא תלויים ועומדים עד יום הכיפורים. יכול להיות שיצא מפיו, אבל לא נודע לו שיש ל"ב רתיבות ב"היום הרד" כנגד ל"ב נתיבות שבהם נברא העולם ונגד ל"ב ציץ במעשה ששת ימי בראשית, וכנגדן ל"ב רתיבות מן נעשה אדם עד זכר ונקיבה בראם, וכן עוד הרבה מאוד חיבר מורי רבינו דהחסיד ז"ל, וכתב טעם וסוד על הכל, וחברם יחד בקרסים ובלולאות, על כן ירא ה' יזהר מלהוסיף ומלגרוע.

How severe was the complaint of the German sages against the French sages led by Rabbenu Tam, to whom the secrets and mysteries of the prayers apparently had not been handed down!

However, some attempted to bridge the gap between the mystical claims of the Hasidei Ashkenaz[10] and the halachic arguments of the French sages.

---

9   Ms. Brit. Mus. 534; ms. Munich 393, 35a, and see editors' n. 58, ibid.

10   This approach to the liturgical text is especially clear in R. Yehudah ha-Hasid's *Sefer Gematriyyot* (edited by Y. Y. Stal, Jerusalem: 2005), and further in *Sefer ha-Rokeah ha-Gaddol*, by R. Elazar of Germaiza (edited by B. S. Schneersohn Jerusalem: 1967), and other works from this school of thought.

For a further understanding, or at least description, of this attitude towards prayer, I shall cite from Gershon G. Scholem's classic work, *Major Trends in Jewish Mysticism* (New York: 1946, 100–101):

> The Hasidic literature on the subject of prayer is comprehensive and to a large extent still in our hands. It shows that the number of words which constituted a prayer and the numerical values of words, parts of sentences, and whole sentences, were linked not only with Biblical passages of equal numerical value, but also with certain designations of God and the angels, and other formulas. Prayer is likened to Jacob's ladder extended from the earth to the sky; it is therefore conceived as a species of mystical ascent and appears in many of these "explanations" as a "highly formalized process full of hidden aspects and purposes." ...
> The enormous concern shown for the use of the correct phrase in the traditional

R. Avraham b. R. Azriel, in his *Arugat ha-Bosem* (ed. Urbach, vol. 3, 474), suggested the following:

היום הרת עולם – there are thirty-two words in this *piy-yut*, corresponding to the thirty-two ways in which the world was created, as is noted in *Sefer Yetzirah* [1:1]. One should not say ותוציא לאור משפטינו קדוש [leaving out the word היום], for then a word will be missing, as is explained in *Siddur Rashi,* Seder Rosh ha-Shanah.[11] Instead, we should say: ותוציא לאור משפטינו הא־ל קדוש.	היום הרת עולם – יש בו ל"ב תיבות כנגד ל"ב נרתיבות שבהן נברא העולם, כדאירתא בספר יצירה. ואין לומר "ותוציא לאור משפטינו קדוש", שאז חסר תיבה, כאשר מבואר בסידור רש"י בסדר ר"ה, אלא אומרים "ורתוציא לאור משפטינו הא־ל קדוש", וכו'.

Here we find a compromise: The suggestion of the French sages to omit the word "today" is accepted, but in order not to change the number of words, another word, הא־ל, is substituted.

---

texts, and the excessive pedantry displayed in this regard reveals a totally new attitude towards the function of words. Where the Merkabah mystics sought spontaneous expression for their oceanic feeling in the prodigal use of words, the Hasidim discovered a multitude of esoteric meanings in a strictly limited number of fixed expressions. And this painstaking loyalty to the fixed term does indeed seem to go hand in hand with a renewed consciousness of the magic power inherent in words.

See further on this issue Joseph Dan, *The Esoteric Theology of Ashkenazic Hasidim* [*Torat ha-sod shel hasidut Ashkenaz*] (Jerusalem: 1968 [Hebrew]), 14–17, on R. Elazar of Worms's *Sodot ha-Tefillah* (The Mysteries of the Liturgy) and 79–83, on the transfer of these esoteric traditions and the "chain of traditions" associated with them. More recently, *Sodot ha-Tefillah* has been attributed to R. Shem Tov bar Simhah, a disciple of R. Elazar of Worms. See Daniel Abrams, "*Ketuvei – Yad Hadashim shel Sefer ha-Sodot shel R. Shem Tov bar Simhah ha-Pulmus …*," *ve-ha-mekorot she-hayu be-yado." Asufot* 10 [1995]: 49–70; and see, most recently, S. Immanuel, *Mehqerei Talmud* 3 (part 2 [2005]: 593–603], and the important material edited by S. E. Stern, in *Moriah* 30/2–4, 2009, pp. 3–8. See also the very insightful article of Talya Fishman, "Rhineland Pietist Approaches to Prayer and the Textualization of Rabbinic Culture in Medieval Northern Europe" (*Jewish Studies Quarterly* [2004]: 311–331, with its copious references to the relevant literature; and also I. Ta-Shma, *The Early Ashkenazic Prayer: Liturgy and Historical Aspects* (Jerusalem: 2003, 43–53 [Hebrew]). A deeper insight into this mystical attitude towards prayer will give us a greater understanding as to the vehemence of the controversy between Hasidei Ashkenaz and their French contemporaries. (See above preceding note.)

11   This is not in *Siddur Rashi* as we have it; see editor's notes there.

However, this was not sufficient to satisfy the complaint of R. Yehudah he-Hasid, since he emphasized the importance not only of the number of words, but also of the number of letters. Such a substitution as suggested in *Arugat ha-Bosem* yields one fewer letter in *Ha-yom harat olam*. It seems, therefore, that another version was created to meet this objection: the substitution of the word אִיוֹם ("Awesome One") for הַיּוֹם ("today"), both of which have the same four letters.[12] In addition, the word sounds almost identical to הַיּוֹם; indeed, if the tradition of R. Yehudah he-Hasid was transmitted orally, it would have been easy to connect the new version with the old tradition (since the letter *heh* was hardly pronounced), and thus to justify it or even, perhaps, to see it as R. Yehudah he-Hasid's original wording.

This new version may be found in a special group of manuscripts, as may be seen from the variant readings in *Mahzor le-Yamim Noraim, Rosh ha-Shanah* (edited by D. Goldschmidt, 244, line 5. Jerusalem: 5730, and editor's notes, ibid.). When we examine the various readings listed there, we see that the version הַיּוֹם is found in ten manuscripts, eight from a group stemming from western Germany (see Introduction, 51–52), and two from *Minhag Tzarfat* (ibid., 53); thus this version was known in France, but was later eliminated. There are another thirteen manuscripts following the French version (ibid., 53–54) in which the word is missing, and they reflect Rabbenu Tam's emendation. The change to אִיוֹם can be found in manuscripts originating in the area of Asti, Fossano, and Moncalvo, in the Piedmonte region of northern Italy, to which French refugees went (see Goldschmidt, 13).[13] These manuscripts are

---

12 On this subject, see I. Ta-Shma, *Tarbiz* 39 (1970): 184–194, and additional comments by S. Z. Havlin, ibid., 40 (1972): 23–25, and further discussion and references in my *Minhagei Yisrael* 2 (Jerusalem: 1981, 183–184).

13 Further on *Mahzor AF"M* see D. Goldschmidt, *Mehkerei Tefillah u-Piyyut* (Jerusalem: 1979), 80–121. A somewhat similar example of a variant reading which may have developed out from the mistaken hearing (?) of a word which was substituted with a very similar-sounding word, we find in the *El Adon piyyut* (of Shabbat *shaharit*). There some versions have דעת ותבונה סובבים הודו, while others have סובבים אותו. *Hodo* and *Oto* sound much alike. The kabbalists were adamant that "wisdom and understanding surround His splendor" (*hodo*) and not "surround Him" (*oto*). For, they argued, one cannot speak of these attributes surrounding Him. Furthermore, it has been pointed out that this phrase echoes verses in Psalms 148:13: הוֹדוֹ עַל אֶרֶץ וְשָׁמָיִם "His splendour is upon earth and heavens," and Proverbs 3:19–20: ה' בְּחָכְמָה יָסַד אֶרֶץ, כּוֹנֵן שָׁמַיִם בִּתְבוּנָה, בְּדַעְתּוֹ תְהוֹמוֹת נִבְקָעוּ – "The Lord by wisdom hath forwarded

not earlier than the eighteenth century (ibid., 54). It is clear, therefore, that this is a new version.

Urbach (ibid., 97–99) points out that R. Yehudah he-Hasid did not actually write a commentary to the prayer book, but rather many pamphlets (*kuntresim*) and responsa which his disciples collected and used to support their position when stating what was the "correct, authentic" version. It was, presumably, such pamphlets that the Tur mentions (referred to above in chapter 15, near note 2):

לשון אחי ה"ר יחיאל ז"ל: דורשי רשומות הם חסידי אשכנז אשר היו שוקלין וסופרין מספר מנין
תיבות התפילות וברכות וכנגד מה נתקנו . . . וכו'. ובשו"ת הרא"ש ד, כ: . . . כי יש לי קונטריס מעשה
ישן וכתוב בו כל הברכות של כל השנה וסכום כמה תיבות יש בכל ברכה וברכה וכנגד מה נתקנה.

It was against this that R. David Abudarhim inveighed.

The kind of forceful "editorial" activity that we have seen among Hasidei Ashkenaz, and also by R. Tam of France, also may be found in other areas during other periods of time. We learn of such goings-on in a responsum of R. Menahem Meiri, the 14th-century Provençal scholar (*Magen Avot*, sec. 1):

שאנו נוהגים לומר אל מלך נאמן, בין בסוף ברכת אהבת לקריאת שמע, והם מוחים בדבר, ולא עוד
אלא שטוענים עלינו שהוא הפסק בין הברכה למצוה, ומזקיקים לחזור ולברך.

מנהג קדום בארצות הללו מימי קדם, בימי הרבנים הגדולים, וכן בארץ צרפת ובאשכנז,
שאומרים אחר ברכת אהבת עולם כשבאים להתחיל בקריאת שמע, אל מלך נאמן.

ובאמת, לא היה מנהג זה, לא בארץ המערב [ו] בארץ ישראל, ולא בארץ [המזרח], וגם לא
בארץ קטלוניא אשר היתה מקדם בכלל ארץ ספרד. וכבר הגיע לידינו מחזור[י]ם מארץ קטלוניא,
כתובים מזמן קדם קדמתה, שלא היה [מנהג זה], כי היה מנהגם כארץ ספרד ברוב הדברים או בכלם.
ובימי הרב ר' זרחיה הלוי, שיצא בבחורתו מעיר גירונדא, וזכה ללמוד במגדל לוניל, ועמד שם
זמן רב, וחזר ובא לו לשם, והנהיג לשם כל בני הקהל כמנהג הארץ הלזו, ונקבע במחזורותיהם כדרך
שהוא קבוע במחזורים שלנו.
ובהגיע תור הרב הגדול ר' משה בר' נחמן ז"ל, ראה שמקודם לא היו נוהגים כך, ושבכל

---

the earth; by understanding hath He established the heavens. By his knowledge the depths are broken up . . . ." (See *Kenesset ha-Gedolah* of Tzuberi, 1/2, Tel-Aviv 1976, 442; *Baer Sidddur*, 211.) However, *Siddur Otzar ha-Tefillot* (674) points out (*Iyyun Tefillah*) that אותו is the reading in *Seder Amram Gaon, Mahzor Vitry, Mahzor Roma, Abudarhim*, etc. Hence, it seems clear that this was the original reading. And perhaps the kabbalists, finding this formulation unacceptable, changed it to a very similar-sounding word with the same number of letters, giving us a roughly parallel example to the one discussed above.

ארץ ספרד לא היה אומרים אותו, ונתקשה בעיניו על שהיו אומרים אותו, מצורף, למה שהיה הרב בר מחלוקתו של הרב ר' זרחיה ומגיה על ספרו, עד (שחב) [שהיבר] מזה ספר נכבד קראו "ספר מלחמות".

והעיד הרב ז"ל, ששאל בזה [את] הרב המופלג רבינו מאיר מטוליטולא, ושהרב ז"ל השיבו שהוא טעות, ושאין אומרים אות[ו] בכל ספרד, ולא בארץ ישראל. ונתבטל המנהג על פי הרב, ונמחק מן המחזורים.

והחזיק הרב טובה לעצמו, ונתן שבח והודאה לאל, על שנתבטל השבוש הזה על ידו. ונתן טעם לדבריו מפני שברכת "אהבת [עולם]" היא "ברכת מצות שמע", ואין להפסיק בין הברכה לעשיית הדבר שעליו בירך, ועניית אמן אחר הברכה הוא הפסק.

והביא ראיה על זה ממה שאמרו בירושלמי של ברכות פרק אין עומדין (פרק ה' הלכה ד'): הפורס על שמע, והעובר לפני התיבה, והנושא את כפיו, והקורא בתורה, והמפטיר בנביא, והמברך על אחת מכל מצות האמורות בתורה, לא יענה אמן אחר עצמו, ואם ענה הרי זה בור. והיתה ראיה זו פשיטא בעיניו, שעניית אמן זה הוא הפסק, עד שחתך את הדין מכחה, שכל שאומר אל מלך נאמן הרי הוא כאומר אמן, וכמו שאמרו ז"ל: מאי אמן אל מלך נאמן, ואף כשאמרו שלא במקום אמן כל שכן שהוא הפסק, שהרי יש בו ריבוי תיבות יותר מבאמן. וא"כ כל שאמרו, בין במקום אמן בין שלא במקום אמן, הרי הוא בור וטועה, ושהוא הפסק, וצריך לחזור ולברך.

ובזמנ[י]נו זה באו הנה הנה תלמידים מקובלים משנות הרב, והיו מתמיהים עלינו על שהיינו מחזיקים במנהג זה, ובאמרנו להם יום יום, שכך נהגו בארצות האלו בזמן כמה גאונים וכמה רבנים שהיו בארץ הזאת לאלפים ולמאות, רבני אלפין ורבני מאוון, הכל היה כאין בעיניהם. סוף דבר קשתה יד לשונם עלינו, חזקו ידיהם בלשונם הגבירו.

ואני בראותי כי גבהו דבריהם אמרתי אענה אף אני חלקי, ונכנסתי עמהם במשא ומתן. ושאלתי את פיהם, זו מנין לכם שיהא הפסק עד שיהא צריך לחזור ולברך. ואם מפני שהרב ז"ל אמרה, באמת יודע אני על הרב ז"ל שהיה מופלג בחכמה ומופלא שבבית דין, שלא לחלוק עליו ולשנות אחר דבריו, ומכל מקום אף אנו נהגנו בזה על פי רבנים גדולים שאין גבוהי כמותם, אוקי גברי בהדי גברא ואוקי מנהגא אחזקיה, אלא הביאו ראיה.

We see, then, how the Provençal communities had a certain tradition as to their version of the prayer. When Nahmanides, in Spain, became a major influence on the pupils, he made them remove this text from the prayer books. It was the goal of the Meiri, in his work *Magen Avot,* to restore the old local traditions to their former esteem and re-introduce their traditional readings into their prayer books.

A somewhat similar controversy raged in the time of R. Yaakov Emden (1697–1776), between him and R. Shlomo Zalman Hanau (Reza).[14] Consider,

14 Ironically enough, R. Yaakov Emden's *Siddur*, *Amudei Shamayim* (Altona: 1745–1748) was actually printed in accordance with the text of R. Zalman Hanau's *Siddur* (*Shaarei Tefillah*, *Beit Tefillah*, Yaznitz 1725). See Emden's *Luah Erez*, part 1, sec. 117, 45, when he himself sadly admits to this fact, saying: "I too erred in this . . . and did not have the strength at the outset to correct all the errors . . . ." See editor's note 155, for additional places in which he apologized for such errors, referring also to Emden's *Sheilat Yavetz*, part 2, sec. 17. See further the comments of R. Yaakov Hayyim Sofer, in his *Maamar Yaakov* (Jerusalem: 2002), 124–126. On the relations between R. Yaakov Emden and R. Zalman Hanau, see Penkover's article in *Mikra u-parshanut* 4 (1997): 127–128. His *siddur* suffered even more in later years when it was reprinted, as it were, under the name of *Siddur Beit Yaakov*. R. Hayyim Eliezer Shapiro of Munkacz wrote concerning this edition:

> . . . But recently in the new editions they corrupted it including in the text a mixture [of readings] in such a fashion that it is impossible to know what is of the Gaon [R. Yaakov] and what is of others. And though they indicated in most places [their additions] in brackets, they sometimes placed his words in brackets, so that there is such a mess and muddle throughout that one can not know what came from whom. And I do not know who gave permission to R. Yudkis of Berdichev to do this, especially since they included many *zemirot* (songs) to which he objected . . . .

See further on his *Siddur* in *Minhagei Yisrael*, vol. 2, 167, 303 (with bibliography); vol. 7, 61; vol. 8, 299, and *Tiferet Tzvi*, vol. 2, 376. There he points to serious halachic pitfalls that face one who relies on this edition of R. Yaakov Emden's *Siddur*. Thus, on page 16, we read that one who has had an emission must immerse himself in a *mikveh* (*tevilat baal keri*). However, in *Orhot Hayyim* (Spinka), by R. Nahman Kahana (Sighet: 1898, vol. 2), there is an essay at the end called *Over Orah*, by the Aderet (R. Eliyahu David Rabinowitz Teomim) who writes (sec. 88) that the editor created a great stumbling-block in the *siddur* of R. Yaavetz in Warsaw, in that he printed the section "Seder Baal Keri" against the opinion of all the early and late authorities . . . and this was copied from a small tract called *Taharot Yisrael* [by R. Aviezer b. R. Yitzhak Isaac of Tiktin, Vilna: 1866], which in turn is based on *Mekor ha-berachah*, a commentary on the first four chapters of Mishnah Berachot [by the same R. Aviezer, Lvov 1851]. And how great are the (cautionary) words of the Hatam Sofer (who warns against the use of a printed book) with an approbation. "And furthermore, besides this he did much damage in the print of the main text of the *siddur*." He further refers us to what R. Hayyim Eliezer Shapira wrote in his *Maamar Nusah ha-Tefillah*, sec. 10 (printed in his *Hamishah Maamarot*, Beregsas: 1922, reprinted Jerusalem: 1951, 164):

> The *Siddur* of the Gaon Yavetz, which is famous for its accuracy . . . . However, recently they corrupted it in the new editions, adding to it in such a manner that

for instance, the following passage in his *Sulam Beit El* (the introduction to his *Siddur Beit Yaakov*, 3:7):

> One must realize that one hundred and twenty elders and prophets (the Men of the Great Assembly) carefully considered each and every word of the texts of the eighteen blessings (as well as the rest of the blessings) and weighed them in their holy minds, and instituted the blessings with great consideration and exactness. In any case, it is a very wonderful thing that for the first three blessings, we – all the people of Israel in all the places of their dispersion – say exactly the same words. Even if they have been separated from each other as far as east is from west, they have guarded against any change in them. Not the slightest thing has been added, no word has been lost or changed, because they knew that this [text must be preserved] strictly.
>
> This is what Rabbi Yehiel said: "The Hasidei Ashkenaz are interpreters of lists, who counted and recorded the numbers of words of the prayers and the blessings, and what they symbolize. They said there are 197 words in the first three blessings: the first has 42 words, the second has 51 words . . . ." His [Rabbi Yehiel's] reward is secure [for having preserved this count], and he did not labor in vain! Whether he was correct in all that he recorded, or some of it, or even if none of it is correct, in any event the reward for his good intentions will not be withheld from him.
>
> And may God forgive Rabbi David Abudarhim, who mocked this practice and said that this counting is only valuable for the one who makes it, but to no one else, since he realized that not all Israel have the same *nusah,* word for word. But even if this is true, [Rabbi Yehiel] gained himself merit for his good intentions and helped others by listing the words in each blessing. There is no doubt that the Men of the Great Assembly who wrote them were very particular about the number of words, even granting that they did not intend these numbers to symbolize anything. In any case, they were certainly exacting about the language, that it be a clear text that would be equally understandable to all of Israel, as the Rambam wrote.
>
> If, over the course of time, and through the many copyings that were done during times of persecution, and through "pouring from vessel to vessel," the texts changed between the distant places from east to west, that is the fault of the scribes and the copiers. Nevertheless, this only caused the *nusah* to be

---

it is no longer possible to know what is by the Gaon and what is by others . . . .
I do not know who permitted this to be done, especially as they included songs and all sorts of things to which the Gaon was specifically opposed.

Fragment of an Oxford Ms. from the school of Hasidei Ashkenaz on the "correct" forms of the liturgy with numerological guidelines.
(See S. E. Stern, *Moriah* 30, 2009, p. 5)

divided into two forms [Ashkenazic and Sephardic] . . . . One version is definitely incorrect . . . . Since we do not know clearly who possesses the first, true
tradition, each [group] keeps its own version, and justifies it as best as it can . . . .

*If only the earlier generations had written the numbers of words of the prayers
and blessings in books, as they knew it!* They would certainly have helped themselves, and those who came after them, just like the work of the Masoretes on
the Bible . . . . It is not a worthless endeavor, and the *Zohar,* too, was involved
in this . . . .

In the mid-nineteenth century, Rabbi Yaakov Zvi Meklenburg, in his
Siddur Tefillat Yisrael (Königsberg: 1855, with the commentary *Iyyun Tefillah*),
alters passages in the *selihot* which seem to address angels as conveyors of
prayers and requests to God, so that these requests might be formulated as addressed, without intermediaries, directly to Him. These reformulations were
mandated by his understanding that the appeal to or through intermediaries
was halachically unacceptable. (See D. Goldsmidt's discussion in his *Seder
Selihot,* Jerusalem 1965; 11–12.)

See in detail in my *Netivot Pesikah* (Jerusalem: 2008, 58–62). Most recently, we have seen such a discussion concerning *Siddur Ish Mazliah* (see D.
Yitzhaki's articles in *Or Yisrael* 25 [2002]: 217–226, and in his introduction to
R. Yaakov Emden's *Luah Erez,* 29 et seq., and so also in R. Shlomo Toledano's
Divrei Shalom ve-Emet, vol. 2 [Jerusalem: 2005, introduction 21–22], where
he decries R. Ovadia Yosef's attempt to create a unified Sefardic custom and
liturgical version, which has caused many North African [Moroccan] Jews to
reject their own authentic tradition for that put forward by R. Ovadia Yosef.
He argues forcefully that such communities should return to their ancestral
traditions, which are, in any case, well authenticated in the testimonies of early
authorities.) (See ibid. 7–15, 25 etc., and cf. vol. 1, Jerusalem: n.d., 2000 [?], pass.
See additional material on this issue in B. Lau, *From "Maran" to "Maran": The
Halachic Philosophy of Rav Ovadia Yosef* [Israel: 2005] [Hebrew], 348–351.)

Such debates and controversies were always part of Jewish synagogue life,
and the dynamism of liturgical development and presumably this phenomenon will continue on into the forseeable future.

APPENDIX 2

Seven Versions of *Birkat Nahem*

In chapter 19, note 6 above, we called attention to the instructive case of the reformulation of *Birkat Nahem*. After the reunification of Jerusalem, the development of the Jewish Quarter and opening up of the Western Wall plaza, it was no longer felt that one could say that the "city was in mourning, destroyed, defiled and desolate . . . without her children . . . without inhabitants." Therefore, new formulations were suggested. Incidentally, the same problem exists in other liturgical passages, such as in the *piyyut* of *Neilah, Ezkerah Elokim ve-ehemayah*," (ed. Goldschmidt, 663) where we read:

בראותי כל עיר על תילה בנויה, ועיר הא־להים מושפלת עד שאול תחתיה: When I see every city built up on its hill, while the City of God is . . . downcast [or humiliated] most deeply. (Cf. Deut. 32:22 and Isaiah 57:9.) Here, we cite seven different versions of *Birkat Nahem*, in what was clearly a political-ideological exercise.[1]

1. The Traditional *Nahem*:[2]

Comfort, O Lord our God, the mourners of   נחם ה' א־להינו אר־ת אבלי ציון
Zion, the mourners of Jerusalem, and the city   ואת אבלי ירושלים ואת העיר

---

1   See chap. 19, n. 6 above for the bibliographic sources of this appendix. The translations of nos. 1–3 are those found in Wachs's article, and nos. 4–7 are my own, (hence, the slight inconsistencies in translation).

2   We are referring to the *Nahem* prayer for Tishah be-Av. There is another version found in *Mahzor Vitry* (229, sec. 269) in his *Hilchot Tishah be-Av*, which has slight variations and a different ending. See Levine, 73. There are also some differences between the current version in *Nusah Ashkenaz* and that of *Nusah Sefarad* (Levine, 72). All the versions are based on Y. *Berachot* 4.3, 8a., (=Y. *Taanit* 2.2 65c). which reads as follows:

that is in mourning, laid waste, despised and desolate. She is in mourning because she is without her children. Her homes have been destroyed. She is despised in the downfall of her glory; she is desolate through the loss of her inhabitants. She sits with her head covered like a barren, childless woman. Legions devoured her, idolaters took possession of her; they put thy people Israel to the sword and killed wantonly the faithful followers of the Most High. Because of that, Zion weeps bitterly, Jerusalem raises her voice. How my heart grieves for the slain! How my heart yearns for the slain! Thou, O Lord, didst consume her with fire, and with fire Thou wilt in future rebuild her, as it is written, "I will be to her, saith the Lord, a wall of fire round about; and I will be in the midst of her" (Zacharia 2:9). Blessed art Thou, O Lord, Comforter of Zion and Builder of Jerusalem.

האבלה והחרבה והבזויה והשוממה האבלה מבלי בניה והחרבה ממעונותיה והבזויה מכבודה והשוממה מאין יושב והיא יושבת וראשה חפוי כאשה עקרה שלא ילדה. ויבלעוה לגיונות וירשוה עובדי זרים ויטילו את עמך ישראל לחרב ויהרגו בזדון חסידי עליון. על כן ציון במר תבכה וירושלים תתן קולה. לבי לבי על חלליהם מעי מעי על חלליהם. כי אתה ה' באש הצתה ובאש אתה עתיד לבנותה כאמור "ואני אהיה לה נאם ה' חומת אש סביב ולכבוד אהיה בתוכה". ברוך אתה ה' מנחם ציון ובונה ירושלים.

2. Abraham Rosenfeld's version:[3]

Comfort, O Lord our God, the mourners of Zion, the mourners of Jerusalem and the holy city that weeps for Thy people Israel, who was thrown to the sword, and for the most pious who were

נחם ה' א-להינו, את אבלי ציון ואת אבלי ירושלים ואת העיר הקדושה, המבכה על עמך ישראל אשר הוטל לחרב, ועל

א"ר אחא בר יצחק בשם ר' חייא דציפורין: יחיד בט"ב צריך להזכיר מעין המעורה. רחם ה' אלקינו ברחמיך הרבים ובחסדיך הנאמנים עלינו ועל עמך ישראל ועל ירושלים עירך ועל ציון משכן כבודך ועל העיר האבילה והחרבה וההרוסה והשוממה הנתונה ביד זרים הרמוסה ביד עריצים וירשוה לגיונות ויחללוה עובדי פסילים ולישראל עמך נתת נחלה ולזרע ישורון ירושה הורשתה כי באש היצתה ובאש אתה עתיד לבנותה, כאמור, "ואני אהיה לה נאם ה' חומת אש סביב ולכבוד אהיה בתוכה".

On this version and its parallel in JT *Taanit*, see L. Ginzberg, *A Commentary on the Palestinian Talmud*, vol. 3 (New York: 1941 [Hebrew], 308), who discusses the different readings in detail. See Ritba on *Taanit* ad fin., who points to the variations between the Yerushalmi version and that in our *siddurim* (as Ginzberg noted, ibid.). Compare *Seder Rav Amram Gaon*, (ed. E. D. Goldschmidt, Jerusalem: 1971, part 2, sec. 98, 132); *Siddur Rav Saadya Gaon* (edited by I. Davidson, S. Assaf and B. I. Joel, 318–319. Jerusalem: 2000 [see Wachs, 248]).

3 Seder *Tefillat Zikaron* (translated and edited by Abraham Rosenfeld. Jerusalem: 1981).

slain in arrogance; and for the mighty ones of Israel who suffered martyrdom for the sanctification of thy Divine name. Indeed, Zion weeps bitterly, and Jerusalem raises her voice: "O my heart, my heart (grieves) for those who were slain! O my innermost heart, my innermost heart (yearns) for those who were slain!" Our Father who art in heaven, avenge Thy city which Thou hast given to us as an inheritance, and gather the remnants of Israel out of all the countries whither Thou hast driven them and they shall dwell therein, and there shall be no more extermination, as it is said: "Jerusalem shall be inhabited without walls, for the multitude of men and cattle therein. And I will be to her a wall of fire round about, saith the Lord, and I will be for a glory in the midst of her." Blessed art Thou, O Lord, Comforter of Zion and Rebuilder of Jerusalem!

חסידי עליון שנהרגו בזדון, ועל גבורי ישראל שמסרו נפשם על קדושת השם. ציון במר תבכה וירושלים תתן קולה. לבי לבי על חלליהם, מעי מעי על חלליהם. אבינו שבשמים, נקום את נקמת עירך אשר נתתה לנו לנחלה, וקבץ את שארית ישראל מכל הארצות אשר הדחת אתם שם, וישבו בה, וחרם לא יהיה עוד, כאמור "פרזות תשב ירושלים מרוב אדם ובהמה בתוכה. ואני אהיה לה, נאם ה', חומת אש סביב, ולכבוד אהיה בתוכה". ברוך אתה ה' מנחם ציון ובנה ירושלים.

3.   Prof. E. E. Urbach's version:[4]

Lord our God, with abundant compassion and enduring kindness, take pity upon us, upon Your people Israel, and upon Your city Jerusalem which is being rebuilt upon its ruins, restored upon its ravage and resettled upon its desolation. For her most saintly martyrs who were wantonly slaughtered, for those of Your people who were murdered and for her sons who gave their lives and spilled their blood for her sake, Zion moans and wails, "My heart, my heart cries for the dead, my recesses weep for the dead." Over the city which You liberated from the hands of villainous legions and gave to Your people in perpetuity, spread Your shelter of peace as a peaceful river in fulfillment of that which is stated, "And I shall be unto

רחם ה' אלהינו ברחמיך הרבים ובחסדיך הנאמנים עלינו ועל עמך ישראל ועל ירושלים עירך הנבנית מחרבה והמקוממת מהריסותיה והמיושבת משוממותה, על חסידי עליון שנהרגו בזדון ועל עמך ישראל שהוטל לחרב ועל בניה אשר מסרו נפשם ושפכו דמם עליה. ציון במר תבכה וירושלים תתן קולה. לבי לבי על חלליהם מעי מעי על חלליהם. והעיר אשר פדית מידי עריצים ולגיונות ולישראל עמך נתתה נחלה ולזרע ישרון ירושה הורשתה נטה עליה סוכת שלומך כנהר שלום לקיים

4   *The Holy City: Jews on Jerusalem* (edited by A. Holz, 108–109. New York: 1971).

her a wall of fire round about, saith the Lord,
and I will be for a glory in the midst of her."
Blessed art Thou, O Lord, Comforter of Zion
and Rebuilder of Jerusalem!

מה שנאמר, "ואני אהיה לה נאם
ה' חומת אש סביב ולכבוד אהיה
בתוכה". ברוך אתה ה' מנחם ציון
ובונה ירושלים.

4. Rabbi Goren's version:[5]

Comfort, O Lord our God, the mourners of Zion
and the mourners of Jerusalem, and the city that is
in mourning, laid waste and destroyed. Zion shall
weep bitterly and Jerusalem shall give voice. My
heart, my heart [goes out] to their corpses, my innards, my innards to their slain. And to your people Israel you have given inheritance, and, to the
seed of Jeshurun you have granted possession. Stir
her up, Lord our God, from her dust, and awaken
her suffering land. Extend to her like a river of
peace and like a rushing stream flooding the honor
of the nations. For Thou O Lord, didst consume
her with fire and with fire shalt Thou rebuild her,
as it is said, "For I, saith the Lord, will be unto her
a wall of fire round about, and will be the glory
in the midst of her" (Zachariah 2:9). Blessed art
Thou, O Lord, Comforter of Zion and Builder
of Jerusalem.

נחם ה' א-להינו את אבלי
ציון ואת אבלי ירושלים
ואת העיר האבלה החרבה
וההרוסה. ציון במר תבכה
וירושלים תתן קולה, לבי
לבי על חלליהם, מעי מעי
על הרוגיהם. ולישראל
עמך נרתתה נחלה וזרע
ישורון ירשה הורשת. נערה
ה' אלקינו מעפרה והקיצה
מארץ דויה. נטה אליה כנהר
שלום וכנחל שוטף כבוד
גוים, כי אתה ה' באש הצתה
ובאש אתה עתיד לבנותה,
כאמור", ואני אהיה לה נאם
ה' חומת אש סביב, ולכבוד
אהיה בתוכה". ברוך אתה ה'
מנחם ציון ובונה ירושלים.

5. The version of Rabbi David Chelouche:[6]

Comfort, O Lord our God, the mourners of Your
Temple and Mount Zion, which dwells desolate
without her children. The bondwoman lords it
over her mistress, the children of Hagar have built
on it their mosque, and we cannot go up to see
and prostrate ourselves before you in the House
of Your choice, the wayside habitation, the great
and holy dwelling-place which is called by Your
name, by reason of our manifold sins that have

נחם ה' א-להינו את אבלי
מקדשך ואת הר ציון ששמם
מבלי בניו הוא יושב, שפחה
תירש גברתה, בני הגר בנו עליו
מסגדם, ואין אנו יכולים לעלות
ולראות ולהשתחוות לפניך
בבית בחירתך בנוה הדרך
בבית הגדול והקדוש שנקרא
שמך עליו, בעוונותינו שרבו

---

5 *Siddur la-Hayyal le-Chol ha-Shanah* (1970), 217.
6 D. Chelouche, *Hemdah Genuzah* (Jerusalem: 1976), sec. 21:8.

piled up and our transgressions that have grown
upwards to the heavens. My heart, my heart [goes
out] to Mount Moriah, my innards, my innards,
to the Holy of Holies wherein tread the unclean.
For Thou, O Lord, didst consume her with fire,
and with fire shalt Thou rebuild her, as it is written, "For I, saith the Lord, will be unto her a
wall of fire round about, and will be the glory
in the midst of her." Blessed art Thou, O Lord,
Comforter of Zion and Builder of Jerusalem.

למעלה ראש ובאשמורתינו
שגדלו עד לשמים. לבי לבי
על הר המוריה מעי מעי על
קדש הקדשים שטמאים הלכו
בו. כי אתה ה' באש הצתה
ובאש אתה עתיד לבנותה,
ככתוב, ואני אהיה לה נאם ה'
חומת אש סביב ולכבוד אהיה
בתוכה. ברוך אתה ה' מנחם
ציון ובונה ירושלים.

6. The version of Rabbi Hayyim Mendel Lewites:[7]

Comfort, O Lord our God, the mourners of
Zion and the mourners of Jerusalem with Your
great mercies and Your faithful grace, for us,
for Israel, for your city Jerusalem and for Zion,
the dwelling place of your honor. And to your
people Israel you have given inheritance, and
to the seed of Jeshurun you have granted possession. Extend our borders so that all peoples
of the earth may recognize and know that Your
city is our city and the place of the Temple. For
Thou dist consume her with fire, and with fire
shalt Thou rebuild her, as is said, "For I, saith
the Lord, will be unto her a wall of fire round
about and will be the glory in the midst of her."
Blessed art Thou, O Lord, Comforter of Zion
and Builder of Jerusalem.

נחם ה' א-להינו את אבלי ציון
ואת אבלי ירושלים ברחמיך
הרבים ובחסדיך הנאמנים
עלינו ועל ישראל ועל ירושלים
עירך ועל ציון משכן כבודך,
ולישראל עמך נתת נחלה
ולזרע ישורון ירושה הורשת,
ותרחיב את גבולנו ויכירו
וידעו כל באי עולם כי ערך
עירנו ומקום מקדשנו. כי אתה
ה' באש הצתה ובאש אתה
עתיד לבנותה, כאמור, "ואני
אהיה לה נאם ה' חומת אש
סביב ולכבוד אהיה בתוכה".
ברוך אתה ה' מנחם ציון ובונה
ירושלים.

7. The version of Mr. Yosef Ben-Brit:[8]

Comfort, O Lord our God, the mourners of Zion,
and the Temple Mount which is in mourning,
bereft of the Temple and without Jewish prayer

נחם ה' א-לוהינו את אבלי
ציון וירושלים, ואת הר הבית
האבל מאין מקדש ומאין

---

7   "Ha-Evkeh ba-Hodesh ha-Hamishi?" Tzemihat Geulatenu: Kovetz Maamarim be-Hal-
    achah, be-Aggadah u-ve-Hagut ha-Yehudit. Jerusalem: 1984, 20–24.

8   "Tefillat 'Nahem' – min ha-lev o stam shigrah." Amudim 36/10 (Tammuz 5748):
    408–411.

upon it. Therefore, Zion shall weep bitterly and Jerusalem shall give vent to her cries. My heart, my heart [goes out] to her corpses, my innards, my innards to her slain. Extend to her like a river of peace and a rushing stream flooding the honor of the nations. For Thou, O Lord, didst consume her with fire and with fire shall Thou rebuild her, as it is said, "I will be to her, saith the Lord, a wall of fire round about, and I will be the glory in the midst of her" (Zachariah 2:5). "Praise ye the Lord, for it is good to sing praises unto our God; for it is pleasant, and praise is comely. The Lord doth build up Jerusalem, gathereth together the outcasts of Israel. He healeth the broken in heart, and bindeth up their wounds" (Psalm 147: 1–3). "Praise the Lord, O Jerusalem! Praise thy God, O Zion, For he hath strengthened the bars of thy gates; He hath blessed thy children within thee" (ibid., 12–13). "Save, Lord! May the King hear us when we call" (ibid., 20:10). Blessed art Thou, O Lord, Comforter of Zion and Builder of Jerusalem.

תפילה יהודית עליו. לכן ציון
במר תבכה וירושלים רתתן
קולה. לבי לבי על חלליה,
מעי מעי על הרוגיה. נטה
אליה כנהר שלום וכנחל
שוטף כבוד גויים. כי אתה
ה' באש הצתה ובאש אתה
עתיד לבנותה, כאמור: "ואני
אהיה לה, נאום ה', חומת אש
סביב ולכבוד אהיה בתוכה.
הללויה כי טוב זמרה לאלקינו
כי נעים נאוה תהילה. בונה
ירושלים ה', נדחי ישראל
יכבץ.⁹ הרופא לשבורי לב
ומחבש לעצבותם. שבחי
ירושלים את ה', הללי
אלוקיך ציון. כי חזק בריחי
שעריך ברך בניך בקרבך. ה'
הושיעה המלך יעננו ביום
קראנו". ברוך אתה ה', מנחם
ציון ובונה ירושלים.

It should be noted that in all these different variations the beginning (the *petihah*) and the finale of the benediction (the *hatimah*) are identical, and have not been in any way altered or modified. And as to the central part of the prayer-benediction (the *toref* or *guf*), there too the basic theme has not been changed, though additions have been inserted and different emphases have come into play. Here again, their acceptance or non-acceptance was primarily a political-ideological issue, though it was often couched in halachic terminology.¹⁰ However, the willingness by several prominent rabbis to make such

---

9   In Psalm 147:2, the Hebrew has יכנס, but in Isaiah 56:8, we read: נאם ה' א-להינו מקבץ נדחי ישראל (Levine ibid., 88, n. 33).

10   R. Ovadia Yosef (Responsa *Yehaveh Daat* 1, Jerusalem: 1977, sec. 43, 120–122, strongly objected to any change in this prayer, arguing that it was composed in the time of the Men of the Great Synod (*Anshei Kenesset ha-Gedolah*), "and their

changes, even in an ancient and wholly traditional *berachah*, is significant for us, and therefore pertinent to our argument.[11]

---

words are based on golden foundations with hidden celestial secret [meanings] . . . ." See most recently R. Hayyim Navon's article, entitled "*Nusah ha-tefillah bi-metziut mishtanah*" (*Tzohar* 32 [2008]: 57–66), which deals also with the prayers for Israel Independence Day (*Yom ha-Atzmaut*). His tentative conclusion is that minimalistic change to suit new situations may be acceptable. For a somewhat similar example of the political-ideological subtext in a liturgical passage, see J. Tabory, "The Piety of Politics: Jewish Prayers for the State of Israel," in *Liturgy in the Life of the Synagogue* (225–246). Of course, the main difference between these two cases is that *Nahem* is an ancient benediction while the prayer for the state of Israel is a totally new literary creation.

11 These changes also reflect an awareness of the necessity that liturgical texts must also be relevant. And this sensitivity to the need for relevance and an honest portrayal of reality may always be found in the comment of the *Zohar* (1.157a) on the phrase על הארץ הטובה – "on the good land," in the second blessing of the Grace after Meals (*ve-al ha-kol*): אי בארעא דישראל מברכינן, לבר מארעא מנלן? – If in the Land of Israel we bless, outside Israel from where do we know [that one blesses]? In other words, how do we bless "the good land" when it is destroyed and barren? The *Zohar* gives a mystical explanation that justifies reciting this phrase even in the barren and destroyed Israel, and this explanation was taken up by the kabbalists (see *Tzelota de-Avraham*, vol. 2, 518–519).

The *Ha-Siddur ha-Meduyak* Affair

In 1986, there appeared in Bnei Brak a new Sefardi *siddur* entitled *Ha-Siddur ha-Meduyak – Ish Matzliah*, meaning "The Exact Siddur." This "exact" version based itself on the emendations of the great Tunisian rabbis, R. Shaul ha-Cohen and R. Matzliah Mazuz, the Rosh Yeshivah of Yeshivat Kisse Rahamim. At the end of this *siddur* appeared a section called לאוקומי גירסא – *Le-okumei girsa*, meaning "to correct the reading(s)," in which a long list of (mainly grammatical corrections) are tabulated (second ed., 1986, 3–43). This prayer book, which was tremendously successful and immediately ran into several further editions with runs of many thousands of copies, received the approbations of R. Shlomo Amar, R. Ovadiah Yosef, R. Shmuel ha-Levi Vozner, R. Dov Kook, R. Shimon Hai Aluf, R. Yoram Aberjel, R. Neeman (Mazuz). It was also viciously attacked by the anonymous author of *Kovetz li-Gedor Peretz* (2004), with a special section entitled לעקומי גירסא – *Le-akumei girsa*, i.e., "to distort the reading." This was an enlarged and "improved" version of an earlier such polemic pamphlet entitled Responsum *Le-hoshvei Shemo*.[1]

However, R. Yosef Caro himself, in his work *Avkat Rochel* (edited by R. David Avitan, sec. 28, 137–138. Jerusalem: 2002), wrote that minor changes in prayer readings are permissible when there are variant traditions, since these matters are not issues of *issur ve-heter* – that which is forbidden or permitted. This responsum is further cited by the Hidah, R. Hayyim Yosef David Azulai, in his work *Tov Ayin* (Jerusalem: 1961, sec. 7, 131), in a long responsum on

---

1 These anonymous pamphlets were published by "*Agudat Mishmeret ha-Kodesh*," whatever that may be.

changes in prayer readings. The Hidah, who accepts the *Avkat Rochel's* ruling, is further cited by R. Yosef ben Naim in his work *Sheerit ha-Tzon,* vol. 2 (edited by M. Amar, sec. 260, 364, Lod: 2005), who also follows this guideline.[2]

The Hidah also cites this responsum of R. Yosef Caro in his work *Yosef Ometz* (Jerusalem 1961, sec. 10, 20a), where he states once again: "From here (i.e., Caro's responsum), it is clear that it is permissible to change a word, or words [here and there], as I wrote in my book *Tov Ayin.*" However, he then continues to clarify his position by limiting these changes to sporadic individual cases, but not when such grammatical emendations would affect many passages throughout the prayer book and also run counter to what is broadly accepted throughout the communities. In such cases he is adamant that such changes are totally unacceptable, and he even takes to task the Tosafot Yom Tov, R. Yomtov Lipmann Heller, for stating that one should say *hei ha-olamim* and not *hai ha-olamim* (ibid., 20b),[3] and he "mourns this orphan generation

---

2   Presumably, it is for this reason that in vol. 1., sec. 123, 354–355, he writes that in the *Kaddish*, he decided to keep to his – albeit minority – tradition of saying בעגל ובזמן קריב, as opposed to the more common בעגלא.

3   Here I should like to call attention to Dan Rabinowitz's note in his Seforim Blog, in an article entitled "Bibliography: Why It is Important." There he writes as follows:

> An egregious error due to lack of bibliographical information can be found in the Machon Yerushalayhim edition of the *Shulhan Aruch.* Included in this edition is the commentary of R. Menachem Mendel Auerbach, *Ateret Zekenim.* In *Orah Hayyim,* no. 54, R. Auerbach discusses whether the word *"Hai"* – *het, yud* – should be punctuated with a *patach* or a *tzerei.* R. Auerbach states "one should have a *tzerei* under the letter *heh* ... and this in accord with what R. Shabbatai writes in his *siddur.* However, the Maharal of Prague says to use a *patah.*" Now, when R. Auerbach references R. Shabbatai and his *siddur,* the Machon Yerushalayim edition includes an explanatory note: "*Siddur ha-Arizal* in the *Baruch she-amar* prayer." Thus, according to Machon Yerushalayim, R. Auerbach is quoting the *Siddur ha-Arizal* compiled by R. Shabbatai Rashkover. That, in and of itself, is a bit odd as this *siddur* is more interested – as the title implies – in the Ari and his kabbalistic ideas, rather than in grammar. Therefore, to use it in a discussion of grammar, which the quote in question is dealing with, is a bit odd! Setting that aside, there is a more fundamental mistake here, as the *siddur* compiled by R. Rashkover was only published for the first time in Koretz in 1795. R. Auerbach lived from 1620–1689. Thus, he was dead for over one hundred years prior to the publication of the *siddur* of R. Rashkover. Moreover, *Ateret Zekenim* was first published in 1702 in Amsterdam, also long before the *siddur* in question was ever published. The Rashkover's *siddur* was only first

which rejects that which is primary (*ikar*) and seizes upon the secondary

---

written in 1755 and not published until 1797. What is particularly striking about this example is that if one actually examines Rashkover's *siddur*, he doesn't even have a *tzerei* in the word in question!

Instead, the *siddur* in question from "R. Shabbatai" is that of R. Shabbatai Sofer, the well-known grammarian. As this R. Shabbatai is a grammarian and wrote his *siddur* specifically in order to correct and highlight the proper grammatical readings – see the lengthy introduction to this *siddur*, where R. Shabbatai bemoans people's disregard of proper grammar – it makes perfect sense to quote this *siddur* from this "R. Shabbatai." This is not the only place R. Auerbach quotes R. Shabbatai, one quote in particular is important as it dispels who the "R. Shabbatai" Auerbach is referring to. In *Orah Hayyim*, no. 122, Auerbach gives R. Shabbatai's full name in another discussion about proper grammar. Auerbach refers to "I also saw this in the *siddur* of R. Shabbatai of Przemysl." R. Shabbatai of Przemysl is otherwise known as R. Shabbatai Sofer (1565–1635) and that is who is referred to earlier as well.

On R. Sofer, see Stefan C. Reif, *Shabbethai Sofer and His Prayer-Book* (Cambridge and New York: Cambridge University Press, 1979).

We should also call attention to the *siddur* called *Shaarei Tefillah* (Yaznitz: 1725), by the great grammarian R. Shlomo Zalman Hanau (called by his acronym RZ"H, רז"ה), who "corrected" the "corrupt" versions of the prayer book in accordance with the right forms of grammar. His *siddur* ignited a fierce controversy, and among his vehement opponents was R. Yaakov Emden. This controversy continues to this day. See for example R. David Yitzhaki's aggressive article *Magihei Siddur ha-Tefillah be-Ashkenaz: Ha-Medakdek RZ"H ve-Ziyufav*" (*Tzefunot* 3/3 (II) [1991]: 75–81), who accuses the RZ"H of falsifications and forgery. See, even more recently, a series of articles in *Ha-Maayan* (48/4 [2008]: 70 et seq., ibid., [49/1]: 53–64), in which RZ"H and Satanov are called "the wicked ones of Israel," in that "they caused grave damage to the version of the liturgy [affecting] many Jewish people." In the latter article, R. Raphael Benyamin Posen shows that the RZ"H was highly respected by his contemporaries, and great rabbinic scholars of subsequent generations (54–55, n. 3), including R. Yitzhak Elhanan Spector. To his references we may add the *Peri Megadim, Eshel Avraham* 582:4, who calls him *Ha-Medakdek ha-Gaddol*, "the great grammarian, Rabbi Shlomo ha-Cohen Zalman Hanau, z"l." On Satanov, see Posen ibid., 55 et seq. See further on this issue what I wrote in *Netivot Pesikah* (Jerusalem: 2008, 58–62), citing, inter alia, R. Yaakov Hayyim Sofer, *Maamar Yaakov* (Jerusalem: 2002, 120 et seq.), who demonstrated the dangers of trying to apply what appear to be normative grammatical rules to our liturgical texts.

Further on *hai* and *hei* see R. Yaakov Babani. *Yashresh Ya'akov* (Nuremberg [Altona]: 1768), where he has a comprehensive discussion about this word and its punctuation, and *Ha-Siddur ha-Meduyak, Le-okumei girsa*, 14; and R. Yaakov Yosef Schechter, in his article "*Luah erez le-ha-Gri Emden z"l*" (*Yeshurun* 2 [1997]: 534–535, n. 17). See also the extended discussions of R. Yaakov Verdiger, in *Tzelota de-Avraham*, vol. 3 (Jerusalem: 1893, 371–375), citing, inter alia, *Tosafot Yom Tov*, by

(*tafel*) . . . and [suggests] that they know the truth and that all Israel are mistaken." Therefore, in the Hidah's view, there are limitations to what and how much can one change, "correct" and amend.

As mentioned earlier, *Ha-Siddur ha-Meduyak* was repeatedly attacked by the anonymous pamphleteer, who made cynically selective use of citations from prominent authorities, such as the Hidah and others, to demonstrate forcefully that no changes may be made in the "accepted version" of the *siddur.* The pamphlet reprints in full the scathing review of R. David Yitzhaki, which appeared in *Or Yisrael* (25 [2002]: 217–226). Of course, R. Yitzhaki himself, who found errors among the suggested emendations, is himself not averse in principle to emendations, as is evident in his masterly edition of R. Yaakov Emden's *Luah Erez* (Toronto: 2001).

The pamphlet's author (or were there perhaps more than one?) gives his arguments what appear to be greater force and credence by including critiques of two other publications in his booklet: *Tikkun Soferim ha-Meduyak* and *Ha-Tehillim ha-Meduyak,* in which the arguments center around the "sanctity" and accuracy of the Masoretic text, which, of course, is a far different and much more problematic issue, and for which there is no difficulty in finding a host of authorities who would not sanction a single emendation of the sanctified canonic text.[4]

The acrimony in these criticisms reminds us of a passage that circulated in early medieval Europe that describes the encounter between a (Christian) cleric and a particular demon known as Tutivillus in some versions. When asked about the bulging sack on his back, the demon gleefully responds that he

---

R. Yom Tov Lippmann Heller on M. Tamid 7.4, *Sheilat Yavetz,* by R. Yaakov Emden, responsum 141, *Aruch ha-Shulhan, Orah Hayyim* 54:1, etc. He ends by saying that as yet there is no determination which is the more correct version. See also *Tiferet Tzvi,* vol. 2, 378.

This work was recently republished and edited by Moshe Didi and David Stabon (Kiryat Sefer: 2005), and the discussion there is on 72–76 (=37b–39b, in the earlier editions). This edition also contains an introduction, which discusses the authorship of *Yashresh Yaakov,* (5–12). The editor believes the author was "R. Yaakov Bashan, but he requested R. Yaakov Babani to sign as author out of fear of his antagonists" (ibid., 12).

4   See further what I wrote on this issue in my *Darkah shel ha-Halacha* (Jerusalem: 2003, 226, n. 362).

has filled it with syllables and slurred utterances and verses of Psalms that the clergy had stolen from God when they enunciated their prayers incorrectly.[5]

However, what appears to be a devastating critique of the *siddur* was most convincingly countered on every point in *Kuntres Ish Matzliah*, published in *Va-yaan Shmuel* (3 [2000]: 283–340).

We shall not go into the arguments and counter-arguments that underlie this polemic discussion, but merely point out that a leitmotif that change and innovation are unacceptable seems to run through all the various critiques. Thus, for example, an approbation by R. Shmuel ha-Levi Vozner – the same rabbi who gave his *haskamah* to the *Ha-Siddur ha-Meduyak* – is cited on page 3. I shall quote part of it:

> The meaning of the great rabbis' words is clear – the *masorah* (i.e., tradition), both in matters of prayer and in everything related to parts of the Torah – is the basis of our existence – and that which the earlier authorities did not emend, even though they were fully conversant with the rules of Hebrew grammar, we may not alter or correct (except that which seems clearly to be a scribal error or a copyist's mistake, etc.) . . . .
>
> It is distressing to believe that learned rabbis lend support to this dangerous approach. The guiding principle in all these matters is in the aphorism of the Hatam Sofer, of blessed memory, that *"hadash assur min ha-Torah"* – "Innovation is biblically prohibited."[6]

To this we reply with an equally compelling statement by Rav Kook: *"Ha-yashan yithadesh ve-ha-hadash yitkadesh"* – "The old shall be renewed, and that which has been innovated shall become sanctified." He goes on to say: "Together they shall constitute torches to light up Zion."[7]

---

5   See Talya Fishman, ibid., (app. 1, n. 9), 313, referring (ibid., n. 1) to M. Jennings, "Tutivillus: The Literary Career of the Recording Demon" (*Studies in Philology* 74 [1977]: sec. 5); M. T. Clanchy, *From Memory to Written Record* (Cambridge MA: 1979, 187); *Sefer Hasidim* (edited by Wistinetzki-Freimann, Frankfurt 1924, sec. 733).

6   See what I wrote on this position in *Darkah shel ha-halacha*, 222–229 (with bibliographic references).

7   *Iggerot ha-Rayah*, vol. 1 (Jerusalem: 1962, 214; discussed in *Darkah shel Halachah*, 106).

APPENDIX 4

Corrupt Versions or Alternate Versions?

At times, we may find that scholars have argued persuasively that our standard version of a particular prayer is not its original form, and that the original one was corrupted at an early date. The question that then arises is: Should we try to go back to the original "correct" version, or should we retain our current accepted one even though it is not really correct? It should also be noted that usually these "incorrect" versions make perfect sense as they stand. We raise this question without offering a solution, and to clarify the issue further, we shall cite two examples.

1. Birkat Magen Avot

This prayer, which is recited towards the end of the Friday night service, is an abbreviated version of the Sabbath eve *Amidah*. It serves as a kind of *hazarat ha-shatz*, or cantor's repetition. This becomes clear where we set out a comparison between the *Amidah* and *magen avot* in the following table:

מגן **אבות בדברו**	א־להי אברהם, **יצחק, יעקב** . . . מגן אברהם	אבות (1)
מחיה מתים במאמרו	מי כמוך בעל גבורות . . . בא"י מחיה המתים	גבורות (2)
הא-ל **הקדוש** שאין כמוהו	אתה קדוש . . . בא"י הא-ל הקדוש	קדושה (3)
המניח לעמו ביום שבת קדשו	[ויכלו/ישמח/אתה אחד . . .]	קדושת היום (4)
לפניו **נעבוד** ביראה ופחד	**והשב את העבודה** לדביר ביתך . . .	עבודה (5)

הודאה (6)	מודים אנחנו לך .... נודה לך ונספר תהלתך ... הטוב שמך ולך נאה להודות	ונודה לשמו בכל יום תמיד מעין הברכות. א"ל ההודאות, אדון השלום
שלום (7)	שים שלום/שלום רב בא"י מקדש השבת ויכל/וזכר למעשה בראשית	מקדש השבת ומברך שביעי ומניח בקדושה לעם מדושני עונג זכר למעשה בראשית

At what we have indicated as line 6, we find the phrase מעין הברכות, which may roughly be translated as "an abstract, or synopsis, of the benedictions," and indeed this prayer is clearly a synopsis of the *Amidah,* as we have shown in the above chart.

Magen avot was examined by several scholars, who noted that the Yemenite version has a slightly different reading: מעון הברכות (*meon ha-berachot*, instead of *me-ein ha-berachot*.)[1] Indeed, the difference between a *yod* and a *vav* in manuscripts is hardly noticeable. In addition, this alternative reading is to be found in a number of Genizah fragments. Gedalyahu Alon[2] devoted a careful study to this alternative reading, and demonstrated most convincingly that this was indeed the original (Palestinian) version. In order to prove this point, he cited various testimonia from early manuscript sources,

---

1   S. Assaf, *Toratam shel Geonim ve-Rishonim*, 1: *Mi-Sifrut ha-Geonim* (Jerusalem: 1933, 77, n. 4); S. Lieberman, *Midreshei Teman* (Jerusalem: 1940), 9; H. Brody, *MGWJ* 54 (1910): 500.

2   *Mehkarim be-Toldot Yisrael*, vol. 2 (Israel: 1958, 128–134). As an example of a witness to the reading, see ms. Oxford Heb. D.55.33–34, in the version of *birkat ha-shalom* at the end of the *Amidah* prayer. It reads as follows:

ברכינו אלקינו ושמ[רינ]ו וחנינו ושלומך שים עלינו וסוכת שלומך פר[וס ע]לינו. ברוך אתה ה' מעון הברכו[ת]. ....

See U. Ehrlich, "*Tefillat Shemoneh Esreh Shelemah al pi Minhag Eretz Yisrael.*" *Kobez al Yad* 16 (28): 15. This text was already cited and discussed by J. Elbogen in his *Studien zur Geschichte des jüdischen Gottesdienstes* (Berlin: 1907, 46). Ehrlich (ibid., note 46) makes some slight corrections to his reading.

Since we have mentioned *birkat ha-shalom*, it is worth noting the version cited by Fleischer in his article "*Ketaim mi-Kovtzei Tefillah Eretz-Yisraeliim min ha-Genizah.*" *Kobez Al Yad* 13 (1996); 23 (2005): 149.

אתה הוא ה' אלקינו צדקות [אהבת צדק] ושלום תטע בתוכנו. ב[רוך] אתה ה' [עושה ה'] שלום.

See also Fleischer's nn. 40, 41, ibid.

midrashim and *piyyutim*. Also, following earlier scholars,[3] he showed that this phrase has been displaced from its original position and that this section of the prayer should read: מעון הברכות. מעון הברכות א‑ל ההודאות אדון השלום is a name-attribution (*kinui*) of God, literally meaning the "residence of the blessings" – i.e., the source of all blessings. It may even be conjectured that the first stage of the change was from מעון (*maon*) to מעין (*maayan*), the well-spring or source of blessings, which has roughly the same meaning, and that this was later misunderstood to be מעין (*me-ein*), "the synopsis" of the blessings, and this by way of a comparison with the common Talmudic phrase מעין שבע (*me-ein sheva*) – a synopsis of the seven blessings of *birkat ha-mazon* (Grace after Meals), as in JT *Berachot* 8, 11d, and JT *Pesahim* 9:37a.[4] Under the influence of this mistaken understanding of the phrase, its location was changed to its current position.

Should we then seek to restore *magen avot* to its original form, or should we leave it in its widely accepted present state, which makes sense as it stands?

2. Yismah Moshe

The second example comes from the prayer *yismah Moshe*, which is found in the Sabbath *mussaf Amidah*. Aharon Mirsky, in his monumental work *Ha-Piyyut*,[5] examined this prayer in detail, pointing out that it raises three puzzling questions:

Most blessings of this type begin with אתה, such as אתה יצרת, אתה אחד, אתה ברכתנו, etc. But this one does not.

Other blessings of this category refer to the essential nature of the holy day (*kedushat ha-yom*). Thus, אתה קדשת refers to the holiness of the Sabbath; in אתה אחד we read: יום מנוחה וקדושה לעמך נתת referring to the Sabbath as a day of rest and holiness; and תכנת שבת refers to the *mussaf* offering. But *yismah Moshe* does not speak of the reason for keeping the Sabbath, or that God gave us the Sabbath. It merely tells us that Moses was delighted that God called him a loyal servant and that he received the tablets of the Law from Him.

---

3   Brody, ibid.
4   Cf. BT *Berachot* 16a, 29a: מעין י"ח; ibid.: מעין כל ברכה וברכה ibid., 37ab; 44a מעין שלש; ibid., 40a, *Sukkah* 46a: מעין ברכותיו, etc.
5   pp. 88–92.

Normally, the biblical verses that come after the prayer (introduced by the phrase וכן כתוב ובתורתך – "and so it is written in your Torah") are already prefigured in the prayer itself, so that they follow on naturally from the preceding section. Thus, in אתה קדשת we read: וברכת מכל הימים וקדשת מכל הזמנים, and then there follows: וכן כתוב בתורתך: ויברך א־להים את יום השביעי ויקדש אותו .... Since *yismah Moshe* tells how God gave Moses the tablets of the Law which contain the commandment to keep the Sabbath, we would have expected that the verses that follow come either from Exod. 20:8–11, or from Deut. 5:12–15, which give the fourth commandment dealing with the Sabbath. But instead, the verses that follow come from Exod. 31:16–17, which, although they refer to the Sabbath, are in no way related to the Ten Commandments.[6] Mirsky concludes that what we have here is the remnant of a longer *piyyut* (a *kerovah*), most of which has been lost, and which was written in an alphabetic acrostic form. Only the middle three lines, beginning with the letters *yod, kaf* and *lamed,* have survived. See the chart overleaf for his reconstruction.

Were we to have the remaining sections, we might possibly understand the connections with the following verses. Or perhaps this *piyyut* originally had quite a different context, unrelated to the verses that follow.

But in order to clinch his argument, he had to posit that the third line began with a *lamed* – i.e., with the words לוחות אבנים, (tables of the Law), whereas in our *siddurim* the version is שני לוחות אבנים, *two* tablets of the Law. According to Mirsky, the word שני was added at a later date, altering the scansion of the verse, and therefore not a part of the original text.

Such a conclusion had already been suggested by Menachem Zulay, who found a manuscript which indeed read לוחות אבנים, without the word שני. Later on, Wieder discovered three additional such manuscript testimonies,[7] giving considerable more credence to Zulay's and Mirsky's conjecture.

Should we then erase the word שני from our *siddurim*? As stated above, I

---

6   This was noted by the Aderet, Rabbi Eliyahu David Rabinowitz Teomim, in his *Lishkat ha-Shavim* 19 (first published anonymously in the journal *Kenesset ha-Gedolah* 3 [Warsaw: 1891], and then republished in *Tefillah le-David* [Jerusalem: 2004, 124–125]). Incidentally, the Aderet made many suggestions of changes and emendations throughout the liturgical texts, as may be seen throughout this volume.

7   *Hitgabshut*, vol. 1, 298; vol. 2, 576, n. 8.

א ...	מ ...
ב ...	נ ...
ג ...	ס ...
ברוך אתה ה' מגן אברהם	ברוך אתה ה' המחזיר שכינתו לציון
ד ...	ע ...
ה ...	פ ...
ו ...	צ ...
ברוך אתה ה' מחיה המתים	ברוך אתה ה' הטוב שמך ולך נאה להודות
ז ...	ק ...
ח ...	ר ...
ט ...	ש ...
ברוך אתה ה' הא-ל הקדוש	ת ...
ישמח משה במתנת חלקו כי עבד נאמן קראת לו	ברוך אתה ה' המברך את עמו ישראל בשלום
כליל תפארת בראשו נתתו בעמדו לפניך על הר סיני	
לוחות אבנים הוריד בידו וכתוב בהם שמירת שבת	
וכן כתוב בתורתך ושמרו וכו'	
א-להינו וא-להי אבותינו וכו'	
ברוך אתה ה' מקדש השבת	

קראת לו	כי-עבד נאמן	במתנת חלקו	ישמח משה
על הר סיני	בעמדו לפניך	בראשו נתת	כליל תפארת
שמירת שבת	הוריד בידו וכתוב בהם		לוחות אבנים

leave these questions open as a subject for further consideration.[8]

---

8   There are undoubtedly examples of what appear to be errors in our standard versions of the prayer book, some more obvious, some less so. Thus, for example, already the Maharshal (R. Shlomo Luria, 1510–1573), writes in his famous responsum no. 64:

אבל קודם למנצח איננו מתחיל אלא "תהלה לדוד" ומסיים ב"תהלת ה' ידבר פי", ואיננו מוסיף "ואנחנו נברך וכו'", כי אין כאן מקומו אלא בפסוקי דזמרא כדי לשלשל ההודיות ....

He is referring to the second *ashrei* (Psalm 145), which comes after the Torah readings, and he regards the last verse (taken from Psalm 115) as being out of place (and only in place in *pesukei de-zimra*). Therefore, he declines to say it (see the note in *Seder Avodat Yisrael*, i.e., the *Baer Siddur* (69); but note, however, that it is not altogether clear that this is really an error.)

It has also been pointed out that in the statement appearing before the prayer *Ribon kol ha-olamim*, in the *shaharit* prayer before the *korbanot*, which reads:

לעולם יהא אדם ירא שמים בסתר **ובגלוי** ... וכו'.

the word ובגלוי is superfluous and mistaken. (See Verdiger, *Tzelota de-Avraham*, vol. 1, 73, in *Va-Yaas Avraham* ad loc.; E. Landeshut, apud *Siddur Hegyon Lev* [Königsberg: 1825]; Klatzki, *Erech Tefillah*, 18.)

On the other hand, there are examples of what were thought to be errors, which actually are valid alternative versions. So, for example, in the Passover Haggadah, the blessing over the second cup of wine ends: ונאכל שם מן הזבחים ומן הפסחים (in accordance with M. *Pesahim*, 10.6). But some versions have מן הפסחים ומן הזבחים (in accordance with the Mishnah in the Yerushalmi, ibid.). Furthermore, in some Haggadot it is stated that this second version should be said when Passover begins directly after the Sabbath. It was suggested that this directive is based on a misinterpretation of the initial letters במש"ב. which stood for במשנה שבירושלמי – "in the Mishnah in the Yerushalmi," but that this was erroneously understood to represent במוצאי שבת – "at the close of the Sabbath." However, this is quite incorrect, for the suggestion to use the alternative reading on that particular night was the novum of R. Yaakov Weil (fifteenth century Ashkenaz) for persuasive halachic reasons, and is not to be found in Haggadot prior to this time. (See M. M. Kasher, *Haggadah Shlemah* [Jerusalem: 1956, 143, n. 10], and ibid., 68–69 in the apparatus.)

Similarly, in the Grace after Meals (*birkat ha-mazon*), there are the famous alternative versions, one for regular weekdays and one for Sabbaths and holidays, namely: מגדיל and מגדול. The former is from Psalm 18:51, while the latter is from 2 Samuel 22:51. It has been suggested that the difference between weekdays and special days again is based on an erroneous misinterpretation of the initial preceding the word מגדול, namely: בש"ב. This was mistakenly understood to represent בשבת – "on the Sabbath," whereas in fact it represented ב. שמואל ב. (Presumably, according to this view, the other holidays were added later.) Now, however, attractive this suggestion may be, it is incorrect. For the division of the book of Samuel into two distinct parts (1 and 2 Sam.), which was introduced by the Christian Hebraist Stephen Langton (d. 1228), following the Septuagintal division, appears first in Hebrew manuscripts around 1448 (*Sefer Shmuel*, edited by Yehudah Kiel, 3, n. 2. Second edition, Jerusalem: 1981), whereas these alternative readings predate this division. (In the Rambam's *siddur* we find *migdol*, and in *Mahzor Vitry*, *magdil*; see Goldschmidt, *Mehkarei Tefillah u-Piyyut*, 71, 216.) See also *Siddur Baer*, 561–562; *Tzelota de-Avraham*, vol. 2, 555–556.

Likewise, also in the Grace after Meals, towards the end of *birkat rahem*, we read: כי אם לידך המלאה הפתוחה הקדושה והרחבה. Avraham Verdiger, in *Va-Yaas Avraham* (*Tzelota de-Avraham*, vol. 2, 520–521), rightly pointed out that הפתוחה הקדושה makes little sense, and therefore declared it a mistaken version, which should read מלאה הגדושה "full and overflowing." He cites a book (without identifying it) which claimed that the Baal Shem Tov had written this correction in the margin of his *siddur*. However, *Sheruta de-Tzelota* (by R. Yaakov Verdiger), ibid., points out that the early testimonies have לידך הקדושה והמלאה והרחבה, which makes good sense and requires no correction. (He also cites a Sefaradi version which contains לידך המלאה והרחבה. העשירה והפתוחה Thus, rather than correcting קדושה to גדושה – a small and attractive

emendation – one should probably just restore the words to their earlier order, הקדושה והמלאה etc.

Finally, it is interesting to note the explanation given in *Le-okumei girsa*, 7 no. 10, for the reading in the *piyyut Yedid Nefesh* by R. Eliezer Azikri, אנא א־לי חמדת לבי – *hemdat libi*. The original reading as found in the author's autograph copy was מחמד לבי – *mahmad libi*. Rabbi Mazuz suggests that the printers "corrected" it so as not to mention the name Muhamed. He ends by saying that the Ashkenazic version, אלה חמדה נפשי, is definitely a mistake.

APPENDIX 5

The *Piyyutim* Controversy

In chapter 8, note 1 and near chapter 11, note 1, we touched upon the issue of the insertion of *piyyutim* within the matrix of the established prayer version, and particularly within the *Amidah,* and even within the first three and last three benedictions. We referred to the fact that this was a source of considerable controversy in which leading geonim and rishonim took opposing positions. While we cannot cover the whole scope of this chapter in the history of our liturgy, the evidence for which is found in all too numerous polemic texts, we shall here cite in extenso a long section from the *Shibolei ha-Leket* of R. Tzidkiyah ben R. Avraham ha-Rofeh, the thirteenth century Italian authority, which gives us a representative picture of the issue. We shall quote this passage, section 29, from S. K. Mirsky's edition (New York: 1966, 209–218 [with his notes]), and provide a brief summary of the salient points in English:

דין אם מותר להתפלל קרובות ופיוטים בתוך התפילה

כח. אמר רב יהודה[1] לא ישאל אדם צרכיו לא בשלש ראשונות ולא בשלוש אחרונות, אלא באמצעיות.

וכתב רבנו חננאל[2] זצ"ל: קים להו לרבנן דליחיד, אבל שאילות ששואלין הציבור כגון זכרינו לחיים שרי, דהא ג' אחרונות כולהי שאלה נינהו ושרו, דשאלות ציבור הן. ועוד כתב, דאסור לכל מאן דמשני או מוסיף או גורע בג' ראשונות מן המטבע שטבעו חכמים בברכות. ואילו החזנין שמניחין מטבע הברכות ואומרין קרובות לאו שפיר עבדי. אבל המאריך והמקצר באמצעיות לית לן בה.

והרב ר' אברהם בן עזרא זצ"ל כתב בפירוש קוהלת:[3] אל תבהל על פיך, אל יוציא פיך מלים

---

1   ברכות לד, א.

2   פיר"ח נספח לאוצה"ג מס' ברכות עמ' 42, ור' הערות שם על כל הראשונים שהביאו פיסקא זו בקיצור או בשינויים.

3   ה, א.

לפניו⁴ בבהלה, ולבך אל ימהר, כי אם תבינו, כי הלב כמו אובד ותועה בעסקי העולם, על כן אמר משיח יי' (שמואל ב, ז כז) מצא עבדך את לבבו.⁵ ודע כי האלהים נצב עליך ורואה אותך ושומע את דבריך, כי הוא בשמים, בגובהי גבוהים,⁶ ואתה על הארץ, ואין למטה ממך, על כן יהיו דבריך מעטים, שלא תסתכן, כמו שהיה כהן גדול ביום הכיפורים מתפלל תפילה קצרה ויוצא. אמר אברהם המחבר, הנה נא הואלתי לדבר בעבור היות כבוד המקום מלא כל מקום, ולא יוכל האדם להישמר בכל מקום, הוכן לו מקום שיהי לו קבוע לתפילתו והוא חייב לכבודו. גם הוא האדם להודות ולשבח לאלהיו בכל רגע, כי חסדו עימו בכל חלקי הרגע, שיחיינו ויתענג בהרגשות. רק בעבור היות האדם מתעסק בעסקי העולם הושם לו זמן שיתפלל בו, והם עתים ידועות, ערב ובוקר וצהרים. כי מי שיש לו עינים ידע עת צאת השמש ועת נטותו ועת בואו. על כל כשיתפלל האדם חייב שישמור פתחי פיו, ויחשוב בליבו שהוא עומד לפני מלך אשר בידו להמית ולהחיות. על כן אסור לאדם שיתפלל ויכוין בתפילותיו פיוטים לא ידע פירושם,⁷ ולא יסמוך על המחבר הראשון,⁸ כי אין⁹ אשר לא יחטא, או המעתיקים חטאו.¹⁰ והטוב בעיני, שלא יתפלל אדם כי אם התפילה הקבועה, ויהיו דברינו מעטים ולא ניענש בדין.

ובשם רבינו גרשם זצ"ל מצאתי: מה שהורה לכם החבר שלא להתפלל קרובות בתוך התפילה בחגים ובמועדים ובראש השנה ויום הכיפורים, ואפי' זכרינו לחיים, לפי שאינו מעניין מגן, שאילה זו נשאלה לפני רב כהן צדק זצ"ל והשיבו:¹¹ לשאול אדם צרכיו בג' ראשונות וג' אחרונות ולומר זכרינו לחיים במגן, כמנהג שלנו אתם עושין כי הוא מנהג ישיבה, שאנו שואלין¹² במגן זכרינו, ובאתה גיבור מי כמוך, ובמודים וכתוב לחיים, ובשים שלום בספר חיים, מראש השנה עד יום הכיפורים. ואם הא דרב יהודה דאמר אל ישאל אדם צרכיו וכו' הלכה היא, אם כן אנו עושין שלא כהלכה, אלא אין אנו חלוקין על הלכה זו, **דרב יהודה לא דיבר אלא בצרכי יחיד**, כדאיתה במסכת ע"ז.¹³ היה לו חולה בתוך ביתו, או היה צריך לפרנסה כול', אבל צרכי ציבור שואלין, כגון זכרינו לחיים ובספר חיים.

ועוד השיב רב נטרונאי גאון זצ"ל,¹⁴ שאומרין פיוטין באבות וגבורות ובכל תפילה שלכל רגל ורגל מעניינו, ומרבין בו דברי אגדה ובחנוכה¹⁵ ובפורים, אם אומרין בכל ברכה וברכה מעין אותה ברכה, ובראש השנה ויום הכיפורים דברי ריצוי וסליחות, ובתשעה באב דברי חורבן

---

4 לפנינו: "בביתו בבהלה".
5 בפסוק: "מצא עבדך את לבו להתפלל".
6 לפנינו: "בגבהי מרום הגבוהים".
7 שם: "עיקר פירושם".
8 שם: "ברצונו הראשון".
9 שם: "אין אדם".
10 הראב"ע מאריך הרבה והמלים "והטוב בעיני" וכו' הוא סוף דברו שם.
11 במחז"ו סי' שכו (עמ' 365) כתוב בסתם: "ובתשובות הגאונים כך הושב ולשאול אדם צרכיו" וכו'. כמו לפנינו, והשווה להלן בשבה"ל סי' רפו: "ובשם רב עמרם ורב כהן צדק גאונים ז"ל מצאתי" וכו', ובס' הפרדס (מהדו' עהרענרייך עמ' רכג–רכד) ובשע"ת סי' קנא, ובהגהות "איי הים" שם.
12 במחז"ו שם במשובש: "ממנהג אתם עושי' מה הויא מנהג ישיבה שאנן שואלין", ועוד הרבה שיבושים נפלו שם.
13 ח, א, ובתוד"ה אם בא, ור' הגה"מ ה' תפילה פ"ו אות ג'.
14 ח"ג סי' נ', ובאוצה"ג לברכות, התשובות, סי' קעח, עמ' 70, ובנסמן בהע' שם.
15 שם: ובט"ב, וזו טעות מוכחת, שכן תשעה באב נזכר להלן, גם שם, ובאוצה"ג לא העיר על כך.

הבית, הרשות בידו. ועיקר שאומרין בכל ברכה וברכה מעין פתיחתה וחתימתה שלברכה, ובאמצע אומר דברי אגדה ודברי שבח שלהקב"ה שפיר דמי.[16] וגם יש לנו ללמוד מן הפייטים הראשונים שהיו חכמים גדולים. הרי ר' ינאי שהיה מן החכמים הראשונים[17] ופייט קרובות לכל סדר וסדר שלכל השנה.[18] וגם ר' אלעזר ביר' קליר[19] היה מן החכמים הראשונים ופייט קרובות לכל הרגלים והזכיר באבות וגבורות דברי אגדה ועניינים הרבה. וגם רבינו קלונימוס[20] שהכם גדול היה [פייט קרובות לכל הרגלים והזכיר בם אגדה ועניינים הרבה, ור' משולם בנו ידענו שחכם גדול היה][21] ופייט קרובה לצום כיפור, ובתוך הברכה אמר עניינים הרבה, ובסוף סמוך לחתימה הזכיר מעין הברכה. ויש ללמוד מהן ולא לבטל קרובות שהן שבח הקב"ה. עד כאן תשובת רבינו גרשום מאור הגולה זצ"ל.[22]

וכן כתב אחי ר' בניִמן נר"ו שאין לנו למעט בקרובות ופיוטים שהן מיוסדין על שבח המקום [ויש בהן מעניינו של יום כדאמרינן[23] ברוך יי' יום יום (תהלים סח, כ) כל יום ויום תן לו מעין ברכותיו][24]. ומצינו שהקב"ה חפץ בתפילתן של ישראל, דאמרין בבראשית רבא:[25] ר' שמואל בר חייא בר יודן אמר על כל קילום וקילוס שישראל משבחין להקב"ה משרה שכינתו עליהן שנ' (תהלים כב, ד) ואתה קדוש יושב תהילות ישראל. ואיתא נמי בפסיקתא דשמיני עצרת:[26] יספת לגוי

16   עד כאן תשובת רב נטרונאי ומיכאן ואילך לשון רבנו גרשם.

17   ינאי נמנה בין "המשוררים הקדמונים" ע"י רס"ג בהקדמתו הערבית לס' האגרון הרכבי זכל"ר, ה, עמ' נ.

18   שי"ר, תולדות ר"א הקליר, הע' 19 הביא לשון שבה"ל (עפ"י הקצר): "הרי ר' ינאי שהיה מן החכמים הראשונים ופייט קרוב"ץ לכל סדר וסדר של כל השנה" וכו', וכתב: "מלשוננו נראה ברור שר' ינאי פיטן היה קודם ר"א קליר, אך מי הוא ר' ינאי זה ואנה נזכר עוד", וב"תשובות למשיגים", סי' יז, נתן תודה לציון שנודע לו על ידו מעט יותר על ר' ינאי וסים כי איטלקי היה ובזמן הקליר. בשנת תרע"ט הוציא ישראל דאוודיזאן את ספרו "מחזור ינאי", בנוויארק, ובשנת תחר"ץ הוציא מנחם זולאי בהוצאת שוקן בברלין את ספרו "פיוטי ינאי", ועתה ברור מה פירוש "שפייט קרובות לכל סדר וסדר של כל השנה", וכי מקומו של ינאי הוא בארץ ישראל או סמוך לה, במקום שהיה נהוג מחזור הקריאה של ג' שנים (מגילה כט, ב), ר' מאמרי "למהותו של מדרש תנחומא", סורא, כרך ג', עמ' 93–119).

19   ר' עליו יוסף מרקוס, חורב, חוברת א, כרך א, עמ' 21 "הפיטן הזה, שלפי דברי ש. י. רפופורט לא נמצא חכם בעמנו אשר רבו הספקות כל כך על זמן היותו, על ארץ מולדתו, ועל עצמו, מי הוא זה ואיזה הוא ושער זה היום עמדו חכמנו נבוכים לפני בעיה זו הולכת ונפתרת עתה". לדעתנו חי בטבריה בימי מלחמות הביצנטינים עם הפרסים סמוך לחתימת התלמוד, עי"ש. [ראה עתה מאמרו של עזרא פליישר "לפתרון שאלת זמנו ומקום פעילותו של ר' אלעזר בירבי קיליר", תרביץ נד, תשמ"ה, עמ' 385–412. ד. ש.].

20   ר' עליו ועל ר' משולם בנו, לאנדסהוטה, עמוד העבודה מעמ' 265 ואילך; דוד קאסטעל, מבוא לתשו' גאונים קדמונים דף יא, ע"ב "ר' קלונימוס אבי ר' משלם"; גנז"ש ח"ב עמ' 204, שם עמ' 272.

21   המוסגר בארכיים, לפי הנדפס, ובכ"י שלפני לא נזכר ר' משולם כלל, רק אבי, ור' דאוודיזאן בהקדמתו לספרו מחזור ינאי מה שהביא בשם א. מרקס על נוסח התשובה בכ"י.

22   ב"ארחות חיים ח"א, הלכות תפילה סי' נ'ז באה התשובה בקצרה ובעבוד. וע"ע לענין הנידון, גאוניקה ח"א, עמ' 122–123; עפנשטיין, בייטרעגע עמ' 39–40 (מונטסטריפט שנה 52 עמ' 596–597).

23   ברכות מ, א; סוכה מו, א.

24   המוסגר הוא בכ"י עה"ג. ובשולי הדף כתוב שם: "ובמסכת יומא בפרק אמ' להם הממונה, ההוא דנחית קמיה דר' אבא כול' ופירש רבינו שלמה זצ"ל שליח ציבור שמסדר בתפילתו סדר עבודתיו שלכנ'ד גדול אל שם ונשלמה פרים שפתינו. הנה שמומיח מדבריו שמותר לומר קרובות בתוך התפילה. אליה — אולי זהו ר' אליה חתן ר' ישעיה מטראני, שבנו ידוע בשם ר' ישעיה ב"ר אליה, בן בתו של ר' ישעיה הזקן.

25   פמ"ח, ז (טהעאדאר 482) ושם: "ר' שמואל בר חייא רב יודן בשם ר' חנינא אמר על כל שבח ושבח" וכו', ור' מ"י שם.

26   פסדר"כ ל' (דף קע ע"ב).

יי' יספת לגוי נכבדת (ישעיה כו, טו) אומות העולם אתה נותן[27] להם ימים טובים הן אוכלין ושותין
ופוחזין, ונכנסין בבתי תיאטראות[28] ובבתי קרקסאות ומכעיסין אותך,[29] אבל ישראל[30] אתה נותן
להם ימים טובים והן אוכלין ושותין,[31] נכנסין לבתי מדרשות ולבתי כנסיות ומרבין בתפילות ומרבין
בקרבנות,[32] לפיכך צרך[33] הכת' לומר ביום השמיני עצרת.

ועוד מצינו שגם בימי רבותינו נהגו בקרובות ופיוטים כדאיתה בפסיקתא דסוכה[34]: כד דמך ר'
אלעזר ביר' שמעון היה דורו קורא עליו מי זאת עולה מן המדבר כתמרות עשן מקוטרת מור ולבונה
מכל אבקת רוכל (שה"ש ג ו). מהו מכל אבקת רוכל? דהוה קריי ותניי, קרוב ופייטן.[35]

וכן מצאתי שהשיב רבנו תם זצ"ל[36]: כף רגל חמש מאות וחמש עשרה ישרה לכסא. בתלמוד
ירושלמי בפרק הרואה[37] ראיתי: אמר ר' יהושע בן לוי[38] מן הארץ ועד לרקיע מהלך חמש מאות שנה
אמר ר' ברכיה בשם ר' אבהו בשם אבין סומקא[39] גדול מזה, רגל אחד[40] מרגלי החיות מהלך חמש
מאות וחמש עשרה שנה. מה טעם? דכת' (יחזקאל א ז) ורגליהם רגל ישרה, כמנין ישרה, בוא וראה
כמה הקב"ה גבוה. ומשם ייסד הקלירי, כי רוב דבריו על פי תלמוד ארץ ישראל,[41] וחולק על תלמודנו
במסכת חגיגה,[42] ובימיו היו מקדשין על פי הראייה, ומארץ ישראל היה מעיר אחת ששמה קרית
ספר. וראיות יש, כדאיתא בפסיקתא[43] כדדמך ר' אלעזר בי' שמעון פתח עליה ההוא ספדנא מי זאת
עולה כול', מכל אבקת רוכל, דהוה קריי ותניי קרוב דרוש ופייטן, בעל דרשות וקרובות ופיוטין. נראה
לי דר' אלעזר ביר' שמעון הוא ר' אלעזר קלירי, דמצינו בפסיקתא[44] שבתחילה היה מוליך משואות
ואוכל מלא תנור פת, פעם אחת הוליך החמורים עם משאם על הגג, ושמעתי שעל אכילתו
קרוי קלירי. ובההיא שעתא פייט קרובות הללו, בשעה שהיה משתכר היה קונה עוגות משכרו, ושוב

---

27   שם: מרבה.

28   שם: "טרטיאות". הכתיב בשבה"ל מדוייק ונ"ל שהמעתיקים סירסו מלה זאת בכוונה כדי לכנות דבר מתועב להם.

29   שם נ': "בדבריהם ובמעשיהם".

30   שם נ': "אינן כן".

31   שם: "ואוכלים ושותים ושמחים ונכנסין לבתי כנסיות ולבתי מדרשות".

32   שם: "ומרבים במוספסין ומרבים בקרבנות".

33   כן בכ"י ומדויק, ובנדפס בשבה"ל ובפסדר"כ: צריך.

34   פסדר"כ דף קס ע"ב, ושם הפיסקא שם: ולקחתם לכם, וכן נמצא בויק"ר פ"ל.

35   שם: "קרוי ותנוי ופייטן ודרשן", ור' שם הע' כ"ד ולהלן בלשון תשובת ר"ת. והמלה קרוב היא מל' קרובות, ור' תו'
     חגיגה יג, א, ד"ה ורגלי החיות: 'תנא קרא קרובץ ופייטן'".

36   עי' תו' חגיגה יג, א, ד"ה ורגלי החיות, ומחז"ו סי' שכה, עמ' 363.

37   ברכות פ"ט ה"א, י"ג ע"א.

38   בירו' לפנינו: "דאמר לוי".

39   שם: "ואמר רבי ברכיה ורבי חלבו בשם ר' אבא דמוקה", ובשבה"ל הנדפס: אבן סומקא.

40   בירו': "אף טלפי החיות מהלך ה' מאות שנה וחמש עשרה, מניין ישרה", בשבה"ל הוסיף כנראה: מה טעם וכו',
     בדרך פירוש.

41   השווה שבה"ל ה' מילה סי' ז: "כמו שיסד הקלירי בשמונה עשרה של חנוכה – ואע"פ דבתלמודא דידן – דרוב
     פיוטים של הקלירי על פי הירושלמי ועל פי האגדות".

42   יג, א, ותו' שם ד"ה ורגלי החיות.

43   ר' לעיל הע' 34 ובשו"ת רשב"א ח"א תס"ט: "והקליר אומרים עליו שהוא ר' אלעזר בן ערך שאמרו עליו שהוא
     תנוי והוא קרוי והוא פיטוי", נראה שגירסתו בפסיקתא היתה במקום ראב"ש: ארב"א, ר' מחז"ו עמ' 362 הע' ו,
     ו"עמודי העבודה" עמ' 26–27.

44   פסדר"כ, ויהי בשלח, דף פ"א ע"א, ובע' קפ"ז שם, והשווה אוי"ז ח"א סוס"י יט ומחז"ו עמ' 363.

נעשה תלמיד חכם. תדע שבימיו היו מקדשין על פי הראייה, שלא תמצא בכל פיוטיו קרובה ליום
טוב שיני. ואם תאמר ארחץ בניקיון כפות,[45] שליום טוב שיני של סוכות. כתוב במחזורים ישנים,
קלירית זאת אומרים ביום טוב שיני, ואחות אשר לך כספת[46] שעשה הוא ליום טוב ראשון, שלשמיני
עצרת, תדע שמזכיר טל בברכת מחיה המתים, כטל תחייה להחיותם, ואילו היה ליום טוב אחרון
שלשמיני עצרת היה מזכיר בגשם נדבות להחיותם.[47]

ומקראות שבמשנתינו במגילה פרק בני העיר[48] שאמר שקורין ביום ראשון והוא מזכירן
בקרובותיו בהזכרת פסוקין ככת', ולא אותן פסוקין שאומר התם בגמרא שאומר ליום טוב שיני.
וכל מי שאומר שעושה אומן כמותם, אינו אלא טועה. ואפילו[49] תאמר שלא עשה אותן ר'
אלעזר ביר' שמעון, ותאמר שעל ידי שכינה נתפקח ואחר היה, מכל מקום יש לך לומר שמקרית
ספר היה ובימיו היו מקדשין על פי הראייה. ובהרבה מקומות חולק על תלמודינו ותופש לו שיטת
תלמוד ירושלמי[50] **ותלמוד** ממנו **בצרכי רבים דשייכי לומר. והא דאמרינן אמר רב יהודה אל ישאל
אדם צרכיו לא בשלש ראשונות ולא בשלש אחרונות, בשלש ראשונות דנראה כעבד שמסדר שבח
לרבו [בשלש אחרונות דנראה כעבד שקיבל פרס מרבו והולך לו]**[51] **הנהו צרכי יחיד קאמר, וצרכי
דקתני מוכיח דצרכי עצמו משמע, כדאמר בפרק קמא דעבודה זרה: אע"פ שאמרו לא ישאל אדם
צרכיו לא בשלש ראשונות ולא בשלש אחרונות, אם יש לו חולה בתוך ביתו אומר בברכת חולים, ואם
צריך לפרנסה אומר בברכת השנים, דהיינו צרכי יחיד. אבל בג' ראשונות צרכי רבים הן, לפיכך האריכו
בהן יותר מבקדושת היום שזהו שבח שכל ישראל צריכין לומר רחמים.** הא למדת שבימי תנאים היה,
שלא מצינו אמוראין שבארץ ישראל חולקין על תלמודנו באותן הדברים שהוא חולק. ועל דא אנא
סמיך לומר פיוטים ויוצרות וזולתות ואופנים, ולא כאז מבראשית הוכתרה, כאשר אפשר לפנים,[52]
אבל קרובות דצרכי ציבור נינהו, וכן זוכרנו לחיים, וככן שנא מזכירנו שביעלה
ויבוא. ומבני פריצי עמנו יתנשאו להעמיד חזון ונכשלו[53] ירקב שמם כי לא המה. אך מתוך שראו

---

45   ר' עמודי העבודה עמ' 35 מס' 70.

46   שם עמ' 43–44 סי' 158.

47   הרב חיד"א ב"ברכי יוסף", או"ח סי' קי"ב ד', מביא קושיית צורבא מרבנן מתוס' חגיגה יג, א, שהוא קיצור מתשובת
ר"ת שלפנינו, שהקליר לא חיבר פיוטים ליו"ט שני, על תוס' מגילה כה, א, ד"ה מפני "שיסד הקליר בקדושתא
שאנו אומרים ביום שני של פסח", ותירץ ש"אנו אומרים", אין הכוונה שהוא תיקן, ור' מעדני יו"ט על הרא"ש,
ברכות פ"ה סי' כא, אות ג', ור' גם מחז"ו עמ' 363 הע' 1 שתירוץ כן מדעתו. ותירוץ זה הוא באמת על פי תשובת
ר"ת גופו שלפנינו על הפיוט "ארחץ בנקיון כפות": "קלירית זו אומרין ביום טוב שיני", ופלא שלא העירו על כך.
ולענין אם חיבר הקליר פיוטים ליו"ט שני ר' תולדות הקליר לשי"ר, הע' ו.

48   ל, ב המלים: ומקראות – וכל, חסירות במחז"ו שם.

49   במחז"ו שם: "ואפילו תאמר שלא היה ר' אלעזר בר' שמעון ותאמר שעל ידי עוגה נתפקח בעשותו פתיחת הלב
ואחר היה ח".

50   שם: "ותלמוד ממנו דבצרכי רבים שרי להאריך באמצע הברכה ואינו הפסק". מן המלים: והא דאמרינן עד המלים:
הא למדת, חסר במחז"ו בודאי מטעות הדומות, שכן המימרא של רב יהודה היו בלי ספק בתשובת ר"ת,
ואע"פ ש"בשבה"ל כבר הביאה בראשית הסימן הוא חוזר עליה כאן מפני שזה מגוף התשובה.
בכ"י שלפני עה"ג.

51

52   חסר במחז"ו ור' להלן הע' 73 על אות מבראשית, ולפי"ז יש לקרוא: "ולא כאות מבראשית הוכתרה", פיוט בברכת
המזון, מפני שברכת המזון היא מן הברכות שאמרו בהן לקצר, והמלים: "כאשר אפשר לפנים", היינו להלן לפי
התוספתא. בנדפס: "ולא כמו".

53   מליצה עפ"י דניאל יא, יד. ור' תשו' פירקוי בן באבוי, גנ"ש מעמ' 546, ואוצה"ג לברכות, התשובות סי' קעט וסי'

בהלכות גדולות⁵⁴ ; אית מרבנן דלא אמרי זכריני וקרובות, החזיקו בתרמית. אך ההלכות גדולות ורבינו חננאל זצ"ל פסקו⁵⁵ **אל ישאל אדם צרכיו בג' ראשונות ובאחרונות, דוקא צרכי יחיד, אבל צרכי רבים דכל ישראל שרי**, דהא כל ג' אחרונות צרכי רבים נינהו. ואת⁵⁶ שליחיד אינו יכול לומר לפי שדומה כמסדר שבח לפני רבו, ויכול לשאול צרכי רבים, דהיינו שבח הרב, שרבים צריכין לו, שכן מצינו בעבודה והודאה ושים שלום, כולם צרכי רבים הן. והא דא⁵⁷ לעולם אל ישאל אדם אלא אם כן יש לו חולה בתוך ביתו, לאו דוקא: אלא⁵⁸ יתפלל אלא בבית שיש בו חלונות, וכן: אל⁵⁹ יוציא אדם עצמו מן הכלל, וכן: אלא⁶⁰ יהלך אדם במקום סכנה, וכמו: אל⁶¹ יטיל אדם אימה יתירה, וכמו: אלא⁶² ישאל אדם צרכיו בלשון ארמי, כגון אלה הדברים לאו דוקא. ודוק ותשכח. מכל אילו תלמוד שמצוה להרבות בכבודו שלמקום. וכבר נחלקו⁶³ **על הקרובות ר' יוסף טוב עלם עם ר' אליהו הזקן, ועלתה בידם מותר מותר, משום דמצוה מן המובחר, ועל ידם אדם מכוין את לבו לשמים. ובג' ראשונות תיקנו יותר משאר ברכות.** ואפילו באמת ואמונה והשכיבנו מותר, שלא כפירוש רבינו שלמה זצ"ל, שפירש אחת ארוכה, אמת ואמונה, ואחת קצרה השכיבנו.⁶⁴ ושמעתי מאבא מארי ששמע מרבותיו שכשפטיט ר' אלעזר וחיות אשר הנה מרובעת פנים בכסא, ליהטה האש סביביו. ומפי רבותיו גאוני לותיר שמע כן.⁶⁵ וגם ר' שמעון⁶⁶ הגדול שהיה מלומד בניסים היה אומרם בכל יום וגם רבינו סעדיה שמעפי שמכן אנו חיים שמסר לנו סדר העיבור, **פירש שמצוה ומותר.**⁶⁷ ופירוש משנה דפירקא קמא דברכות לא כפירוש רבינו שלמה זצ"ל דמוקי לה אאמת ואמונה והשכיבנו, דמאי שנא הני, ומאי אורכין וקוצרין איכא בהני, ומאי שנא הנך דלעיל, ומאי טעמא, אלא הכי פירושא: בין ארוכה בין קצרה, אכל ברכה וברכה קאי.⁶⁸ ועל הראשונות פירש כן, כדאמרין בפירקא קמא, ובפרק

קפף (עמ' 70–71).

54 דו"ו ו ע"ד, ועי' בהגהות רא"ש טרויב שם, ובמחז"ו 364 ובע' שם. וע"ס העתים עמ' 251 ובע' ל"א שם.

55 הובאו בשבה"ל לעיל בראש סימן זה. בתו', ברכות לד, א, ד"ה אל: "ר"ח ורבי האי", ור' טואו"ח סי' תקפ"ב ובב"י וב"ברכי יוסף" שם אות ד', ובטואו"ח סי' קי"ב, ובע' שלפני זה, ובהגהות איי הי"ם שע"ת סי' קנ"א, ובגנז"ש ח"ב עמ' 513.

56 במחז"ו פיסקא זו משובשת בזה"ל: "ועם מה שעובד מבקש מרבו יכול לשאול צרכי חביריו שהן רבים דהיינו כבוד הרב שרבים צריכים לו", וצריך תיקון לפי שבה"ל שלפנינו, ולא העיר ע"ז שם. בנדפס: ואם.

57 ע"ז, ח, א, ובתו' שם. וכל הפיסקא מן הה"ג ור"ח ז"ל פסקו היא באו"ז ח"א סי' כ, והשווה הגה"מ פ"ו מה' תפילה אות ג'.

58 ברכות לד, ב.

59 שם מט, ב.

60 שבת לב, א: תענית כ, ב; אל יעמוד אדם במקום סכנה.

61 גיטין, ו, ב.

62 שבת יב, ב; סוטה לג, א.

63 השווה הגהות אשרי, ברכות פ"א סי' יב.

64 ברכות יא, א, רש"י ותוס' שם ד"ה אחת ארוכה ואחת קצרה.

65 שי"ר, תולדות הקליר, הע' 32, כותב ע"ז שכל הפיוטים מיוסדים על מדרשים, אבל מה סתירה יש לשמיעת ר' מאיר חתנו של רש"י מרבותיו.

66 במחז"ו: ר' שמעון ב"ר יצחק.

67 זה חסר במחז"ו, ולענין היחס של ר"ת לסדור רס"ג, ר' סה"י סי' מ"ה מקי"נ, עמ' 82: "וכמה ברכות מצאנו בסדר רב סעדיה", וראב"ע בפירושו לקהלת ה א, שהזכיר בשבה"ל לעיל משבח פיוטי רס"ג "שלא חבר מחבר כמו הם". ור' מבוא למחז"ו עמ' 47.

68 הכוונה שאפשר להאריך בברכות ק"ש בפיוטים באמצען, ופירוש אחת ארוכה ואחת קצרה, כמו אחת בתולה

186

החולין[69] אחת בתולה ואחת בעולה. ומקום שאמרו לקצר אינו רשאי להאריך, ההיא משנה בברכת
הפירות ובברכת המצוות, כדמפרש בתוספתא דברכות[70] ובירושלמי,[71] כלומר הני בין קצרות בין
ארוכות, אבל אחריני מקום שאמרו לקצר אינו רשאי להאריך ולהאריך אינו רשאי לקצר, כגון ברכת
הפירות וברכת המצוות. והכי פירושה דמתני': בשחר מברך שתים לפניה ואחת לאחריה, ובערב
מברך שתים לפניה ושתים לאחריה, אחת ארוכה ואחת קצרה, בין ארוכה ובין קצרה, כל ברכה
וברכה. והוה ליה למימר: אחת ארוכה ואחת קצרה, אלא דהוה משמע הנך בין ארוכות בין קצרות,
הא כל שארא לא, דאיכא נמי טובא דרשאי להאריך ולקצר.[72] מקום שאמרו להאריך אינו רשאי
לקצר, לקצר אינו רשאי להאריך, פי' בברכת המזון אות מבראשית,[73] דהא מברכות שאמרו לקצר
הוא דאינו רשאי להאריך. והא דמני בתוספתא,[74] לקצר ולחתום ולשוח, מיפרשי נמי התם. אבל
במקום ארוכה אינו בכלל שאמרו אינו רשאי לקצר, דהיינו רישא, והוה ליה למימר: ארוכה
לא יעשנה קצרה קצרה לא יעשנה ארוכה. ומאי שנא הני, אמת ויציב, אמת ואמונה והשכיבנו, הא
הך מקום שאמרו בשתים שלפניה, המעריב ערבים ואוהב עמו ישראל, לא איירי מידי. ועוד מאי
שנא דאמרינן שלערבית ובשלשחרית ושתק, ומאי טעמא? ועוד דלא מדכר להו בתוספתא, ובשביל
שנזכרו במשנה לא היה נמנע מלהזכירם בתספתא. ועוד, כמה ברכות יש ארוכות מקצרין וקצרות
מאריכין. ותמה על עצמך לפי דברי השמחים ללא דבר פעותות תועים בפשוטות. וכי לא ידעו גדולי
הדור הא דלא ישאל אדם צרכיו. ועוד שהאריכו בהם יותר מאמצעיות. אלא פשוט כיום שנכון
להרבות בשבחו שלמקום[75] ובצרכי ציבור. ובג' ראשונות יותר, כגון זוכרינו, ומי כמוך, ובכן תן פחדך,
וסדר הקדושה בכולי עניין, שבאותן ברכות שיחיד שואל צרכיו דומה שמסדיר שבח שבח לפני
רבו. וזהו שבחו שמרבים בעניוֹת[76] שלתורה ובצורכי כל ישראל, כגון ג' אחרונות, רצה והודאה ושים
שלום, וברכת כהנים כלולה בהן. והכי פירושא דתוספתא: למה אמרו אחת ארוכה ואחת קצרה?
פי' דרך תוספתא באלף מקומות ליקח קצת מן המשנה לזכרון דברים, למה אמרו[77] אחת ארוכה
ואחת קצרה, כלומר, בין ארוכה בין קצרה, מקום שאמרו להאריך אינו רשאי לקצר, לקצר אינו רשאי

---

69 ואחת בעולה.

70 יבמות מא, א.

71 פ"א, 8: "אלו ברכות שמקצרין בהן המברך על הפירות ועל המצות, ברכת הזימון וברכה אחרונה שבקרית שמע,
אלו ברכות שמאריכין בהן ברכת תעניות" וכו'. ר"ל גינצבורג, גנו"ש ח"ב עמ' 521–520, חשב שפירוש זה הוא של
רס"ג ולא של ר"ת, מפני שקרא: "ופירש משנה דפירקא קמא דברכות לא כפירוש רבנו שלמה זצ"ל", היינו שרש"ג
פירש, אבל כבר העיר הר"ש ליברמן בתוס"ר ח"א (עמ' 10 הע' 1) שכתוב: "ופירוש וכו', היינו שר"ת פירש, כמו
שהביעו כל הראשונים, עי"ג הערותיו לתוספתא ברכות עמ' 5.

72 פ"א ח"ח, ג ע"ג.

73 ר' סה"י לר"ת סי', ס"ג י"ב, מקי"נ, עמ' 146, ור"ל גינצברג גנו"ש ח"ב עמ' 521, ור"ש ליברמן תוספתתא לברכות
עמ' 7–6.

73 "אות מבראשית הוכרתה" הוא פיוט שחיבר ר' מאיר הכהן לברכת המזון בשבת נשואין, סי' תצ"ז במחז"ו, ור' שם
עמ' 365 הע' ת, ולעיל הע' 52.

74 ברכות פ"א שם ור' ר"ש ליברמן עמ' 7 הע' 27, שכן הוא הסדר הנכון בתוספתא: אלו ברכות שמקצרין בהן (6)
אלו ברכות שאין חותמין בהן (7) אלו ברכות ששוחין בהן (8). בנדפס דתני.

75 המלה: "של" היא בכ"י בסוף השורה ומנוקדת בסגול תחת השי' ובפתח תחת הל' להראות על חיבור שתי המלים
ועל הקריאה הנכונה, והחיבור של המלה "של" עם שלאחריה הוא תדיר בכה"י. בנדפס בטעות: פשוט ביום וכו'.

76 נקוד בכ"י פתח תחת הב' ותחת הנ' וחולם על הו', והכוונה בקריאות ובתפילות.

77 היינו במשנה.

להאריך, פי' והוצרך להוציא רוב ברכות מן הכלל,⁷⁸ לפי ששינינו במשנה אחת קצרה, לחתום אינו
רשאי שלא לחתום, על אילו ברכות שמקצרין בהן, שמברכין על הפירות ועל המצות, ברכת הזימון
וברכה אחרונה שלזימון.⁷⁹ הא למדת שאין אומר אות מבראשית⁸⁰ והכי פירושא: אילו ברכות
שמקצרין בהן, כגון שאינו רשאי להאריך אבל שרי לקצר, ואילו שמאריכין בהן, ברכת תענית וברכות
של ראש השנה וכו', שאינו רשאי לקצר. ואילו שאין חותמין בהן כול', ומפרש כל סדר שבמשנה:
להאריך אינו רשאי לקצר, לקצר אינו רשאי להאריך, לחתום, לחתום אינו רשאי שלא לחתום, לפתוח בברוך
אינו רשאי שלא לפתוח, לשוח אינו רשאי שלא לשוח. הא למדת שמקצרין ומאריכין דתוספתא,
פירושא הוא להאריך אינו רשאי לקצר. הרי למדנו שבכולן מקצרין ומאריכין חוץ מאותן שפרשה
התוספתא. ועוד ראיה גדולה דפירוש אחת ארוכה ואחת קצרה שפירש רבינו שלמה זצ"ל ליתא,
דהא בהיה בהיה קורא⁸¹ אמר רב פפא קא סברי במערבא: ואמרת אליהם אינה אינה התחלה, עד אמר רב חייא
בר אבא⁸² אמר⁸³ אני ה' אלהיכם⁸⁴ צריך לומר אמת, פי' דלילה לא אמר⁸⁵ אני ה' אלהיכם⁸⁶ אין צריך
לומר אמת. ופריך תלמודא. והא בעי לאדכורי יציאת מצרים,⁸⁷ דאמר הכי מודים אנחנו לך כול',
ולא היו אומ' אמת ואמונה כלל בשלא אמר אני יי' אלהיכם. מכל הפנים למדת שאפילו אחת ארוכה
ואחת קצרה כדפרישית. עד כאן דברי רבינו תם זצ"ל וכולם נכוחים למבין וישרים למוצאי דעת.⁸⁸

The discussion begins with the statement of Rav Yehudah (in BT
Berachot 34a) that a person should not make any requests in the first three or
the last three benedictions of the *Amidah*. The Meiri then quotes Rabbenu
Hananel as saying that it is our tradition that this statement only refers to

---

78 שהרי ברוב ברכות מותר להאריך באמצען ולמה הוציאה המשנה אלו מן הכלל שאין להאריך בהן.

79 היינו באלו הקצרות אין להאריך.

80 היינו הפיוט הזה שהיו שאמרו אותו בברכת המזון בשבת של נישואין. ור' או"ז ח"א סי' כ: "הי' אומר ר"ת שאין
   לומר אות מבראשית הזוכרת בברכת הזן והשיב עליו רבינו יצחק בן אחותו זצ"ל דברכת הזן לא הוה ברכת (המזון)
   [הזימון] דאין זה אלא נברך שאכלנו משלו, אבל ברכת (המזון) [הזן] יכול להאריך". וע" בנסמן בתוספתא לר"ש
   ליברמן עמ' 7–8 ובהע'.

81 ברכות יד, ב. בנדפס בטעות: דהא בהא קורא.

82 שם: חייא בר רב.

83 בשבה"ל הנדפס בטעות: מה.

84 דהיינו פרשת ציצית – רש"י.

85 בשבה"ל הנדפס בטעות: לאמר.

86 לפי שאין מצות ציצית בלילה.

87 שהרי שנינו מזכירין יציאת מצרים בלילות.

88 כמה מן הראשונים הביאו תשובה זו של ר"ת אם היא בארוכה או בקצרה, ואציין בזה, נוסף על הנזכרים בהערות לעיל:
   תוספ' ר' יהודה "ברכה משולשת" ג' ע"ב, ד"ה אחת, תוספות הרא"ש שם ח ע"א, ד"ה אחת, תר"י על הרי"ף
   ברכות (ד' ווילנא ה ע"א) ד"ה מתני' בשחר, חידושי הרשב"א לברכות יא, א, וס' המכחים עמ' 32, וס' המנהיג,
   דיני תפילה, סי' נ"ח ואבודרהם (השלם עמ' עא) ומאלה שדנו על ענין הפיוטים בתפילה, שו"ת רמב"ש, מהדו'
   רא"ח פריימן סי' מא (אם ראוי לעמוד בתפלת רבנו סעדיה וכדומה לה) עמ' 328–329 סי' ש"ס, עמ' 39–40;
   (השווה מו"נ ח"א פנ"ט) וטואו"ח וב"י סי' קיט, וסי' תקפב, ומן האחרונים שדנו בעניין הפיוטים שו"ת "חות יאיר"
   סי' רל"ח, ועל הפולמוס סביב אמירת פיוטים אצל משכילי רוסיה מאוסף מכתבי מ"א פרידלנד, תלפיות כרך ח'
   חוב' ג–ד עמ' 459–483.

private supplications, but communal requests, such as זכרנו לחיים, and so on, are permitted. He continues that one may not alter the version of these benedictions that were established by the sages, and those cantors who do so and add *kerovot* (a form of *piyyutim*) are not doing the right thing. However, in the middle benedictions one may lengthen or shorten at will.

He then goes on to cite R. Avraham ibn Ezra, the great *paytan*, who inveighs strongly against those who add *piyyutim* in their prayers, particularly when they do not understand the meaning of the text.

On the other hand, he says he found in the name of Rabbenu Gershom that he was asked if it is correct that one may not add *kerovot* in the liturgy of the festivals and even brief additions like זכרנו לחיים, which is not really in consonance with *birkat magen*. He replies that this question was put before R. Cohen Tzedek, who responded that one may do so, that this is the custom of the yeshivah, and that only private requests are prohibited (as above).

Rav Natronai Gaon stated that one recites *piyyutim* in the first benedictions and throughout the liturgy in all festivals, Days of Atonement and fast days. The main point is that these insertions should relate to the *petihah* and the *hatimah* of the benedictions. Between them one may add words of *aggadah* and praise to the Lord, as we may well learn from the great early *paytanim* such as Yannai, R. Elazar ha-Kallir, Rabbenu Kalonymus, etc. All this he found in the responsum of Rabbenu Gershom Meor ha-Golah.

Furthermore, his brother, R. Binyamin, asserted that one should not be sparing in including *kerovot* and *piyyutim*, and he goes on to say that God delights in Israel's prayers, citing a passage in *Genesis Rabbah* 48:7 (ed. Theodor-Albeck, 482), in the name of R. Shmuel bar Hiyya bar Yudan, who said that for every single utterance of praise that Israel heaps upon the Lord, He causes His *Shechinah* to hover over them, as is said (Psalm 22:4), "But Thou art holy, O Thou that inhabitest the praises of Israel."

He also found that Rabbenu Tam responded that communal supplications are permitted and only private ones are prohibited. Hence, additions related to communal needs are found throughout the liturgy, as are *piyyutim*. He cites testimonies to prove this point, concluding that it is a mitzvah to give abundant praise and honor to the Lord. He even states that the *kerovot* of R. Yosef Tuv Elem and R. Eliyahu ha-Cohen cause us to have greater intent (*kavanah*) in our prayers, and it is, therefore, a superior mitzvah (mitzvah *min*

ha-muvhar) to recite them. He then continues to strengthen his argument referring to various rabbinic sources.

In conclusion, this long passage gives us an indication of the nature of the controversy that raged over the centuries throughout various communities as to the legitimacy of inserting requests, passages and *piyyutim* of various kinds within the body of benedictions and other sections of the liturgy. Thus, for example, the Maharashdam, R. Shmuel de Medinah (1506–1589), writes in his responsum no. 35 (*Orah Hayyim*) that "the absence [of piyyutim] is better for us than their declamation, particularly since in our day, hardly anyone knows what they mean." This was during the period after the expulsion of the Jews from Spain (in 1492), when there was a great deal of confusion in mixed communities with competing and conflicting versions of the liturgy, where this again became a crucial issue, as indicated in the beginning of this responsum. (See also Y. D. Gilat's article, "*Lo titgodedu*" (*Bar-Ilan* 18–19 [1981]: 89–95). On the other hand, see the responsum of Radbaz, R. David ben Zimra (part 3, no. 532) who lambasts those who removed the *piyyutim* from their services.

We may add the fascinating document that Prof. M. A. Friedman published from the Genizah, a letter written in approximately 1213, probably from Fostat in Egypt, to R. Samuel ha-Levi, a physician in the sultan's service, who had requested that the sultan forbid the additions of *piyyutim* in the liturgy. Our author begs his opponent to rescind the request, extolling the use of *piyyutim* which, he claims, is completely legitimate halachically and serves to enhance communal prayer. He complains bitterly against those who wish to undermine hallowed traditions and argues forcefully for the preservation of the *piyyutim* as a part of the synagogue liturgy. (See his article, "*Zaakat shever al bitul amirat ha-piyyutim – bakashah lifnot la-sultan*" [A cry of anguish over the nullification of *piyyutim* – a request to approach the Sultan], *Peamim* 82 [1989]: 128–147.)

This document should be seen in its direct opposition to the responsum written by the contemporary R. Yosef Rosh ha-Seder from 1211. He lists a whole series of compelling reasons why the *piyyutim* should be done away with. For example, they lead to confusion regarding the real intent of the prayer or blessing, disturb *kavvanah*, lengthen the service so that people are distracted from prayer, alter the structure of benedictions, and so on. (See M. A. Friedman, *Hitnagdut le-tefillah u-le-minhagei tefillah Eretz-Yisraeliim*

be-sheelot u-teshuvot she-min ha-genizah (mi-teshuvot shel R. Yosef Rosh ha-Seder, Knesset Ezra) (Jerusalem: 1995, 64–102, and especially 98–100.) In the final instance, the overall consensus is that these insertions are permitted, as is clearly demonstrated throughout our liturgy.

However, this controversy contains a deeper level, one which was touched upon by the late Prof. Ezra Fleischer in his important article *"Bein arai le-keva be-tefillot ha-rabbim be-Eretz Yisrael ha-kedummah"* (published in *Sefer ha-Zikkaron le-Rabbi Yitzhak Nissim zt"l, ha-Rishon le-Tziyyon*, vol. 5 [Jerusalem: 1985, 7–33]). This study discusses the relationship between fixed-version prayers and changing ones in early Eretz Yisrael – i.e., between the fixed version and the piyyutic ones. On page 8, he writes as follows:

> The fixed versions and the *piyyut* actually represent two opposing viewpoints as to the essential nature of prayers, which in truth are two opposite "humors" in the nature of humanity. The one viewpoint speaks in the name of the love of the fixed, the known, the regular and the usual; the other in the name of the love of change, of alternation, of surprise which provokes curiosity. The tension between these two viewpoints is probably the catalyst in human culture, and its existence and development depends on the right balance between these two elements, the one which aims, in vain, to preserve past accomplishments, while the other seeks, also in vain, to exchange them for new values and new aims.

He goes on to explain that it was not the intention of the *paytanim* to undermine the fixed version of the liturgy, but rather to enrich it. However, these two opposing forces inevitably developed into the controversy described above.

He makes another important distinction (ibid., n. 10), not always recognized by students of liturgy, between *fixed* version (*nusah kavua*) and a *uniform* version (*nusah ahid* – discussed in chapter 16, near note 2), pointing out that even nowadays, while we do not have a uniform version of the liturgy, we do have a fixed version (i.e., a standard established structure etc.). See also "The Dynamic Process of Change in Our Liturgy" above.

APPENDIX 6

The *Avodah* Prayer – An Example of the Complex Development of a Benediction

It will, I believe, be revealing to trace the development of one benedictional prayer in order to demonstrate the numerous and extreme changes that it underwent, the problems that its reformulation faced, the ideological dilemmas and controversies that the smallest differences reveal, and, in general, the dynamism of its developmental process.

The example I have chosen to discuss is the first of the last three benedictions of the *Amidah, birkat ha-avodah,* more commonly now called *retzeh,* which we briefly touched upon above (Talmudic Sources Forbidding Change . . .). This prayer has been exhaustively analyzed in *Tzelota de-Avraham* 1 (302–305, in R. Mordechai Spielman's *Tiferet Tzvi,* vol. 2, Brooklyn, NY: 1985, 146–149), and in Luger's *Tefillat ha-Amidah* (173–183). Here we shall give an abbreviated version of this prayer's history:

Rashi on BT *Berachot* 11b writes that during the time of the (Second) Temple, the benediction was as follows:

Find favor, Lord our God, in the sacrificial service (*avodah*) of Your people Israel, and the fire offerings of Israel and their prayer. Blessed . . . Who accepts the sacrificial service of His people Israel with favor.	רצה ה' א-להינו עבודת עמך ישראל ואישי ישראל ותפילתם תקבל ברצון. ברוך . . . המקבל עבודת עמו ישראל ברצון.

Or possibly the ending (*hatimah*) was: שאותך לבדך ביראה נעבוד – "You, Whom alone shall we worship in awe."

In BT *Yoma* 68b, Rashi writes that the High Priest on Yom ha-Kippurim would say:

Find favor in Your people Israel, and favor the sacrifice in the sanctum of Your house (Temple). Blessed art Thou … Whom alone we shall serve … etc.

רצה בעמך ישראל ותרצה העבודה בדביר ביתך. בא"י שאותך לבדך ביראה נעבוד.

This latter *hatimah,* … שאותך לבדך, which is also found in Midrash Psalms 29.2 (ed. Buber 232), and in *Yalkut Shimoni* on 1 Sam. 2, has been preserved in the Ashkenazic rite of *birkat kohanim,* when the priests bless the people on festival days.

After the destruction of the Temple, this blessing was altered since sacrifices were no longer offered, and the *hatimah* became: המחזיר שכינתו לציון – "Who restores His presence to Zion," a version found throughout the early authorities. However, in *Leviticus Rabbah* 7:2 (ed. Margaliot, 151), the formulation is: רצה ה' א-להינו ושכון בציון עירך – "Find favor, Lord our God, and dwell in Your city, Zion." And this, indeed, is the Palestinian version of the prayer as we learn from numerous Genizah fragments.

See also J. Mann (HUCA 2 [1925]: 306–307), where a fuller version from a Genizah fragment contains the following formulation:

Find favor, Lord our God, and dwell in Zion, Your seat, as before. Speedily shall Thy servants serve Thee (i.e., with sacrifices – *ya'avducha*) and in Jerusalem may we prostrate ourselves before Thee. Blessed art Thou … Whom we will serve in awe.[1]

רצה ה' א-להינו ושכון בציון כמאז מהרה יעבדוך עבדיך ובירושלים נשתחוה לך. בא"י שאותך ביראה נעבוד.

The *Rokeah* (sec. 322) states that the rabbis instituted that this prayer should be recited three times daily (*shaharit, minhah* and *aravit*) in a formulation that runs as follows:

"Please, return Your divine presence to Zion Your city, and the order of the sacrificial service to Jerusalem."

אנא השב שכינתך לציון עירך וסדר העבודה לירושלים …

Our current version was further elaborated to include Rashi's version: רצה ה' א-להינו בעמך ישראל ובתפילתם as mentioned above.

First, then, we ask that our prayers, which took the place of sacrifices after the destruction of the Temple, be accepted favorably. Then we continue

---

1   See editor's note in *Lev. Rab.,* ad loc., as to whether this text is an indication that one should bow down at this point.

to request: והשב את העבודה לדביר ביתך – "and return the sacrificial service to the sanctum of Your Temple."

Here we may add that it has been suggested that the more correct version is the Ashkenazic one, also found in *Zohar Pekudei* 347a: רצה... בעמך ישראל ובתפילתם, "and *in* their prayer," rather than the Sefardi ולתפילתם שעה – "and *to* their prayer hearken," for this latter request was already made in the previous benediction, שמע קולנו – "Listen to our voice."

Still another version of this prayer is preserved in some of the rites for the festivals. Its text is as follows:

And may our requests be as pleasant to You as a burnt offering and a sacrifice. Please, Merciful One, in Your great mercy restore Your divine presence to Zion and the order of sacrifices to Jerusalem. May our eyes see Your return to Zion with mercy, and let us serve You there in awe as in past years. Blessed art Thou, O God, Whom we will serve in awe.

ותערב עליך ערתירתנו כעולה וכקרבן. אנא רחום ברחמיך הרבים השב שכינתך לציון וסדר העבודה לירושלים. ותחזנה עינינו בשובך לציון ברחמים, ושם נעבדך ביראה כימי עולם וכשנים קדמוניות. בא"י שאותך לבדך ביראה נעבוד.

This looks very much like a composite version, but, while it expresses the same basic yearning for the return of the Divine Presence to Zion and the reestablishment of the sacrificial ritual, it still has a very different form from our רצה formula.

Luger has identified multiple variations in Genizah manuscripts of the Palestinian version of this prayer. He brings an early version in *Pesikta de-Rav Kahana* (ed. Mandelbaum, 353): רצה, א־להינו, ושכון בציון עירך ויעבודך בירושלים, which is similar to that which we found in *Leviticus Rabbah*. A further version found in the Genizah is:

רצה ה' א־להינו ושכן לציון. יעבדוך עבדיך בירושלים נשתחוה לך ברחמים בנו ותרצינו. בא"י שאותך ביראה נעבוד.

A longer and more complex version has:

רצה ה' א־להינו בעמך ישראל ושכון בציון מהרה יעבדוך בניך בירושלים ואתה ברחמים תחפוץ בנו ותרצינו, ותחזנה עינינו בשובך לציון ולירושלים עירך ברחמים כמאז...

An even fuller version runs as follows:

רצה ה' א-להינו בעמך ישראל ולתפילתם שעה והשב העבודה לדביר ביתך ושכון בציון עירך בימינו. יעבדוך בניך בירושלים ואישי ישראל ותפילתם תקבל ברצון ותהי לרצון תמיד עבודת ישראל עמך. אנא למענך קבלינו ורצינו ורצה נא את תפילתנו, ותחזנה עינינו בשובך לציון ברחמים כמאז . . .

These two compound versions end with the *hatimah*: המחזיר שכינתו לציון.
There were additional variations, such as:

עולות נעלה זבחים נקריב שלמים נגיש ואתה ברחמים תחפוץ בנו ותרצינו. בא"י שאותך ביראה נעבוד.

And during the *mussaf* of Shabbat Rosh Hodesh, we find the following after *Yaaleh ve-yavo*:[2]

אז תחפוץ זבחי צדק עולה וכליל, אז יעלה על מזבחך פרים, ואתה ברחמים תחפוץ בנו ותרצינו. בא"י שאותך ביראה נעבד . . .

An interesting passage may be found in the commentary of the Rosh on Mishnah *Tamid* 5:1:

Since they did not have time to pray the full eighteen benedictions, they would pray, "Grant that the sacrifice be a sweet savor," and they would not say "and return the sacrificial service to the sanctum of Your Temple," nor did they end "and return Your divine presence to Zion," but "that we may serve You alone in awe. Blessed art Thou Who dwelleth in Zion."	כי לא היה להם פנאי להתפלל י"ח ברכות והיו מתפללים "רצה שיהא קרבן ריח ניחוח", ולא היו אומרים "והשב את העבודה לדביר ביתך", וגם ל"א היו מסיימים "ומחזיר שכינתו לציון" אלא "שאותך לבדך ביראה נעבוד. בא"י שוכן בציון".

This is a completely new ending, and שאותך נעבוד, which we have seen to be an alternate *hatimah*, has here been incorporated into the main body of the benedictory formula. Note, too, the shortening of the prayer for lack of time, as noted above.

Two different literary formulations seem to emerge from this medley of versions: one that mentions the yearning for the return of the sacrificial ritual in the Temple in Jerusalem, ending "Who restores His divine presence to Zion," and the other with its emphasis is that God return to dwell in Zion, and that we should be able to serve Him in awe.

There was also a long-standing controversy as to the meaning of the

---

2   See Fleischer, *Tefillah u-Minhagei Tefillah*, 37.

phrase [3] ואישי ישראל in our רצה version. Tosafot on BT *Menahot* 110a write:

> There are conflicting midrashim. Some say that the souls of the righteous are
> offered [by the Archangel Michael on the celestial altar],[4] while others say that
> they are fiery sheep. This is what is stated in the eighteenth benediction, in the
> *avodah*: ואישי ישראל ותפילתם מהרה באהבה תקבל ברצון – "and the fire-offering of
> Israel and their prayer may You rapidly accept with love and favor."

In the *Ein Yaakov* ad loc., there is an addition:

> What does he [i.e., Michael] offer? Can you imagine that there are oxen and
> sheep there? Clearly what he offers is nothing other than souls of the righteous.

The Tur on *Orah Hayyim* 120 writes:

> And even though there is no [Temple] service nowadays, we pray that our
> prayers, which come in place of sacrifices, be favorably accepted before the
> Lord.

He appears to understand אישי ישראל as denoting that which prayer came
in their place, so that אישי ישראל are, in fact, the three daily prayers that were
instituted to replace the sacrificial offerings.[5]

In the *siddur* of R. Shimshon of Germaiza (Jerusalem: 1972, 109), we
read:

This is the version of *retzeh*: "And the fire-offering and their prayers accept favorably with love." We do not read "speedily," for the souls of the righteous are offered by Michael *daily* on the celestial altar. And the prayer was formulated with this notion in mind.... Therefore, Rabbenu Yitzhak ben Asher Halevy[6] did	וז"ל רצה. ואישי ישראל ותפילותם באהבה תקבל ברצון. ולא גרסינן "מהרה", דהא נשמת צדיקים שמקריב מיכאל בכל יום על מזבח של מעלה נתייסדה תפילה זו ...

---

3   On the term אישים, see further in *Tiferet Tzvi*, ibid., 150–152.
4   This motif is found throughout rabbinic literature. See, e.g., *Zohar* 1.80a, 81a;
     Zohar 2, 159a, 247a; *Zohar* 3, 121b, *Zohar Hadash* 25a, *Tikkunei ha-Zohar* 14a; BT
     Zevahim 62a, *Menahot* 110a. See further *Seder Gan Eden*, J. D. Eisenstein. *Ozar
     Midrashim*, vol. 1 (New York: 1915, 88); R. Margaliyot, *Malachei Elyon*, Jerusalem:
     1945, 114–118, 121.
5   So writes the Ba"h, *Bayit Hadash* ad loc.
6   On him, see E. E. Urbach, *Baalei ha-Tosafot* (Jerusalem: 1980), 165–173.

away with saying "speedily"[7] [which might suggest that
we request the speedy death of these righteous people!].

לכן ביטל רבינו ד־לוי לומר
מהרה.

However, the *Mateh Mosheh* of R. Mosheh of Premisle (part 1, sec. 149,
ed. M. Knoblovicz, 87–88. London: 1958) notes that there must be thirty-
four words in this passage, corresponding to the thirty-four priests who offered the ox and the goat . . . and such was the reading of the *Rokeah*, with the
word "speedily." He also notes that R. Yitzchak Halevy eliminated this word;
however, he adds: והשב את העבודה, adding the word *et*, to make up the full
complement of words. However, the *Eliyahu Rabbah*, after citing the *Mateh
Mosheh*, notes that the Tosafot (mentioned above), who bring the tradition
about Michael offering the souls of the righteous, they themselves had the
word "speedily," and therefore he suggests that Michael offers only the souls
of those righteous people who passed away a long time ago. This discussion
continues on in the literature of subsequent generations.

We noted that the Tosafot give two interpretations of אישי ישראל: fiery
sheep or prayers instead of sacrifices, and the souls of the righteous. This controversy gave rise to a discussion as to how to punctuate this passage: אישי
ישראל ותפילת, keeping together אישי ישראל and ותפילתם, meaning the acceptance of prayer now that there is no Temple, or והשב את העבודה לדביר ביתך ואישי
ישראל – "return the sacrificial system to the sanctum of Your temple, and the
fire-offerings," i.e., those fiery sheep we would wish to sacrifice. This latter
view was that of the Gr"a (R. Eliyahu of Vilna) in his *Beur* on *Orah Hayyim*
sec. 120. The Ari, on the other hand, in the *siddur* of R. Koppel is said to have
said: "And when you say ואישי ישראל ותפילתם, concentrate your thoughts on
Michael who offers the souls of the righteous on the celestial altar, which is
hinted at by the final letters of: "ותפילתם . . . ביתך . . . ואישי ישראל" (i.e., the letters
מיכאל – Michael).

We have by no means exhausted all aspect of the history and variety of
the versions of this prayer. But we have been able to see (a) how it was altered
after the destruction of the First and Second Temples; (b) how various versions with different emphases developed; (c) how the text was abbreviated
by those who had little time for lengthy prayers; (d) examples of complex

---

7   On the meaning of מהרה – "speedily" – see *Perush Siddur ha-Tefillah la-Rokeah*,
    vol. 2 (edited by Hershler, 386–387. Jerusalem: 1992).

composite versions incorporating different elements from varying versions; (e) how some authorities eliminated certain words for slightly esoteric reasons; (f) the question of the number of words in this prayer, and (g) how to punctuate parts of it. Finally, we may observe that all these changes and additions are consonant with the basic tenor of the benediction.

This, then, may serve as an example of how complex it is to determine the history of a prayer's literary development, and the many elements that we must take into account in order to understand such development even partially.

APPENDIX 7

"For Your Covenant which You Sealed in Our Flesh"

This phrase is found in all the standard versions of the second benediction of the Grace after Meals, called *birkat ha-aretz* – the blessing over the Land. It is followed by "and for Your Torah which You taught us."

The source of what has been called "the Covenant phrase" is found in a number of early rabbinic sources. Thus in Tosefta *Berachot* 3.9 (ed. Lieberman, 14), according to the printed version and ms. Erfurt, we read: R. Yossi says: "So, too, whosoever has not mentioned the Covenant in the blessing over the Land, we tell him to repeat the blessing." Lieberman, in his *Tosefta Kifshutah,* vol. 1 (New York: 1955), 38, is not completely certain that this passage, which is not found in ms. Vienna, is truly a part of the original Tosefta text, since in JT *Berachot* 1:9 this ruling is cited in the name of R. Ba bar Aha in the name of Rabbi [Judah the Prince].[1] Furthermore, in BT *Berachot* 49a, we read that Rav Hisda, following the opinion of Rav, did not mention the Covenant [or the Torah and *Malchut* – the royal house of David].[2] Furthermore,

---

1 And cf. *Numbers Rabbah* 23:7, ed. *Tanhuma* Numbers *Masaei* 6, ed. Buber 5, where this ruling is cited in the name of "the sages" [שכך אמרו חכמים].

2 The full version of this passage runs as follows:

> Rabbi Zeira said to Rav Hisda, "Come and teach!" Rav Hisda responded: "I have not even learned *birkat ha-mazon* properly, and you want me to teach?" Rabbi Zeira said: "What are you talking about?" Rav Hisda responded: "When I visited the house of the Exilarch and I recited *birkat ha-mazon*, Rav Sheshet uncoiled his neck at me like a snake" [i.e., he was very angry]. "Why?" "Because

earlier on in the same Talmudic discussion (ibid., 48b), we read as follows:

> *Tania* [We have learned in a *baraita*]: R. Eliezer says: Whosoever has not said
> "a desirable, good and spacious land" (ארץ חמדה טובה ורחבה) in the blessing
> over the Land, and "the royal house of David" in the blessing "Who buildeth
> Jerusalem," has not fulfilled his duty. Nahum the Elder says: One must mention
> the Covenant in it [i.e., the blessing over the Land].

In *Hilchot Berachot* 2:3, Maimonides apparently follows the Talmud's
formulation. For he rules that in this benediction one who does not mention
"a desirable, good and spacious land" has not fulfilled his obligation, meaning
that he must repeat the benediction. He then continues to say that "one must
mention the Covenant and Torah," and so on, but does not mandate a repetition of the benedictions for one who did not mention these elements, following the opinion of Nahum the Elder.[3] Moreover, in the story of Rav Zera and
Rav Hisda in BT *Berachot* 49a, it is related that although Rav Sheshet was
angry at Rav Hisda for not mentioning "the Covenant and Torah," he did not
require him to repeat the benediction. When Rav Hisda was asked why he did
not mention them, he replied, as we cited earlier, that he was following the
view of Rav, explaining that "the Covenant" does not apply to women, and
"Torah and the royal house" neither to women nor to slaves.

With this background information we may well understand the rulings
in the *Shulhan Aruch, Orah Hayyim* 187:2:

> In the blessing over the Land, according to the Rosh he should not say "Who
> has given as inheritance to our forefathers a desirable ... land, etc., a cov-
> enant and Torah," for he says "for Your covenant which You have sealed in
> our flesh and for Your Torah which You have taught us," and once is sufficient.
> Maimonides disagrees.

I did not mention '*brit*' [covenant of circumcision], 'Torah' or '[David's] royal
house.' "And why didn't you mention them?" "I followed Rav Hananel in the
name of Rav, as Rav Hananel said in the name of Rav: Whosoever did not say
'Covenant' and 'Torah' and 'royal house' [nevertheless] fulfilled the obligation. I
omitted 'Covenant' because it is not applicable to women, I omitted 'Torah' and
'royal house' because they are not applicable to women and slaves." Rabbi Zeira
exclaimed, "And you rejected all the tannaim and amoraim and followed Rav?!"

3   See *Lehem Mishneh*, ad loc., "*Va-yaas Avraham*" in *Tzelota de-Avraham*, vol. 1, 513–
514; N. L. Rabinovitch, *Sefer Ahavah* 2 (Jerusalem: 1984), 928–929.

Ibid., 3: If he did not mention in the blessing over the Land, the Covenant and Torah – even if he only omitted one of them, he must repeat it.

Rema: Women and servants should not mention the covenant or Torah, for women are not of the covenant (i.e., not circumcised) and slaves do not possess the Torah.[4]

The *Mishnah Berurah,* ad loc., wrote (sec. 9):

Nonetheless, nowadays women too are accustomed to say "for Your covenant which You sealed in our flesh, and Your Torah which You taught us," referring to the covenant of the males sealed in our flesh, and the Torah taught to males … and also [regarding Torah] because women must learn their *mitzvot* in order to know how to perform them.[5]

The view that women should omit mention of the Covenant is surely only in accordance with those who do not require repetition of the benediction if this element is omitted. But surely those who require its repetition would not advise women to omit it. Hence, the suggestion to make this omission is, most probably, in accordance with the view of Rav, Nahum the Elder, Maimonides and those who follow this opinion. Lieberman (*Tosefta ki-fshutah,* ibid.) already pointed out that the early abbreviated versions of the Grace after Meals found in the Genizah contain no mention of the Covenant, Torah or the royal house.[6]

More recently, Avi Shmidman touched upon this issue in an important article entitled "Developments within the Statuary Text of the *Birkat ha-Mazon* in the Light of its Poetic Counterparts" (in *Jewish and Christian Liturgy and Worship: New Insights into its History and Interactions,* edited by A. Gerhards and C. Leonhard, 109–126. Leiden: 2007). There he distinguishes

---

4   See the super-commentaries upon the *Shulhan Aruch, Magen Avraham* and *Beur Halachah,* ad loc., etc.

5   See further *Kaf ha-Hayyim* ad loc., vol. 3, 97b, sec. 20, who cites the Meiri's view on Berachot, ibid., that women recite the entire benediction without omitting a single word because they are a part of the people of Israel, and the benediction refers to the people as well as the land. His view is accepted by the Hidah in *Mahazit Berachah,* sec. 1, etc.

6   He refers us to an article by A. M. Haberman, in *Studies of the Research Institute for Hebrew Poetry in Jerusalem,* vol. 5 (Berlin and Jerusalem: 1939, 45 et seq., especially 50, 60, 66, 67, 68, etc. [Hebrew]).

between "two distinct models of *birkat ha-mazon* recital ... the statutory form of the prayer in which the basic prayer texts remain constant" with a wealth of additional variation, and poetic versions of the prayer, which, although they were composed later, did not come to supplement but to supplant (ibid., 110).[7] He notes correctly that though rabbinic sources specify the overall structure of *birkat ha-mazon,* they "do not delineate a specific prayer text" (109). In discussing the poetic form of the prayer, he notes that the following phrase appears at the end of the second benediction: וזכור לנו מהרה ברית אבותינו, "and speedily recall for us the Covenant of our forefathers." Now whereas in the statutory versions the list of items for which thanksgiving is due always includes the Covenant, usually in the tetracolon meter common to pre-classical Hebrew poetry, it runs thus: ארץ חמדה/טובה ורחבה/ברית ותורה/חיים ומזון. In some cases, this is elaborated in the following form: ועל בריתך ששמת בבשרינו, or שחתמת. "By contrast, among the poetic texts, the mention of the covenant is significantly lacking.... [Therefore] it is likely ... that the covenant phrase [i.e., וזכור לנו מהרה ברית אבותינו] arose as a supplement to the poetic forms of the *birkat ha-mazon* in order to satisfy the rabbinic requirement of the covenant reference" (110).

But what is perhaps more significant for our purposes is that in these early formulations of the covenant phrase, there is no clear identification of the ברית – covenant – with circumcision. The covenant with our forefathers could refer to any of the variety of covenants recorded in the Bible, such as in Gen. 15:18, Exod. 31:16, 34:10, Lev. 26:45, Deut. 4:31, 5:2, and so on. It is true that the Talmud understood the covenant as referring to the specific one of circumcision, which indeed does not apply to women, but only later formulations make this explicit.

Women are certainly included in those other covenants (see the remarkable statement of R. Yair Hayyim Bachrach, in his *Mekor Hayyim*, ed. E. D. Pines, Jerusalem, 1982 p. 96), and women nowadays are deeply involved in Torah study. They were present at Mount Sinai and received the self-same Torah that the men received.[8] It would therefore seem that rather than having

---

7   Cf. E. Fleischer, "Studies in the Problems Relating to the Liturgical Function of the Types of Early *Piyyut.*" *Tarbiz* 40 (1970): 55–60.

8   See the fascinating statement of R. Yair Hayyim Bachrach in his work *Mekor Hayyim* (vol. 1, Jerusalem: 1982, 96) that the sixty myriads who were present at Mt. Sinai

women omit the elements of covenant and Torah, as was suggested by some authorities and not actually practiced from the most part, one could revert to these early non-explicit formulations, such as על בריתך ותורתך, "for Your covenant and Your Torah," or even resurrect the early poetic form ברית אבותינו, "the covenant of our forefathers." Although these suggestions constitute a deviation from the standard and accepted version, they have valid precedents and involve no alterations in either the structure of the benediction or in its general import. On the other hand, the advantages of such a modified version need hardly to be spelled out here.

Finally, I note that in *Shaarei Simcha: Gates of Joy* (ed. A. K. Berkowitz and R. Haut [New Jersey: 2007, 97]) there is a note to ועל בריתך שחתמת בבשרנו: "Some have in mind: ועל מצותך שחתמת בלבנו . . . and for the mitzvot that You sealed in our hearts."[9] While this *mental* addition does not alter the traditional text, it is an admirable attempt to satisfy the desire to make the liturgy more inclusive of women while maintaining the integrity of the standard text. However, here we have suggested going one stage further in this direction without violating normative halachah in any way.

---

included, without doubt, women. He refers us to *Zohar* Leviticus ad init. He then discusses the halachic implicationsof this assumption. (My thanks to my learned colleague Rabbi Shimon Altschul for calling my attention to this source.)

9   See their introduction, xvii.

APPENDIX 8

On R. Meir's Three Benedictions

We have already cited above the statement of R. Meir in BT *Menahot* 13b, namely that one should make three blessings each day, namely: Who made me an Israelite, Who did not make me a woman, and Who did not make me an ignoramus.

היה ר' מאיר אומר: חייב אדם לברך שלש ברכות בכל יום. אלו הן: שעשאני ישראל, שלא עשאני אשה, שלא עשאני בור.

A meaningful example of fluidity in the formulation of benedictions may be found in Moshe Hallamish's book *Ha-kabbalah bi-Tefillah ba-Halachah u-va Minhag (Kabbalah in Liturgy, Halachah and Customs)* (Ramat Gan: 2000, 440–441), where he records some nineteen (!) different versions of R. Meir's first blessing, "Who made me an Israelite":

שלא עשאני כותי	שעשיתני מל ולא ערל	שלא עשאני ערל
שלא עשני ישמעאל	שלא עשני ארמי	שלא עשני נכרי
שלא עשני עובד כוכבים	שלא עשני עכו"ם	שלא עשני עובד גלולים
שלא עשיתני גוי	שלא שמתני גוי	שלא עשני עובד כוכבים ומזלות
שעשני יהודי	שלא עשאני אינו יהודי	שלא עשני גוי כגויי הארצות
שעשני ישראל ולא גוי	שעשיתני ישראל	שעשני ישראל
	שעשני טהור ולא טמא	

We may further add Israel Najara's אשר עשני עברי – "Who has made me a Hebrew." (This may be found in one of his poems. See A. Mirsky, *Shirei R. Yisrael Najara, Mehaber Sheerit Yisrael, Pirkei Shirah* 2 [Jerusalem: 1995, 138]; Hallamish, ibid., n. 19.)

Some of these variations are the result of conventions as to how to write,

or spell out, the term for gentile: עכו"ם, עובד כוכבים ומזלות etc., meaning idolators or simply Gentiles – i.e., non-Jews: ערל, גוי, נכרי, אינו יהודי; some are the result of censorship, e.g., כותי, perhaps עכו"ם, some reflect regional characteristics: ישמעאל, and so forth. טהור ולא טמא – pure and not impure would appear to be parallel to ישראל ולא גוי. The distinction between ישראל ולא גוי and מל ולא ערל (circumcised and not uncircumcised) which seem to be almost identical but appear adjacent to one another in some liturgical manuscripts, may indicate a distinction between gentiles in general, probably here Christians and Moslems, who are circumcised but are not Jewish. But, interestingly enough, the original version of R. Meir which is positively formulated, hardly appears, and the majority of versions follow the formulation in the name of R. Yehudah in Tosefta *Berachot* 6.17 (ed. Lieberman, 38): שלא עשני גוי, and JT *Berachot* 9.2, 13b: שלא עשאני גוי. (Perhaps this is because of the well-known rule in BT *Eruvin* 46b that in a disagreement between R. Meir and R. Yehudah, we follow R. Yehudah's ruling). However, in all these cases the structure and the basic meaning have been preserved.

The phenomenon of alternative versions may also be recognized in זכר ולא נקבה – male and not female (Hallamish ibid., 443) as opposed to איש ולא אשה – a man and not a woman. It may further be noted that Hallamish (ibid., 440) also cites a positive form of the second blessing – "Who did not make me a woman" – in the form of: שעשאני איש – "Who has made me a man," without the negative addendum "and not a woman" (which is perhaps slightly less offensive to those sensitive to such issues).

Hallamish (ibid., 440–441) brings additional benedictions of interest found in early sources. In R. Meir's statement there is also a benediction: שלא עשני בור, who has not made me an ignoramus. But ms. Oxford 1142, from Provence (28a) has: שלא עשני בור, שלא עשני עם הארץ. It appears that this is a conflation of two alternative versions, since the meaning of these two terms are very close to being identical. And in two Paris manuscripts (596 and 616), which are Romaniote versions, and also in ms. Brit. Mus. 11669 from Sicily, we read: שלא עשני בור שאין בו יראת חטא. This is an obvious expansion based on Mishnah *Avot* 2.5, where Hillel says: אין בור ירא חטא – "a brutish man has no fear of sin." (See also Y. Sermonetta, "Nusah ha-Tefillah shel Yehudei Siziliah," in *Jews in Italy: Studies Dedicated to the Memory of U. Cassuto on the Hundredth Anniversary of His Birth* (Jerusalem: 1988), 143.

He also cites another benediction, which is additional to R. Meir's there: שלא עשיתני בלתי מדבר – Who has not made me unable to speak. Perhaps this is parallel to the formulations found in ms. Cambridge Add. 3160: בא"י א-להינו מלך העולם אשר בראת אותי אדם ולא בהמה, and similarly in ms. Parma 1781, 1785, 1768, and ms. Paris 603 (from the fifteenth and sixteenth centuries, from Greece?):

שעשיתני אדם ולא בהמה – Who has made me (created me) a man and not a beast. The classical philosophic categorization is: מדבר, חי, צומח, דומם – "inanimate matter" – what we call mineral; "growing," i.e., plant life; "live" meaning the animal kingdom; and speaking – i.e., humankind. Hence "Who has not made me unable to speak," or perhaps "not a speaking creature" would parallel "and not a beast."

As for the term טמא – "unclean" for a gentile, see A. Büchler's classic article, "The Levitical Impurity of the Gentile in Palestine before the Year 70" (JQR NS, vol. 17/1: 1081), and G. Alon's study in his *Mehkarim be-Toldot Yisrael* (Studies in Jewish History in the Times of the Second Temple, the Mishna and the Talmud), vol. 1 (Israel: 1957), 121–147.

A detailed analysis of these benedictions, often called "the benedictions of self-identity," may be found in an article bearing that title by Joseph Tabory in *Kenishta: Studies of the Synagogue World* 1 (Ramat Gan: 2001, 107–138). On 115–121, he cites classical, Christian and Iranian parallels and how nineteenth century scholars viewed and assessed these apparent parallels as classical influences on Judaism, or "Plato had been influenced by Judaism" (Schopenhauer's view, in his *Die Welt als Wille und Vorstellung* [Leipzig: 1859, vol. 1, 577–588]; Tabory, ibid., 118). He then (121–125) lists the various women's responses to *she-lo asani ishah* in medieval times, noting that the source of *she-asani ki-retzono* is unknown, apparently first appearing in early fourteenth century Spain (Tur *Orah Hayyim* 46 and the roughly contemporary David Abudarhim), and found in Ladino in the fifteenth and sixteenth centuries, as *que me fizo como su voluntad*, or *que fizi me comy la volintady sua*. Yet another response, this time Provençal is קי פיס מי פנה – "Who has made me a woman," i.e., *she-asani ishah*. Yet a third response is found in the Ashkenazic fifteenth century work *Leket Yosher*, which reports that R. Israel Isserlein (1390–1460) said that women say "Who has not made me a brute." A final section (126–138) deals with developments in the modern period (nineteenth century onwards).

More recently, additional discussion on these benedictions may be found

ON R. MEIR'S THREE BENEDICTIONS

in Tzur Shafir's doctoral thesis, *Towards a History of the French Rite of the Prayer that Precedes Prayer* (Ramat Gan: 2006, 232–249).

Finally, we may note that in *Siddur R. Saadya Gaon* (89), there is a comment that "Most of our friends say them [these three benedictions] together every morning after they come out of the toilet," meaning, presumably, that these were private benedictions that were not recited in public.

1. INDEX OF PRIMARY SOURCES

MISHNAH
Shabbat 2, 52
Pesahim 10:6, 179
Avot 2:13, 19

TOSEFTA
Berachot 3:9, 14, 199; 4:4–5, 93; 6:18, 39

TALMUD YERUSHALMI (JT)
Berachot 2:4, 133; 4:3, 8a, 165; 9:1, 12d,
    58, 93; 9:2, 13b, 42; 10:2, 93
Pesahim 9, 37a, 176

TALMUD BAVLI (BT)
Berachot 11a, 96–97; 29b, 136–137; 40b,
    58, 66, 93–94; 48b, 200; 49a, 35–36,
    199; 49b, 80; 60b, 138; 69b, 41
Yoma 68b, 192–193; 69b, 11
Megillah 17b, 29
Taanit 2a, 137; 14b, 64
Bava Batra 16b, 36
Sanhedrin 59a, 38
Menahot 13b, 204; 42b, 42; 43b, 39–40;
    44a, 138

MIDRASHIM
Sifrei Deut. 137
Gen. Rab. 43.7, 421, 86

Num. Reb. 12:11, 86; 23:7, 199
Mid. Sam. 2:10, 25a, 137
Mid. Prov. 19, 86
Mid. Psalms 67, 157a, 137; 29.2, 193
Tanh. B. Exod. 4, 137; Be-Har 1, 86
Seder Eliyahu Rab. 6, 29, 86
Yalkut Shimoni 1 Sam. 2, 193
Yalkut Shoftim 4.4, 705b, 38
Mid. ha-Gadol Gen. 24:1, 36

RAMBAM
Hilchot Berachot: 5, 57, 59; 1:6, 66; 1:9,
    66; 10:16, 87
Keriyat Shema 1:7, 57–58
Tefillah 1:4, 68; 2:19, 68; 4:1, 132; 6:2–3,
    62, 63, 64

SHULHAN ARUCH AND
SUPERCOMMENTARIES
Orah Hayyim 46, 51; 46:9, 94; 54:1, 172;
    119:1, 64; 128:31, 118; 187:2, 200–201;
    192:1, 80
Even ha-Ezer 63:2, 39

2. INDEX OF PRAYER BOOKS

Amudei Shamayim (Emden), 156

ArtScroll, 112

Authorised Daily Prayer Book, 23, 134–136

Avodah she-ba-Lev, 136

Azharot , 151

Baer Siddur (Avodat Yisrael), 48, 87, 91, 179

Daat Kedoshim, 127

Hegyon Lev, 47, 74, 179

Hinah, 34

Kenesset ha-Gedolah, 29, 32, 72, 82, 83, 88, 96, 98, 144, 155

Koren, 112, 113

Likkutei Tefillot, 23

Mahzor [Bnei] Roma, 42, 71, 138, 144

Mahzor le-Yamim Noraim, Rosh ha-Shanah, 143–144, 154, 155

Mahzor Vermaiza, 61

Mishkan T'fillah, 138

Nusah Ahid, 106, 129

Olath Tamid, 129

Otzar ha-Tefillot (Gordon), 22, 48, 155

Prague Siddur 1519, 75

Rinat Yisrael, 112

Seder Rav Amram Gaon, 13, 30, 51, 65, 82, 88, 144, 146

Seder (Siddur) Saadya Gaon, 30, 51, 60, 65, 69, 83, 88, 149

Seder Tefillah li-Yemot Hol u-le-Shabbatot u-le-Khol Moadey ha-Shanah, 129

Sefer Kinot, 128

Shaarei Simcha: Gates of Joy, 139, 203

Shaarei Tefillah: Beit Tefillah, 156, 171

Shaarei Tziyyon, 23

Shabtai (Shabbethai) Sofer, 26, 116, 119, 122, 171

Siddur Beit Yaakov, 157

Siddur Derech Yesharah, 89

Siddur ha-Ari – Kol Yaakov (Koppel), 47

Siddur ha-Arizal – R. Shabbetai Rashkov, 170–171

Siddur ha-Rav Baal ha-Tanya, 102

Siddur ha-Shlah ha-Shalem (Shaar ha-Shamayim), 89

Siddur Habad, 127

Siddur ha-Meduyak, 168–173

Siddur Hanau, 33

Siddur Hechal ha-Berachah – Komarna, 146

Siddur [R.] Herz (Hirz) Schatz (Tihingen), 47, 121, 131

Siddur Ish Matzliah, 168

Siddur Iyyun Tefillah li-Yemot ha-Hol, 133

Siddur la-Hayyal be-Chol ha-Shanah, 164

Siddur Napoli (Naples) 1490, 77

Siddur Raschbam, 95

Siddur Rashi, 145

Siddur Shaarei Shamayim (Emden), 142

Siddur R. Shimshon of Germaiza, 196

Siddur R. Shlomo b. R. Shimshon of
Worms, 147–148

Siddur Tefillah al pi Nusah ha-Arizal, 47

Siddur Tefillah Derech Siah ha-Sadeh,
122

Siddur Torino (Turin) 1525, 49, 76

Siddur Yaavetz, 157

Siddur Zolkiev, 55

Sim Shalom, 11, 139

Tefillah mi-Kol ha-Shanah (Satanov), 80

Tefillah ve-Tikkunim al pi Kitvei ha-Ari,
23

Tefillat Zikaron, 162

Tichlal Etz Hayyim, 45

Tichlal Paamon Zahav, 45

Tihingen – see Siddur R. Herz Schatz

Tzelota de-Avraham, 22, 26, 32, 47, 68,
82, 84, 85, 112, 126, 131, 144, 167, 171,
192, 200

Va-Yeetar Yitzhak (Satanov), 80, 88

3. INDEX OF PRAYERS, BENEDICTIONS AND PIYYUTIM

Ahavah rabbah, 126
Ahavat olam, 126
Alenu, 74–78, 98
Al ha-nissim, 74
Amidah (Shemoneh esreh), 24, 25–32,
    51–52, 60–64, 66–73, 84, 86, 96–97,
    104, 129, 133, 134, 135, 174, 175, 176,
    192, 197
Ashrei, 178
Avodah, 62, 192–198
Ba-meh madlikin, 52
Baruch she-amar, 74
Be-fi yesharim tithalal, 90–91
Be-safah berurah u-vi-ne'imah, 81–82
Birkat ha-aretz, 199
Birkat ha-haftarah, 126
Birkat ha-mazon, 185
Birkat ha-shanim, 28–29
Birkat kohanim, 193
Birkat magen, 86–87
Birkat yotzer, 87
Birkot ha-shahar, 42
Boneh Yerushalayim, 138
El Adon, 84
Eretz hemdah tovah, 200, 202
Et tzemah David, 84
Ezkerah Elokim ve-ehemayah, 161
Grace after Meals, 82, 138–139, 201
Ha-Yom harat olam, 143–147
Hallel, 54–55
Hashkivenu, 29

Havinenu, 118
Honen ha-daat, 126
Kaddish, 170
Kedoshah/gedushah, 179
Kedushah, 98
Kedushah de-sidra, 83
Kedushat shaharit, 83
Keriyat shema, 57, 58, 79
Kiddush, 145
Kol nidrei, 55
Lecha dodi, 112
Magen avot, 174–178
Magen Avraham, 86–87, 174
Magdil/Migdol, 179
Mashiv ha-ruah u-morid ha-geshem/
    gashem, 79–80
Me'ein/Meon ha-berachot, 175–176
Modim anahnu lach, 67
Modim de-rabbanan, 124–125
Mussaf of Rosh ha-Shanah, 88
Nahem, 128, 161–167
Nishmat, 90–91
Pesukei de-zimra, 178
Rahem, 31, 82–83
Refaeinu, 31–32, 64, 68
Retzeh, 192–198
Ribon kol ha-olamim, 178–179
Rosh ha-Shanah and Yom Kippur
    prayers, 63
She-asani kirtzono, 33
Seder Baal Keri, 157

Shelo asani ishah, 112
Shema kolenu, 25–26, 92
Shemoneh esreh – see Amidah
Shomea tefillah, 63–64
Sim shalom, 67
Tahanun, 17, 46–47
Tefillah zakah, 55, 56
Tikanta [Shabbat], 91, 176
Trishagion (Kedushah), 98
U-me-ahavatcha, 30
U-va le-Tziyyon, 73
Ve-al britcha she-hatamta

bi-vesareinu, 202–203
Ve-chiseh David avdecha, 104
Ve-hasieinu, 88–89
Ve-hu rahum, 47
Ve-la-malshinim, 26–27, 92, 146
Ve-li-Yerushalayim, 104
Ve-yatzmach purkanei, 127
Yaaleh ve-yavo, 195
Yedid nefesh, 180
Yekum purkan, 124
Yismah Moshe, 176–179
Yotzer of Shabbat, 81, 88

4. GENERAL INDEX

Abrams, Daniel, 100, 153

Abudarhim, David, 33, 100, 133, 144, 158, 206

Adas Israel, 46

Aderet (R. Eliyahu David Rabinowitz Teomim), 157, 177

Adler, Rachel, 9

Agnon, S. Y. 9, 127

Agudat Mishmeret ha-Kodesh, 168

Aha bar Yaakov, 35, 40

Akum, 45

Alexander of Shklov, 83

Alfasi, Y., 104, 106

Alfasi, Yitzchak (Rif), 96

Alon, Gedalyahu, 175

Amar, R., 101

Amram Gaon, 13, 30, 50, 65, 82, 87, 88, 89, 146

Anshei Kenesset ha-Gedolah (Men of the Great Synagogue), 11, 26

Ari[zal] (ha-Kadosh), 84, 103–107, 121, 125, 146

Arian, Philip, 21

Aristotle, 44

Arugat ha-Bosem, 1, 148–154

Aryei Leib ha-Cohen, 56

Ashkenazi, A., 32

Assaf, S., 30, 42, 175

Ateret Zekkenim, 170

Auerbach, Menahem Mendel, 170–171

Aviezer b. R. Yitzhak Isaac of Tiktin, 157

Avraham b. R. Ezriel – see *Arugat ha-Bosem*

Avraham David b. Asher of Buczacz – see *Daat Kedoshim* (Siddur)

Baal Shem Tov (Besht), 82, 106–107, 127

Babani, Yaakov, 171

Bachrach, Yair Hayyim, 202

Bagno, David, 64

Bans, of Vilna, Grodno, Pinsk, Slutzk, 111

Ben Ish Hai – see Yosef Hayyim of Baghdad

Benayahu, M., 73, 104

Benvenisti, Hayyim, 26, 82

Benyamin Zeev of Slonim, 106

Berkowitz, Adena, 139

Berlin, Naftali Zvi Yehuda (Netziv), 36

Berliner, A., 46, 48, 50, 72, 73

Bernfeld, S., 123

Besht – see Baal Shem Tov

Bleich, Judith, 79, 123

Blidstein, G. J., 67

Blum, Eric, 32

Brodt, Eliezer Yehudah, 142

Brody, H., 175, 176

Brody, Proclamation of, 1772, 108–109

Broyde, M. J., 118, 134

Büchler, A., 206

Carlebach (style minyanim), 123
Caro, Yosef, 59, 100, 103, 125, 168, 170
Censorship, 73–79, 86–92, 131
Changes, recommended, 106
Chazon, E., 17
Chelouche, David, 128, 164
Choriner, Aaron, 122
Clanchy, M. T., 173
Cohen, G. H., 10, 70
Cohen, Hayyim A., 80
Cohen, I. J., 23
Cohen Tzedek, 189
Competing versions, 125–127
Conflated version, 125–127
Cordovero, Moses, 112

Dan, J., 53, 107, 147, 153
Danzig, Avraham (*Hayyei Adam*), 55
Darkhei Noam, 109
David ben Zimra (Radbaz), 72, 190
David ha-Levi, 128
De Sola Pool, David, 10
Didi, Moshe, 172
Dinari, Y., 121
Divrei Kohelet, 89
Dov Baer of Mezridj, 104, 107
Druk, Zalman, 133

Edelmann, Hirsch, 74
Ehrlich, V., 175
Eideles, Eliezer ha-Levi (Maharsha), 38
Einhorn, David, 129
Eisenstein, E. L., 113
Eisenstein, J. D., 196
Elazar of Worms (Rokeah), 53, 91, 112, 153
Eleh Divrei ha-Brit, 12, 13, 123
Elbogen, Ismar, 21, 60, 175
Eliezer ben Natan (Ravan), 61
Eliezer Menahem Min Shah, 133
Eliyahu of Vilna (Gaon of Vilna), 60, 106, 197
Eliyahu Rabbah, 86, 197
Ellenson, David, 130

Ephraim of Bonn, 61
Epstein, Baruch Ha-levi (*Torah Temimah*), 36, 37, 126
Epstein, Yehiel Michel (*Aruch ha-Shulhan*), 12, 118, 134
Eretz ha-Hayyim, 10
Eybeschütz, Yonatan, 133, 142

Falk, Daniel K., 16
Farissol, Abraham, 41–42, 43
Feldman, Emanuel, 34, 38–39
Feminism, 33–40, 143–144, 206
Ferziger, A. 46
Fishman, Talya, 99–100, 153, 173
Fixed prayers, 70–71
Fleischer E., 16–17, 25, 30, 61, 175, 191, 195, 202
Flekeles, Eliezer, 94
Flusser, David, 27
Foremothers, 139
Fraenkel, Yonah, 18
Friedland, Erich, 129, 130
Frimer, Aryeh, 9
Frishman, Elyse, 138
Frumer, Aryeh Zvi, 133

Gaimani, A., 45
Gaon of Vilna – see Eliyahu Gaon
Gamliel, Eliyahu, 79
Gavra, M., 45
Gavriel of Metz, 122
Geiger, Solomon, 89
Gematria, 74, 90, 99–100
Geonim, 23
Gershon Meor ha-Golah, 96
Genizah, 86–87, 175, 194, 201
Ginzberg, L., 68, 125, 137, 162
Gesundheit, B. & Y., 125
Gikatilla (Gikatilia), Yosef, 141–142
Gilat, Y. D., 190
Goldschmidt, Daniel, 71, 82, 143–144, 154, 179
Gordis, Robert, 139

Gordon, Aryeh Leib (*Otzar ha-Tefillot*), 22

Goren, Shlomo, 10, 104, 128, 129, 164

Goy, 45, 94

Grammar, 80, 87

Greek benedictions, 44

Groner, B. Z., 39–40, 51, 62, 99

Guf, 170

Guttmann, Alexander, 12, 13

Gwozdziec, Synagogue, 103, 105

Haberman, A. M., 72, 201

Hafetz Hayyim, 55–56

Hagahot Maimoniyot, 68

Hagiz, Yaakov, 10

Hai Gaon, 88, 94

Halberstam, Hayyim (of Zanz), 106

Halberstam, Yekutiel Yehudah, 18–19

Halivni, E. B., 38

Hallamish, M., 39–40, 104, 127, 204–205

Hanhagot ha-Ari, 104

Hanover, N. N., 23

Harlow, Jules, 11, 134, 139

Hartman, David, 14–16

Hasidah, I. S. I., 42

Hasidei Ashkenaz, 99–100, 121–122, 143–159

Hasidim, 31, 106–110, 111–112, 113

Hatimah, 98, 126, 129, 130, 166, 189, 192, 193, 195

Haut, Rivka 139

Havlin, S. Z., 154

Hayyim Volozin, 134

Hayyot, 83

Hazarat ha-shatz, 98, 174

Heinemann, Josef, 17, 61, 69–70, 96, 123–124

Heller, Yomtov Lipmann, 170, 172

Hemdat Yamim, 55

Hidah (Hayyim Josef David Azulay), 80–82, 168, 170, 172

Hiddushei R. Hayyim ha-Levi, 132

Hildesheimer, 46

Hillel, Yaakov Moshe, 81

Hirsch, S. R., 38

Hirschensohn, Hayyim, 35

Hisda, 35–36

Hoffman, Laurence, 60

Holz, A., 163

Hovav, Meir, 9

Hubka, 103, 105

Idel, Moshe, 83–84, 108–109

Idelsohn, A. Z., 22, 100, 102

Ikkar berachah, 94

Immanuel, Simhah, 100, 153

Issac ben Shlomo Luria – see Ari[zal]

Isaac Tyrnau, 89

Israel Najara, 204

Isserlein, Yisrael (*Terumat ha-Deshen*), 33, 206

Isserles, Moshe (*Rema*), 102, 134

Jacob Koppel of Przemysl, 116, 197

Jacob of Lissa, 13

Jacobson, I., 38

Jacobson, Israel, 123

Jerusalem Day, 10

Joel, Manuel, 129

JOFA, 17

Judah the Pious – see Yehudah he-Hasid

Kadish, Seth, 61, 65, 67, 69, 71, 101, 136

Kahana, Nahman (Spinka), 157

Kahn, D., 73

Kahn, Y. H., 41, 44

Kasher, M. M., 179

Katz, J., 106, 139

Katzenelbogen, Avraham (of Brisk), 106

Kavvanah, 16, 98, 132–136

Kavvanah latzet, 16

Kavvanot, 108–109

Kavvanot ha-lev, 16

Kedushat ha-Shem, 67

Kedushat ha-yom, 176

Kesef Mishneh, 59, 66

Ketzot ha-Hoshen, 133
Keva, 71
Khalatz, Yehudah, 144
Kimelman, R., 23
Kirchheim, Juda Löw, 94
Kitzur ha-Shlah, 89
Klatzki, Yerahmiel, 21, 79, 116, 127, 179
Kochavi, David, 40
Kol Bo, 48, 90–91
Kolbrener, William, 138–139
Kon, Abraham, 137
Kovetz li-Gedor Peretz, 168
Kook, A. I., 35, 173
Kook, Zvi Yehudah, 128
Krauss, Hayyim, 79
Krauss, S., 137
Kreuzer, Uri, 123
Kuntres ha-Sefekot, 133
Kuntres Ish Matzliah, 173

Lamm, Norman, 34, 106
Landau, M. M., 22
Landshuth, 74
Langer, Ruth, 61, 68, 113
Langton, Stephen, 179
Lau, B., 160
Lawot, Avraham David, 102, 104
Le-Hoshvei Shemo, 168
Leket Yosher, 33, 45, 82, 206
Levi Yitzhak of Berdichev, 24, 106
Levine, Yael, 128
Lewites, Hayyim Mendel, 165
Lieberman, S., 37, 39, 42, 94, 175, 199, 201, 205
Loew, Judah (Maharal mi-Prague), 26, 138
Loike, John J., 140
Luah Erez, 72, 156, 160
Luger, Y., 25, 67, 126, 192, 194
Luria, Shlomo (Maharshal), 39
Luzzato, David (Shadal), 71

Magen Avraham, 118, 132
Magid Devarav le-Yaakov – see Dov Baer

of Mezridj
Maharil – see Yaakov Moellin
Maharshal (R. Shlomo Luria), 178
Mahzor Vitry, 32, 67, 91, 96, 126, 144–145, 155, 161, 165
Magdil – see *Migdol*
Maimonides, 23, 46, 57–64, 66–69, 72, 84, 87, 91, 94, 111, 126, 132, 135, 200, 201
Manhig, 48
Mann, J., 30, 44, 127, 193
Mantzpah, 91
Margaliot, Meir, 84
Margaliyot, R., 196
Marx, Dalia Sara, 42
Matbea she-tavu hachamim, 54, 57, 58, 61, 62, 97, 181
Mavo le-Siddur Maharsha, 12
Marzel, Moshe Hayyim, 80
Mateh Mosheh, 197
Mazuz, Mazliah, 168, 180
Medan, M., 31
Me'en ha-Berachot, 175–176
Me'ein sheva, 176
Meir, M., 56
Meir ibn Gabbai, 142
Meir Rabbi, 35–39, 93–95, 204–207
Meiri, Menachem, 80, 97, 155–156, 188, 201
Meiselman, Moshe, 34
Men of the Great Synagogue – see *Anshei Kenesset ha-Gedolah*
Me'on ha-berachot, 175–176
Michtam, 80
Migdol/Magdil, 179
Milhamot ha-Shem, 132
Minhat Elazar – see Shapiro, Hayyim Elazar
Minhat Shai, 80
Mirsky, Aharon, 176–177, 181, 204
Mitnaggedim, 83–84, 106, 108, 109
Mitzvot asei she-ha-zeman geraman, 34
Mosheh of Premisle, 197
Mundshein, Y., 55
Munk, E., 38

Nahman of Braslav, 23
Nadler, Alan, 106
Naeh, Avraham Hayyim, 102
Natronai ben Hilai (Gaon), 13, 51, 146, 167, 189
Navon, Hayyim, 12, 25, 167
Nedavah, 14, 15, 66
Neubauer, A., 53
New prayers, 54–56
Nochri , 45, 94
Nodah bi-Yehudah, 89
Nusah Ashkenaz, 18–19, 22, 47, 58, 79, 106, 127, 129, 161
Nusah Edot ha-Mizrah, 58
Nusah ha-Ari, 103–104, 106, 129
Nusah Haleb (Aleppo), 58–59
Nusah Polin, 129
Nusah Sefarad, 22, 26, 58, 79, 100, 111, 127, 161
Nusah Teman, 58

Oberlander, Baruch, 102, 104
Obligatory prayer, 16
Ofanim, 83
Or Zarua, 82
Orhot Hayyim, 48, 89
Ovadia the Convert, 63
Ovadia Yosef, 128, 133, 160, 166

Paltoi Gaon, 88
Peles, I. M., 94
Perush ha-Tefillot ve-ha-Berachot le-Rabbi Yehudah b. R. Yakar, 87
Perush Siddur ha-Tefillah la-Rokeah, 47
Petihah, 98, 166, 189
Petuchowski, Jacob J., 22, 74, 79, 113, 123, 125, 127, 130
Philipson, David, 123
Pinhas ben Eliezer, 38
Pirko ben Baboi, 51, 68
Piyyut (im), 14, 60–61, 64, 70, 97–98, 112–113, 161, 176–177, 179–180, 181–191
Plato, 44, 206
Pollack, Yehoshua, 132

Popper, W., 73
Posen, R. B., 171
Posner, R., 113
Pri Etz Hayyim – see Vital, Hayyim
Pri Hadash, 88

Qinath ha-Emeth, 122–123

Raavad, 64
Rabbenu (Yaakov) Tam, 51, 152, 154, 189
Rabin, Shmuel, 142
Rabinovitch, Nahum, 65, 68
Rabinowitz, Dan, 56, 170, 171
Rackman, Emanuel, 37
Raffeld, M., 18
Rappel, Yoel, 9
Rayna Batya, 36
Raz-Krakotzin, Amnon, 73
Reform prayer books, 22, 112–113, 138–139
Reif, Stefan C., 21, 112, 113, 114–116, 127, 171
Rema – see Isserles, Moshe
Reunification of Jerusalem, 9, 161
Ritba, 97–98
Rokeah – see Elazar of Worms
Rokeah, David, 26
Rosenfeld, Abraham, 162
Rosh (Rabbenu Asher), 100, 195
Ross, Tamar, 9, 36
Ruah ra, 79

Saadya Gaon, 51, 60, 65, 69, 83, 88, 96, 149, 151, 162
Sacks, Jonathan, 23, 134–136
Satanov, Yitzhak, 79, 80, 88, 171
Satz, Yitzhak, 12, 116
Schammes, Jousep (Juspe), 94
Schechter, A. I., 29
Schechter, Yaakov Yosef ,122
Scheur, Hirsch, 12
Schiff, Shaul, 9
Schiffman, L., 79
Scholem, G., 152–153

Schück, Solomon, 95
Seder Gan Eden, 196
Sefer ha-Batim, 40
Sefer ha-Ittim, 51
Sefer Halachot Gedolot , 68
Sefer Hasidim, 173
Sefer ha-Mahkim, 48
Sefer ha-Manhig, 48, 52, 143–144
Sefer ha-Maor, 132
Sefer Mitzvot Katan (*Semak*), 132
Sefer Nogah ha-Zedek, 122
Sefer ha-Pardes, 52, 88
Sermonetta, 4, 205
Shaar ha-Kavvanot, 19
Shaar ha-kollel, 103
Shaar ha-Kollel – see Lawot, Avraham
   David
Shabbetai Zvi, 90
Shafir, Tzur, 207
Sheliah tzibur, 73
Shear Yashuv Cohen, 128
Shapira, Hayyim Elazar (Muncaczer
   Rebbe), 26, 85, 100–101, 116, 126–127
Shearim, 103
Sheiltot, 13, 14
Shmuel ben Eliezer of Kalvaria, 109
Shmuel ben Hofni, 88
Sheshet, 36, 200
Shibolei ha-Leket, 13, 88, 89, 96, 138, 181
Shik, Moshe, 13
Shilat, Yitzhak, 14, 63, 69
Shiloni, M. M., 66
Shimon ben Zemah ibn Duran, 94, 98,
   101
Shinyever Rebbe, 19
Shmidman, Avi, 201–202
Shlomo ben Aderet (Rashba), 69, 96–98,
   101
Shlomo Min ha-Har, 128
Shomea ke-oneh, 73
Shulhan ha-Tahor, 145
Sithon, Hayyim, 10
Skeat, W. W., 137
Sofer, Moshe (Hatam Sofer), 13, 106, 123

Sofer, Shabtai, 26, 87
Sofer, Yaakov Hayyim, 157, 171
Soloveitchik, Y. D., 14–16, 128, 131, 140
Spanier, A., 127
Sperber , D., 17, 18, 22, 32, 56, 100, 124,
   125, 126, 143, 145, 147, 154, 157
Spielman, M., 64, 74, 88, 89, 104, 131, 157,
   172, 192, 196
Stabon, David, 172
Steinschneider, 34
Stern, Bezalel, 131
Stern, Yosef Zechariah, 95
Sternbuch, Moshe, 133
Sternhart, Natan, 23

Ta-Shma, I., 13, 113, 153, 154
Tabory, J., 18, 21, 136, 167, 206
Tahanun, 17, 46–49
Tahanunim, 17
Tal, S., 21
Tanya (Baal ha-Tanya), 48, 102, 103, 127
Tefillat nedavah, 15
Tehillim ha-Meduyak, 172
Tehinot, 72
Tendler, Moshe D., 140
Teppler, Yaakov Y., 26
Tichlal Etz Hayyim, 45
Tichlal Paamon Zahav, 45
Tiferet Tzvi, 172
Tikkun Soferim ha-Meduyak, 172
Tikkunei ha-Zohar, 84, 196
Tishah be-Av, 10
Toledano, Shlomo, 160
Torah Temimah – see Epstein, Baruch
   Halevy
Toref, 166
Tu bi-Shevat, 54
Tutivillus, 172
Tzalah, Yihye, 45, 98, 144
Tzavaat ha-Rivash, 106
Tzuberi, Y., 32, 72, 73, 82, 96, 144

Urbach, E. E., 61, 128, 153, 155, 196
Uziel, Rabbi, 9

Vaneih, Yitzhak, 45
Va-Yaan Shmuel, 88, 173
Verdiger, Avraham, 22, 84, 179
Verdiger, Yaakov, 22, 171
Vikuha Rabba, 106
Vinograd, Yishayahu, 18
Vital, Hayyim, 82, 102, 103, 108
Vozner, Shmuel; ha-Levi, 173

Wachs, Saul Philip, 128, 162
Weinstock, L., 53
Weiser, R. A., 26, 31, 127
Wermish, Aharon, 34, 38
Wieder, Naftali, 17
Wilensky, M., 109
Wolowelsky, 34, 38

Yaakov Emden. 72, 100, 108, 142, 156, 157, 171–172
Yaakov Moellin (Maharil), 120–121, 145
Yaari, A., 55
Yehoshua ben Levi, 11
Yehoshua ibn Shuaib, 34
Yehudah, 39, 40
Yehudah b. R. Kalonimos, 150
Yehudah he-Hasid, 99, 100, 112, 145, 147, 148, 154, 155
Yehudai Gaon, 68
Yisrael Baal Shem [Tov] (Besht), 82 – see also Baal Shem Tov
Yisrael, Natan, 146

Yitzhak Yehudai Yehiel Safrin of Komarna, 146
Yitzhaki, David, 72, 160, 171
Yohanan ben Reuven of Ochride, 13
Yosef Ben-Brit, 128, 165–166
Yosef ben Moshe (*Leket Yosher*), 33
Yosef Gikatilia (Gikatilla), 125, 140–142
Yosef Hayyim of Baghdad (Ben Ish Hai), 54–55, 80, 112, 121
Yosef Irgas, 125
Yosef of Nemirov, 106
Yosef Rosh ha-Seder, 190
Yosef Tuv Elem, 189
Yudlov, Y., 142

Zalman Hanau (Shlomo ha-Cohen), 156, 157, 171
Zalman of Stuttgart, 120
Zeira, 35
Zemah (Gaon), 14
Zinner, R. G. (Gavriel), 55
Ziskind, A., 79
Ziss, A. A., 145
Zmir Aritzim, 109
Zvi Elimelech, 146
Zohar, 23, 84, 89, 103, 131, 167, 194, 196, 203
Zohar Hadash, 79, 196
Zulay, Menachem, 177
Zunz, L., 21, 50, 72, 73, 74

ABOUT THE AUTHOR

Professor Rabbi Daniel Sperber taught in the Talmud Department of Bar-Ilan University, was the dean of the Faculty of Jewish Studies and serves as the president of the Jesselson Institute for Advanced Torah Studies. The descendant of a line of distinguished Orthodox rabbis, Professor Sperber was born in 1940 in a castle in Ruthin, Wales and studied in the Yeshivot of Kol Torah and Hevron in Jerusalem. He earned a BA in art history at the Courtauld Institute of Art and received a PhD in classics, ancient history and Hebrew studies from University College, London. He also serves as rabbi of the Menachem Zion Synagogue in the Old City of Jerusalem. The incumbent of the Milan Roven Chair of Talmudic Research, he received the Israel Prize in 1992 for his research in Talmud and the history of Jewish customs, and served as the chairman of the Council for Religious Education at the Israel Ministry of Education for a decade.

Professor Sperber has published thirty books and more than four hundred articles on the subjects of Talmudic and Jewish socio-economic history, law and customs, classical philology and Jewish art. Among his major works is a well-known eight-volume series *Minhagei Yisrael* on the history of Jewish customs. Most recently, he has written two books on halachic methodology and rabbinic decision making in confrontation with modernity, and the present work continues these avenues of inquiry.